THE POEMS OF LADY MARY WROTH

THE POEMS OF

Lady Mary Wroth

Edited, *with Introduction and Notes, by*

JOSEPHINE A. ROBERTS

Louisiana State University Press

Baton Rouge

Published by Louisiana State University Press
Copyright © 1983 by Louisiana State University Press
ALL RIGHTS RESERVED
Manufactured in the United States of America

Designer: Barbara Werden
Typeface: Linotron Garamond #3
Typesetter: G & S Typesetters, Inc.

LIBRARY OF CONGRESS CATALOGING IN PUBLICATION DATA

Wroth, Mary, Lady, ca. 1586–ca. 1640.
The poems of Lady Mary Wroth.
Includes index.
I. Roberts, Josephine A.   II. Title.
PR2399.W7A17   1983   821'.3   82-20843
ISBN 0-8071-1707-4 (cloth)
ISBN-13: 978-0-8071-1799-6 (cloth)
ISBN-10: 0-8071-1799-4 (paper)

Louisiana Paperback Edition, 1992
06 08 10 12 14 15 13 11 09 07
8 10 12 11 9

The paper in this book meets the guidelines for permanence and
durability of the Committee on Production Guidelines for Book
Longevity of the Council on Library Resources. ∞

CONTENTS

ILLUSTRATIONS

Frontispiece portrait. Lady Mary Wroth with an archlute; artist unknown. From the collection of Viscount De L'Isle, V.C., K.G., at Penshurst Place, Tonbridge, Kent.

PREFACE

Lady Mary Wroth was one of the most distinguished women writers of the English Renaissance. Although her poems are little known to a modern audience, they were circulated in manuscript among her seventeenth-century contemporaries, including Ben Jonson and William Drummond. Jonson, in fact, wrote a tribute to Lady Mary's poetry in which he stressed its central subject matter, the psychological analysis of love, and claimed that by transcribing her work he became a "much better poet." Her writings include a sonnet sequence, *Pamphilia to Amphilanthus*, in which she examined the conflict between passionate surrender and self-affirmation from the perspective of a female persona. She also composed a variety of other lyric poems which appear throughout the text of her romance, *The Countesse of Montgomery's Urania*, one of the first works of prose fiction to be composed by an Englishwoman. Most recently, her pastoral drama, *Love's Victorie*, has been discovered in unpublished form.

It is fortunate that so many of Lady Mary Wroth's works have survived in the original manuscripts: nearly 75 percent of the collected poems exist in autograph copies, an extremely high percentage for any Renaissance writer. These texts provide valuable information concerning Lady Mary's revisions, as well as her own eccentricities of spelling, grammar, and punctuation. Because the manuscripts of Lady Mary Wroth's poetry have been widely dispersed, this edition seeks to bring together for the first time all of her published, as well as unpublished, poems. I wish to thank the following libraries for permission to consult and reproduce verse from their collections: the Bodleian Library, the British Library, the Folger Shakespeare Library, the Henry E. Huntington Library, the Newberry Library, and the University of Nottingham Library.

As the niece of Sir Philip Sidney, Lady Mary Wroth closely identified herself with the family tradition of writing poetry and serving as a literary patron to numerous aspiring authors. I am grateful to the present owner of the Sidney papers, Viscount De L'Isle, V.C., K.G., who has allowed me to examine and quote from the originals. In addition to preserving the manuscripts and portraits of his collection, he has continued to maintain Penshurst with the same benevolent spirit that Jonson celebrated in the seventeenth century.

While preparing the account of her life, I have also assembled the surviving letters to and from Lady Mary Wroth and wish to thank the following owners of private collections: the Duke of Rutland, the Marquess of Salisbury, the Earl of Denbigh, and Lieutenant Colonel Peter Clifton. I visited the site of Loughton Hall, Lady Mary Wroth's home, which was rebuilt following a fire in the nineteenth century. I truly appreciate the cooperation of the present warden, Arthur Gee, who showed me the records of the house and of the Wroth family. The following archives have furnished biographical material: Cardiff Central Library, Essex County Record Office, Guildhall Library, Greater London County Record Office, Kent County Record Office, National Library of Wales, National Portrait Gallery, and Public Record Office.

In researching Lady Mary Wroth's life and works, I have been assisted by many more individuals than it is possible to name. I am deeply grateful to Peter J. Croft, Librarian of King's College, Cambridge, who is preparing a critical edition of the poems of Sir Robert Sidney, Lady Mary Wroth's father. He has shared with me information concerning a complete manuscript of *Love's Victorie*, which is now in a private English collection. I am also indebted to Margaret A. Beese for providing valuable references concerning Lady Mary Wroth's relationship with William Herbert, Earl of Pembroke, who was the patron of Jonson and the joint dedicatee of Shakespeare's first folio. Miss Beese generously gave me access to her Oxford thesis, a critical edition of Pembroke's poems. Dr. Bent Juel-Jensen kindly allowed me to examine his personal copy of the *Urania*, which contains contemporary manuscript annotations. I wish to thank Margaret A. Witten-Hannah for lending me her excellent unpublished dissertation on the *Urania* and for many helpful insights.

Of the numerous curators and librarians who furnished assistance, I would like to extend particular thanks to G. M. Griffiths, Keeper of Manuscripts at the National Library of Wales; R. H. Harcourt-Williams, Librarian and Archivist to the Marquess of Salisbury; Katharine Pantzer, Editor of the revised *Short-Title Catalogue*; Mary Robertson, Curator of Manuscripts at the Huntington Library; M. A. Welch, Keeper of Manuscripts at the University of Nottingham Library; and Laetitia Yeandle, Curator of Manuscripts at the Folger Library. In tracing the provenance of the unpublished copy of Lady Mary Wroth's romance at the Newberry, I am grateful to Mrs. C. A. Kyrle Fletcher, who shared with me information concerning her late husband's manuscript acquisitions.

For their gracious advice and encouragement, I am especially indebted to the following individuals: Peter Beal, J. Max Patrick, Harrison T. Meserole, William A. Ringler, Jean Robertson, and Gary F. Waller. I have benefited immeasurably from the suggestions of T. Walter Herbert, Dale B. J. Randall, and Craig R. Thompson, who supplied detailed comments on the complete edition. At my own institution, I wish to thank Gale H. Carrithers, Jr., Rebecca W. Crump, Don D. Moore, Lawrence A. Sasek, Donald E. Stanford, and my other colleagues. I am grateful to Beverly Jarrett and Mary Jane Di Piero for their help in bringing this work to print. Claudia Duczer and Elaine Pizzolato aided in typing the final manuscript.

I have received assistance throughout various stages of the project from the National Endowment for the Humanities and the Louisiana State University Council on Research. The Henry E. Huntington and Newberry Libraries generously awarded me summer fellowships, which were instrumental in the preparation of the text.

Most of all, I am indebted to my family and my husband, James F. Gaines, who has remained, as always, a constant source of advice and unfailing support.

Note to the Paperback Edition

The discovery of a copy of Lady Mary Wroth's 1621 *Urania* containing handwritten authorial corrections has led me to revise several passages in the text of this critical edition of her poems. In the textual notes, I indicate the changes with the abbreviation *author's cor.* A comprehensive list of Wroth's manuscript alterations of her prose romance will appear in my forthcoming edition of the complete *Urania*.

I am most grateful to Dr. Charlotte Kohler, who loaned me her personal copy of the *Urania* and generously gave me permission to publish the manuscript changes. I wish to thank M. C. Bradbrook, Katherine Duncan-Jones, Donald W. Foster, and Susanne Woods for suggesting corrections in the first edition. I am deeply indebted to the many Renaissance scholars who have created new audiences for Wroth's poetry.

ABBREVIATIONS AND SIGLA USED IN THE
INTRODUCTION AND NOTES

ABBREVIATIONS

AS	Sir Philip Sidney, *Astrophil and Stella*
Collins	Arthur Collins (ed.), *Letters and Memorials of State in the Reigns of Queen Mary, Queen Elizabeth, King James* . . . (2 vols.; London: T. Osborne, 1746)
CS	Sir Philip Sidney, *Certain Sonnets*
CSP	Calendar of State Papers
DNB	*Dictionary of National Biography*
ELR	*English Literary Renaissance*
Feuillerat	Albert Feuillerat (ed.), *The Works of Sir Philip Sidney* (4 vols., 1912–16; reprint Cambridge: Cambridge University Press, 1962)
HLQ	*Huntington Library Quarterly*
HMC	*Historical Manuscripts Commission*
JWCI	*Journal of the Warburg and Courtauld Institutes*
MLR	*Modern Language Review*
NA	Sir Philip Sidney, *New Arcadia*
N&Q	*Notes and Queries*
OA	Sir Philip Sidney, *Old Arcadia*
OED	*Oxford English Dictionary*
RES	*Review of English Studies*
Ringler	William A. Ringler (ed.), *The Poems of Sir Philip Sidney* (Oxford: Clarendon Press, 1962)
Tilley	Morris P. Tilley, *A Dictionary of Proverbs in England in the Sixteenth and Seventeenth Centuries* (Ann Arbor: University of Michigan Press, 1950)
TLS	*Times Literary Supplement*
Waller	Gary F. Waller (ed.), *Pamphilia to Amphilanthus* (Salzburg: Institut für Englische Sprache und Literatur, 1977)

Sigla

1621	Lady Mary Wroath, *The Countesse of Mountgomeries Urania*, London, 1621
F	Folger Shakespeare Library MS V.a.104
H	Henry E. Huntington Library MS HM 600
N	Newberry Library Case MS fY 1565.W95
No	University of Nottingham Library, Clifton Collection MS CL LM 85/1-5
P	Poems contained in the sonnet sequence, *Pamphilia to Amphilanthus*
U	Poems contained throughout the prose text of the romance *Urania*

INTRODUCTION

I
THE LIFE OF LADY MARY WROTH

LADY Mary Wroth, eldest daughter of Sir Robert Sidney and Lady Barbara Gamage, was born into a family that played a prominent role in the courts of Elizabeth and James I. As a young woman, Lady Mary belonged to Queen Anne's intimate circle of friends and actively participated in masques and entertainments. Yet she violated many of the social conventions of her age by becoming the mistress of her first cousin, William Herbert, Earl of Pembroke, and by bearing him two illegitimate children. Her artistic efforts also aroused controversy when shortly after the publication of her prose romance, the *Urania*, several powerful noblemen accused her of portraying their private lives under the guise of fiction. The course of Lady Mary Wroth's tumultuous life may be traced through the vast correspondence of the Sidney family, which furnishes many details concerning her childhood, education, and later career. Surprisingly, no complete modern biography of the author exists, but because Lady Mary's activities as a courtier strongly influenced her writings, a thorough survey of the life enhances an understanding of her poetry.[1]

Lady Mary's father, Sir Robert Sidney (1563–1626), spent the first twenty-three years of his life largely in the shadow of his more famous brother Philip, who had gained international fame as a statesman, soldier, poet, and patron. Indeed, Sir Henry Sidney advised that Robert should model his life on that of his elder brother: "Imitate hys Vertues, Exercyses, Studyes, and Accyons; he ys a Rare Ornament of thys Age, the very Formular, that all well dysposed young Gentylmen of our Court, do form allsoe thear Maners and Lyfe by" (Collins, I, 246). As a young man, Robert Sidney studied briefly at Oxford and then

---

[1] Although George Ballard described Lady Mary Wroth as a person of "distinguished parts and learning," he excluded her from his collection of biographies because, as he explains in the preface, he was unable to find sufficient information on her life: *Memoirs of British Ladies* (London: T. Evans, 1775), vii. Two later biographical studies of Lady Mary Wroth include Sir Sidney Lee's brief account in the *DNB* and W. C. Waller's article, "An Extinct County Family: Wroth of Loughton Hall," *Transactions of the Essex Archaeological Society*, New Ser., VIII, 156–80. Joseph Hunter also offers a short summary of her life in his *Chorus Vatum Anglicanorum*, 6 vols., British Library Addit. MS. 24492, VI, 338. Margaret A. Witten-Hannah devotes the first chapter of her dissertation on *Urania* to a survey of the author's life: "Lady Mary Wroth's *Urania*: The Work and the Tradition" (Ph.D. dissertation, University of Auckland, 1978), 14–65.

traveled on the Continent under the care of Hubert Languet, the humanist scholar who also served as tutor to his brother.[2]

Despite the many activities in which Sir Philip Sidney was involved, he took a special interest in the education of Robert, whom he fondly addressed as "sweete Robin." In a letter of advice concerning travel on the Continent, Sidney advised his younger brother to read and reflect on Aristotle's *Ethics*. A later letter recommended the study of various historians and advised Robert to continue his interest in music: "Now sweete brother take a delight to keepe and increase your musick, you will not beleive what a want I finde of it in my melancholie times."[3] The elder Sidney also suggested that Robert keep a commonplace book, "a Table of Remembrance," as a record of his reading. Robert eventually followed this advice, for among the Sidney family papers are three bound volumes containing his notes on world history, organized in tabular form.[4]

Although in 1573 a marriage was suggested between Robert Sidney and the daughter of the twelfth Lord Berkeley, this proposal was unsuccessful.[5] Later with the help of his sister and brother-in-law, Henry Herbert, second Earl of Pembroke, Robert Sidney participated in negotiations to marry the wealthy heiress, Barbara Gamage, the only daughter of John Gamage, Lord of Coity in Glamorganshire, by his wife Gwenlleian, widow of Watkin Thomas. Shortly after the death of John Gamage on September 8, 1584, his daughter, then twenty-two years old, had been placed in the custody of her uncle, Sir Edward Stradling, whose home was besieged by suitors. Barbara Gamage's first cousin was Sir Walter Raleigh, who wrote an abrupt letter of warning to Stradling, advising him not to arrange a marriage without the queen's permission: "Sir Edwarde, Her Majesty hath nowe thrise caused letters to be written unto you, that you suffer not my kinsewoman to be boughte and solde in Wales, without her Majesties pryvete; and the consent of my L. Chamberlayne and my selfe, her father's cosen germayne."[6]

Despite Barbara's betrothal to Herbert Croft, grandson of the comptroller

[2] Andrew Clark (ed.), *Register of the University of Oxford* (Oxford: Oxford Historical Society, 1887), Vol. II, Pt. 1, p. 389.

[3] Feuillerat, III, 124, 132–33.

[4] *HMC*, De L'Isle and Dudley, I, items 1227–29, p. lix. Although Sir Robert Sidney's commonplace books contain primarily historical notes, he included as one heading, "Kings and great princes that have bin writers," I, f. 231.

[5] Malcolm W. Wallace, *The Life of Sir Philip Sidney* (Cambridge: Cambridge University Press, 1915), 160–61.

[6] John M. Traherne (ed.), *Stradling Correspondence* (London: Longman, 1840), 22. See the following accounts of Sir Robert Sidney's marriage: Wallace, *Life of Sir Philip Sidney*, 311; Philip Sidney, *The Sidneys of Penshurst* (London: S. H. Bounsfield, 1901), 23–28.

of the royal household, Robert Sidney received permission from Stradling to pursue his suit. Upon learning of this arrangement, Croft complained to the queen for immediate intervention, but he ultimately failed to outwit his rival. The preparations for a wedding between Robert Sidney and Barbara Gamage progressed so quickly that the historian Lawrence Stone has questioned whether Sidney had even met his bride before they were married on September 23, 1584, in Stradling's home.[7] The Sidney Psalter (R. 17.2), now in the Library of Trinity College, Cambridge, records the details of the ceremony; Henry Herbert, who encouraged the marriage through his friendship with Stradling, attended the service as a witness. Only two hours after the sacrament was performed, a messenger arrived with a letter from the queen expressly forbidding the wedding, yet notwithstanding the unusual circumstances surrounding the marriage, the couple eventually received the congratulations of the court. In a letter to Stradling, Francis Walsingham assured him, "But for yt the messinger affirmeth that he came to your house two howres after the mariadge sollempnised, there is no fault layde upon you by her Magestie; the mariadge being generallye well liked of, saving by such here as are partyes in the cause."[8] The Earl of Pembroke continued to intercede on behalf of his brother-in-law, and a month later he arranged for Robert's appointment as a knight of the shire of Glamorgan.

Through his marriage to Barbara Gamage, Sir Robert Sidney gained kinship with some of the most important families in Elizabeth's court. Not only was his wife a first cousin to Raleigh and Charles, Lord Howard of Effingham, but she was also related to Sir George Carey, second Lord Hunsdon, and his wife, who served as patrons to William Shakespeare and Edmund Spenser. Clearly Barbara Gamage's inheritance, which she had acquired only three weeks before the wedding, made her an attractive match for Sidney, but the lady had personal qualities and interests that enabled the union to prosper. She served as the patron of several literary works, for example, and took an active role in the education of her children. The steward Rowland Whyte commented on her diligence: "she sees them well taught, and brought up in learning and qualities fitt for their birth and condition" (HMC, De L'Isle, II, 424).

Robert Sidney accompanied his elder brother on the ill-fated expedition to the Netherlands and was present when Sir Philip Sidney died on October 17, 1586. In the state funeral at St. Paul's, held to commemorate Philip as a

[7] Lawrence Stone, *The Crisis of Aristocracy, 1558–1641* (Oxford: Clarendon Press, 1965), 660.
[8] Traherne (ed.), *Stradling Correspondence*, 30.

national hero, Robert served in the official capacity of chief mourner. Sidney was appointed in 1588 to fill his brother's post of governor of Flushing and spent most of the following decade in the Netherlands. He hired Rowland Whyte, who had accompanied him to Oxford as his confidential advisor and friend, to manage his estate at Penshurst and to keep him informed of events in England.

Although the records of the births and deaths of Sir Robert Sidney's children are incomplete, his servant, Thomas Nevitt, in a 1626 written account of the major household expenses, stated that there were eleven children, but only "sixe of them living untill they came to mens and womens estate."[9] As the eldest daughter, Lady Mary was born on October 18, the date indicated in one of Rowland Whyte's letters, although he unfortunately neglected to mention her age: "this is the birthday of Mistress Mary Sidney, which keapes me heare, and soe till Monday, when I will to court again" (HMC, De L'Isle, II, 488). The parish registers of Penshurst have no record of her birth, but it is likely to have occurred in either 1586 or 1587. If the earlier date is correct, Lady Mary would have been born the day after her uncle, Sir Philip Sidney, died from the wounds he had received at Zutphen. Lady Mary's father attended the bedside of his brother, as did Philip's wife Frances Sidney, but it is uncertain whether Barbara Sidney was also present in the Lowlands at this time.[10] The more likely date of birth is 1587, as implied by Robert's own correspondence; in a letter written on April 20, 1597, Mary is described by her father as "almost ten" (Collins, II, 43).

Of the remaining children of Sir Robert Sidney, one son, Henry, was born and died in Flushing during his father's governorship. The other children included Katherine (1589?–1616), William (1590–1612), Elizabeth (1592–1605), Philip (1594–1620), Robert (1595–1677), Bridget (1597–1599), Alice (1598–1599), Barbara (1599–1643), and Vere (1602–1606).[11] A large

[9] "Memorial of Thomas Nevitt to the Earle of Leicester," dated October 10, 1626, S. Lichfield (ed.), *Sidneiana* (London: William Nicol, 1837), 98. Collins, however, claimed that there were twelve children, I, 120; he erred by including a son named "Philip," who was actually one of the daughters. See the poem to "Mistress Philip Sidney," *Epigrams*, cxiv, in C. H. Herford and Percy Simpson (eds.), *The Works of Ben Jonson* (11 vols.; Oxford: Clarendon Press, 1925–52), VIII, 73–74.

[10] James M. Osborn, *Young Sir Philip Sidney, 1572–1577* (New Haven: Yale University Press, 1972), 515–16.

[11] Sir Robert Sidney's son Henry is mentioned in Augustine Vincent, *A Discovery of Errors in the First Edition of the Catalogue of Nobility, Published by Raphe Brooke* (London: William Jaggard, 1622), 311. The Gamage pedigree, which was prepared in 1608 and preserved in the Sidney family papers, listed six surviving children of Sir Robert Sidney and Barbara Gamage: William, Robert, Mary, Kathryn, Philipp, and Barbara (De L'Isle Papers, Kent County Record Office, U1500, F13, not listed in *HMC*).

group portrait by Marcus Gheeraerts the younger, dated 1596, now on display in the state dining room at Penshurst, shows Barbara Gamage surrounded by six of her offspring; Mary, the tallest child, stands to the right of her mother. In the same room is the full-length portrait (reproduced in the frontispiece) of Lady Mary with an archlute and a smaller painting, possibly of Barbara Gamage and Lady Mary as a young woman.[12] In his poem, "To Penshurst" (*Forest*, ii), Jonson commended Sidney's large household:

> Thy lady's noble, fruitfull, chaste withall.
> His children thy great lord may call his owne:
>   A fortune, in this age, but rarely knowne.
> They are, and have beene taught religion; Thence
>   Their gentler spirits have suck'd innocence.
> Each morne, and even, they are taught to pray,
>   With the whole houshold, and may, every day,
> Reade, in their virtuous parents noble parts,
>   The mysteries of manners, armes, and arts. (ll. 90–98)[13]

Until recently, few scholars interpreted Jonson's reference to "arts" literally because it was generally assumed that Sir Robert Sidney lacked the poetic creativity and taste that distinguished his brother. Yet in 1973 P. J. Croft announced the discovery of a manuscript collection of sixty-six poems by Sir Robert Sidney: thirty-five complete sonnets, eighteen songs, five pastorals, four short epigrams, or *strambotti*, three translations, and an elegy. The poems were never published in Sidney's lifetime but were gathered in a volume and addressed to his sister, the Countess of Pembroke. Although contemporary references to Sir Robert Sidney's poetry are very rare, John Davies of Hereford seems to allude to the verse in a poem included in the collection, *The Scourge of Folly* (1611):

[12] *HMC, De L'Isle*, VI, 552: The Inventory of Penshurst, 1627, refers to a portrait, then located in the bedroom to the parlor, of "the Countesse of Leicester and my Lady Mary Wroth in a frame." The inventory also records the group portrait of the Sidney children, the full-length portrait of Lady Mary, and two paintings no longer at Penshurst: one of Lady Mary as a child, and one of her son, James Wroth. Malcolm Rogers, assistant keeper of the National Portrait Gallery, believes that the lute portrait may be dated *ca.* 1620 by the costume, but he questions whether the face may be too young to represent the author, who would have been thirty-three or thirty-four at the time (Witten-Hannah, "Lady Mary Wroth's *Urania*," 53). The portrait is, however, dominated by the archlute, symbolic of Lady Mary Wroth's commitment to the arts, and the traditional identification is supported by the 1627 inventory. Lionel Cust attributes this portrait to Marcus Gheeraerts the younger: *The Walpole Society*, III, 39.

[13] Herford and Simpson (eds.), *Works of Ben Jonson*, VIII, 96. J. C. A. Rathmell explored the background of the poem in his article, "Jonson, Lord Lisle, and Penshurst," *ELR*, I, 250–60. See also William A. McClung, *The Country House in English Renaissance Poetry* (Berkeley: University of California Press, 1977), 135–38.

> Learning and armes, together with the Muse
> (which trinity of powers Artes heaun sett forth)
> Thy brother did into thy brest infuse
> As to the heire of all his matchlesse worth:
>> Then sith Sir Phillip still in thee abides
>> There's more in thee then all the world besides.[14]

Despite the difficulty of dating Robert Sidney's poems with accuracy, studies of the watermark of the manuscript, now at the British Library (Addit. MS 58435), have indicated that 1596 is the probable *terminus a quo* for the transcription of the poems. At this time, Sir Robert Sidney was stationed in Flushing, where he was often separated from his wife and family.[15]

Throughout much of his daughter's childhood, Sidney remained on the Continent, but he kept in touch by letter. From Flushing, he wrote to his wife, "Farewell, sweete wenche, and make much of little Mall," a nickname for his eldest daughter (*HMC*, De L'Isle, II, 100). Rowland Whyte wrote Sidney of Mary's education: "God blesse her, she is very forward in her learning, writing, and other exercises she is put to, as dawncing and the virginals" (*HMC*, De L'Isle, II, 176). The letters also reveal Sidney's willingness to send for books for his daughter's studies (*HMC*, De L'Isle, II, 321). Rowland Whyte was later proud to report prophetically to Sidney that "Mrs. Mary is grown so tall and goodly of her years, as that your Lordship cannot believe yt, unless you saw yt; and surely will prove an excellent creature" (Collins, II, 152).

As a child, Lady Mary accompanied her mother on frequent trips to the Continent, and the Sidney correspondence suggests that she remained with her family in the Lowlands from June to December, 1590. During this time her brother William was born in Flushing, and it was later necessary to have him naturalized as an Englishman.[16] Lady Mary returned to the Lowlands for a second, extended period from April to December, 1592 (*HMC*, De L'Isle, II, 126–27). When her father proposed leaving Mary and the two older children behind on a third trip in 1597, his eldest daughter became very upset: "every tyme she thinckes of yt [she] doth fall a weeping, and my Lady when she perceves yt doth beare her company" (*HMC*, De L'Isle, II, 261). Her great-

---

[14] Alexander B. Grosart (ed.), *The Complete Works of John Davies of Hereford* (2 vols.; London: Chertsey Worthies Library, 1878), Vol. II, Pt. k, p. 52.

[15] For dating of the text, see Hilton Kelliher and Katherine Duncan-Jones, "A Manuscript of Poems by Robert Sidney: Some Early Impressions," *British Library Journal*, I, 113. Studies of Sidney's life include: J. B. James, "The Other Sidney," *History Today*, XV, 183–90, and Millicent Hay, "Life of Robert Sidney, Earl of Leicester (1563–1626)" (Ph.D. dissertation, Arizona State University, 1979).

[16] Sir Simonds D'Ewes, *A Compleat Journal of the Votes of the House of Commons* (1682), Bill of March 7, 1592, p. 462.

aunt Lady Huntingdon agreed to keep Mary in England, but she later withdrew the offer and suggested that all of the children should travel to the Hague, "where they shall learn the Frensh tongue" (*HMC*, De L'Isle, II, 268). This opportunity to travel in Europe and acquire a second language was likely to have had a strong influence on Lady Mary's subsequent literary activities.

By 1600, Sidney's favor with Queen Elizabeth had begun to increase, for according to Charles Howard, Earl of Nottingham, and Ann Dudley, Countess of Warwick, the queen believed that "now your youthful toyes were out of your brain, you wold prove an honest man" (*HMC*, De L'Isle, II, 440). When Elizabeth honored Sidney with a royal visit to Penshurst, his wife and children entertained the queen with dancing, which he described in a long letter to Sir John Harington.[17] As a young girl, Mary was given a second opportunity to perform before Elizabeth, as Rowland Whyte records: "Mistress Mary on St. Stevens day [26 December] in the after noone dawnced before the Queen two galliards with one Mr. Palmer, the admirablest dawncer of this tyme; both were much comended by her Majestie: then she dawnced with a hym a corante" (*HMC*, De L'Isle, II, 618–19).

Negotiations for the marriage of the eldest daughter had begun as early as 1599, when the eldest son of Sir Thomas Manxfeeld, then fifteen years old, was proposed as a husband either for Mary or her younger sister Katherine.[18] Later, Mary was betrothed to Robert Wroth, the son of wealthy landowner Sir Robert Wroth and Susan Stonard, heiress of John Stonard of Loughton Manor, Essex and Luxborough, Chigwell. The younger Wroth was knighted by James I at Sion House in May, 1603, and in the following year he was married to Mary Sidney at Penshurst on September 27.[19] The bride received a handsome wedding present from her father's captains at Flushing in the amount of £200 "to buy her a chain of pearl, or otherwise employ as she pleased." On behalf of the donors, Sir William Browne wrote, "We all pray for her happiness in the Choice" (*HMC*, De L'Isle, III, 130). In October he acknowledged for all the contributors the safe receipt of "my Lady Wroth's remembrance of very faire gloves" (*HMC*, De L'Isle, III, 140).

[17] Norman E. McClure (ed.), *The Letters and Epigrams of Sir John Harington* (Philadelphia: University of Pennsylvania Press, 1930), 389–90.

[18] *HMC*, De L'Isle, II, 413. Mary's sister Katherine eventually married Sir Lewis Maunsell, the son of Sir Thomas Maunsell of Margam. The surname was variously spelt: Manxfeeld, Mansfeld, Maunsell.

[19] John Nichols (ed.), *The Progresses, Processions, and Magnificent Festivities of King James the First* (4 vols.; London: J. B. Nichols, 1828), I, 166. A detailed account of the Wroth family appeared in *N&Q*, 12th series, X, 434. For information concerning the ancestors of the younger Sir Robert Wroth, see D. O. Pam, *Protestant Gentlemen: The Wroths of Durants Arbour, Enfield and Loughton, Essex*, Occasional Paper (New Series), No. 26 (Enfield: Edmonton Hundred Historical Society, 1973).

Contemporary reference to her marriage also appears in Nathaniel Baxter's poem, *Sir Philip Sidneys Ouránia*, where she is described as the "Ladie M. Agape Wrotha":

> In all the Greeke None but this word is found,
> That doth containe a true description,
> Of vertues Cardinall, which doon abound
> In thine Heroycall disposition.
> *Agape* shewes thy composition:
> Love it is called in our Dialect,
> EROS is Venerie; but this Dilection,
> Chast, holy, modest, divine and perfect,
> Arcadian *Sydney* gave thee this aspect,
> When he forsooke this transitorie Globe,
> To mount the whirling Orbs with course direct,
> Adorning thee with love for marriage Robe.
> Sith famous WROTH *Agape* hath possest:
> *Ouránia* pray's a while to be your guest.[20]

Wroth's father, Sir Robert Wroth (1540–1606), had established a friendship with James I, who had visited his home at Loughton on July 18, 1605, and had stayed for two nights.[21] Upon the death of his father in 1606, the younger Robert Wroth acquired Loughton Hall, as well as the estate of Durrance in the parish of Enfield. The king continued to visit these properties while on hunting expeditions with his friends; an epigram in the collection *Linsi-Woolsie* commemorates Wroth's hospitality: "Thy Durance keeps in durance none, I heare, / Lesse be to pertake of thy bounteous cheere."[22] The shared interest in hunting helped increase Wroth's favor with James I, whose son Prince Henry also visited the lodge. One of the few surviving letters of Sir Robert Wroth, written to his friend Sir Michael Hickes, records his anticipation of a visit from the young prince. James later appointed Wroth as a riding forester, whose chief duty was to lead the king in his expeditions in search of game in the royal forest of Essex.[23] In a poem "To Sir Robert Wroth" (*Forest*, iii) Ben Jonson celebrated the hunting trips undertaken by the king and his host:

[20] Nathaniel Baxter, *Sir Philip Sydneys Ouránia, that is Endimions Song and Tragedie* (London: E. White, 1606), STC 1598, sig. A₄.

[21] Nichols (ed.), *Progresses of James I*, I, 517–18.

[22] William Gamage, *Linsi-Woolsie, or Two Centuries of Epigrammes* (Oxford: Joseph Barnes, 1613), STC 11544, sig. E₁ᵛ.

[23] *HMC*, Salisbury (Cecil), XVII (1605), 364: "The Prince is in very good health, though he has had great riding these four days past; for he has been at Sir Robert Wroth's, where he lay three nights and hunted two whole days, till we were all weary." Sir Robert Wroth's letter

Or, if thou list the night in watch to breake,
  A-bed canst heare the loud stag speake,
In spring, oft roused for thy masters sport,
  Who, for it, makes thy house his court. (ll. 21–24)

Further confirmation of the king's visits to Wroth's estates is provided in Lady Mary's letter to Queen Anne, in which she refers to the financial losses her husband has incurred "by letting the deere feede in his best grounds, to which by his lease hee is nott bound, but is content rather to lose a hundred pounde a yeere, then to trouble them, least itt might hinder the Kings sporte."[24]

Despite her marriage, Lady Mary retained her identification as a member of the Sidney family, as revealed in her coat of arms described by Henry Peacham in his *Compleat Gentleman*.[25]

This forme of bearing, is tearmed a Lozenge, and is proper to women neuer marryed, or to such in courtesie as are borne Ladies; who though they be marryed to Knights, yet they are commonly stiled and called after the Sirname of their fathers, if he be an Earle, or for the greater Honour must euer extinguish the lesse: for example, the bearer hereof is the Lady *Mary Sidney*, the late wife of Sir *Robert Wroth* Knight, and daughter of the right Honourable, *Robert* Lord *Sidney* of *Penshurst*, Viscount *Lisle*, Earle of *Leicester*, and companion of the most noble Order of the Garter, who seemeth by her late published *Urania* an inheritrix of the Diuine wit of her
Y   immor-

Lady Mary Wroth's coat of arms, in Henry Peacham's *The Compleat Gentleman* (1622). Reproduced by permission of the Huntington Library, San Marino, California.

The Sidney coat of arms, also used by the Countess of Pembroke, is mentioned in *Astrophil and Stella*: "Thou bear'st the arrow, I the arrow head" (*AS* 65.14).

Shortly after Mary Sidney's marriage to Wroth, there arose disagreements between the two. In a letter to his wife, Sir Robert Sidney described his unexpected meeting in London with Wroth, who was distressed by the behavior of his new bride:

> Heer I found my son [in law] Wroth, come up as hee tels me to despatch some business, and wil be againe at Penshurst on Fryday. I finde by him that there was some what that doth discontent him: but the particulars I

---

appears in the Lansdowne collection at the British Library: lxxxix. 96, f. 187. William R. Fisher, *The Forest of Essex* (London: Butterworth, 1887), 379–82.
  [24] Cecil Papers, 130/174; *HMC*, Salisbury (Cecil), XXII (1612–1668), 3 (undated).
  [25] Henry Peacham, *The Compleat Gentleman* (London: F. Constable, 1622), STC 19502, 161. The seal on Lady Wroth's autograph letter to the Duke of Buckingham shows her use of the coat of arms (a pheon in a lozenge): Bodleian MS Add. D. 111, ff. 173–74ᵛ.

could not get out of him, onely that hee protests that hee cannot take any exceptions to his wife, nor her cariage towards him. It were very soon for any unkindness to begin; and therefore whatsoever the matters bee, I pray you let all things be carried in the best maner til we all doe meet. For mine enemies would be very glad for such an occasion to make themselves merry at mee.

—*HMC*, De L'Isle, III, 140

Sidney's letter thus provides no specific indication of the difficulty between the newlyweds, but he suggests the need for a private marital adjustment that would spare him any embarrassing ridicule.

Unlike his bride, Sir Robert Wroth appears to have had few literary interests.[26] During his entire career, only one book was dedicated to him—a treatise on mad dogs—whose author Thomas Spackman explained that he honored Wroth because he knew "your place and pleasure is, to keepe many Hounds for Hare and Deare, and Spaniels for land and water."[27]

Regardless of the initial discord of the marriage, her husband's favor with James I helped place Lady Mary in the center of court activities. Her father Sir Robert Sidney also prospered in the Jacobean court and was appointed lord chamberlain to the queen and surveyor-general of her revenues. Through these influences, Lady Mary succeeded in gaining one of the most coveted honors in court, a role in Queen Anne's first masque, which was designed by Ben Jonson in collaboration with Inigo Jones, *The Masque of Blackness*.[28] On Twelfth Night, 1605, she joined the queen and eleven of her friends in disguising themselves as black, Ethiopian nymphs. She took the role of Baryte and walked with Lady Walsingham, Periphere; together they carried "an urn, sphered with wine," a symbol of the fruitfulness of earth. In his official capacity as lord chamberlain to Anne, Sir Robert Sidney was also in attendance, and the family papers record the expensive costume he wore for the occasion: "when the late Queene made a masque att Whitehall wherein the

---

[26] Gifford claimed, "Sir Robert Wroth, the husband of this celebrated lady, was also a poet: fortunately his genius was turned to wit, as hers to love," William Gifford and Francis Cunningham (eds.), *Works of Ben Jonson* (3 vols.; London: Chatto and Windus, 1903), III, 311. Gifford, however, appears to have confused Lady Mary Wroth's husband with his cousin, Sir Thomas Wroth (1584–1672), the author of epigrams: *An Abortive of an Idle Hour, or a Century of Epigrammes* (London: T. Dawson, 1620), STC 26052.

[27] Thomas Spackman, *A Declaration of Such Greivous Accidents as Follow the Biting of Mad Dogges, together with the Cure Thereof* (London: J. Bill, 1613), STC 22977, sig. A$_1$ⁿ.

[28] Nichols (ed.), *Progresses of James I*, I, 489; the text of the masque appears in Herford and Simpson (eds.), *Works of Ben Jonson*, VII, 161–202. The costume designs are reproduced in Stephen Orgel and Roy Strong, *Inigo Jones, The Theatre of the Stuart Court*, (2 vols.; Los Angeles: University of California Press, 1973), I, 88–93. See also D. J. Gordon, "The Imagery of Ben Jonson's *The Masque of Blackness* and *The Masque of Beauty*," *JWCI*, VI, 122–41.

maskers came in like Moores your honour made a sute of Ashe coulor satten cutt with a peach coulor taffetie and laid with silver lace." Although *The Masque of Blackness* was the first in a long series of court entertainments, it was not applauded on all sides. Dudley Carleton, an eyewitness to the performance, wrote to his friend, Sir Ralph Winwood: "Their Apparell was rich, but too light and Curtizan-like for such great ones. Instead of Vizzards, their Faces, and Arms up to the Elbows, were painted black, which was Disguise sufficient, for they were hard to be known; *but it became them nothing so well as their red and white, and you cannot imagine a more ugly Sight, then a Troop of lean-cheek'd Moors.*"[29]

Three years later Lady Mary Wroth also appeared in *The Masque of Beauty*, which featured the "same twelve daughters of Niger" who had appeared previously in *The Masque of Blackness*. An Italian visitor, Antimo Galli, commended the performance of the sequel and specifically praised Lady Mary's gracefulness. Because of the absence of complete records, it is difficult to determine the full range of subsequent entertainments she may have attended, but the prose romance *Urania* is rich in allusions to the visual detail of Jonson's masques, and it is possible that she may have witnessed *Hymenaei* (1606), *The Masque of Queenes* (1609), and *Oberon* (1611). In the *Urania* she refers directly to *Lord Hay's Masque* (1607) by Thomas Campion and probably to *Tethys' Festival* (1610) by Samuel Daniel. Included in the Newberry manuscript of her romance is a description of an imaginary masque presented by a dark-skinned Moor, the King of Tartaria, in which there is a confrontation between the allegorical figures of Cupid and Honor. She also composed an account of a pastoral masque, presented by the seer Lady Mellissea, which is filled with spectacular stage effects.[30]

As a friend to the queen, Lady Mary used her court influence to more practical ends. To provide for the upkeep of the family estate at Loughton, she wrote to Anne requesting her help in obtaining funds for the repair of the building. After thanking the queen for "the infinite favours which from you I have reseaved," Lady Mary expressed her concern that in its present condition Loughton Hall was "soe olde, and in decaye as itt's likely every day to fall

---

[29] Sidney's costume is described in "Memorial of Thomas Nevitt to the Earle of Leicester," October 10, 1626, Lichfield (ed.), *Sidneiana*, 89. Sir Ralph Winwood, *Memorials of Affairs of State in the Reigns of Q. Elizabeth and K. James I* (3 vols.; London: T. Ward, 1725), II, 44.

[30] John Orrell, "Antimo Galli's Description of *The Masque of Beauty*," *HLQ*, XLIII, 13–23. Stanza 70 of the *Rime di Antimo Galli all'Illustrissima Signora Elizabetta Talbot-Grey* (1609) describes Lady Mary. The imaginary masque of the king of Tartaria includes two songs: II. i. ff. 15–15ᵛ. All quotations from the Newberry manuscript are identified by the roman numeral II (designating the second part of *Urania*), the number of the book, and the consecutively numbered folio leaves. Lady Mellissea's pastoral masque is presented as an instructive vision: II. i. ff. 41–41ᵛ.

doune." She then requested, as a personal favor, funds for rebuilding the home since her husband had agreed to add Loughton Hall to her jointure, a promise later fulfilled according to the terms of his will. The queen's answer is not extant, but Lady Mary seems to have been granted her request. By June 30, 1612, the manor house was, according to an official description, "new built."[31]

During the period of her marriage, Lady Mary became known for her literary activities, in the roles of both poet and patron. She emulated the example set by her uncle, Sir Philip Sidney, who had encouraged other writers in their work and had become known as a "general Maecenas of learning."[32] Her father, Sir Robert Sidney, also followed the tradition of the poet-patron and provided support for a number of artists. His interests are revealed in his correspondence with the poet Sir John Harington, in which he urged his friend to "send me verses when you can" and thanked him for his translation of *Orlando Furioso*.[33] Sidney was in frequent communication with Ben Jonson and in 1608 wrote to the Earl of Shrewsbury that he was unable to send him the verses from *The Masque of Beauty* because Jonson was busy writing more for *Lord Haddington's Masque (The Hue and Cry after Cupid)*.[34] Another friend, Henry Wriothesley, third Earl of Southampton, sent him copies of the latest French songs.[35] Indeed, Sir Robert Sidney served as patron for several musical works: Robert Dowland, his godson, dedicated *A Musicall Banquet* (1610) to him, and included as the first song a galliard written in his honor. The musician Robert Jones wrote his *Second Booke of Songs* (1601) in honor of Sidney, and later, when Lady Mary began her career as a poet-patron, Jones dedicated one of his songbooks to her, *The Muses Gardin for Delights* (1610).

Lady Mary Wroth's aunt, Mary Countess of Pembroke, who gave encouragement to such writers as Samuel Daniel, Michael Drayton, and Abraham Fraunce, also left a brilliant intellectual legacy to her niece. According to

[31] Duke of Lancaster, Surveys and Depositions (10 Jac. I), as quoted by W. C. Waller, "Wroth of Loughton Hall," 163. John Nichols gave the following description of the Wroth estate: "The Manor-house is a large handsome mansion, near the church. It commands a delightful and extensive prospect over the surrounding country, and tradition says, that the Princess Anne of Denmark, afterwards Queen, retired to Loughton Hall in 1688, before the revolution commenced in the reign of her father James II." John Nichols, *Progresses of Queen Elizabeth I* (3 vols.; London: John Nichols, 1823), II, 223.

[32] Fulke Greville, *The Life of Sir Philip Sidney*, ed. Nowell Smith (Oxford: Clarendon Press, 1907), 33. For a study of the literary patronage of Sidney and his sister, see John Buxton, *Sir Philip Sidney and the English Renaissance* (2nd ed.; London: Macmillan, 1964), 89–204.

[33] McClure (ed.), *Letters of Sir John Harington*, 389 (undated).

[34] Edmund Lodge, *Illustrations of British History, Biography and Manners* (3 vols. 2nd ed.; London: John Chidley, 1838), III, Appendix, 102.

[35] Collins, II, 102; see A. L. Rowse, *Shakespeare's Southampton* (New York: Harper and Row, 1965), I, 122.

Aubrey, the Countess of Pembroke assembled at her country estate at Wilton a veritable academy: "In her time Wilton House was like a College, there were so many learned and ingeniose persons. She was the greatest patronesse of witt and learning of any lady in her time."[36] The countess' lively mind is demonstrated by her interest in chemistry and her willingness to extend patronage to scientists and physicians. Although she wrote poetry, only a small body of her original work has survived. Her metrical versions of the Psalms and her translations from French and Italian have been preserved, yet the rest of her works had been dispersed by the end of the seventeenth century: "some others are named, but supposed to be lost, or in private hands."[37] Even though Francis Osborne claimed to have "seen incomparable letters of hers," only fourteen of these have survived, and three are included in a volume specifically intended to provide models of elegance in epistolary prose.[38]

Of the remaining correspondence, there is one informal letter extant from the Countess of Pembroke to Lady Mary's mother, Barbara Gamage. Dated September 9, 1590, the letter deals with arrangements for sending a servant to the Sidney household. The countess closes, however, with a possible reference to Mary: "I wisshe it from my hart with my blessing to my pretty Daughter."[39] Because of the absence of records concerning Lary Mary Wroth's christening, we do not know if the Countess of Pembroke served as her godmother, but this letter raises the possibility and suggests that Lady Mary may have been named in honor of her aunt, one of the most distinguished Elizabethan poet-patrons.

Through her involvement in court activities, especially the performance of *The Masque of Blackness*, Lady Mary Wroth became acquainted personally with Ben Jonson. According to the *Conversations* recorded by William Drummond, Jonson claimed that he wrote a pastoral entitled, *The May Lord*, in which Lady Mary, the Countess of Rutland, and several other women were to have parts.[40] He also dedicated one of his finest plays, *The Alchemist* (1612), to Lady Mary,

[36] John Aubrey, *Brief Lives*, ed. Andrew Clark (2 vols.; Oxford: Clarendon Press, 1898), I, 311.

[37] N. H., *The Ladies' Dictionary: Being a General Entertainment for the Fair-Sex: A Work Never Attempted in English* (London: John Dunton, 1694), Wing H 99, 418. For the Countess of Pembroke's surviving poems, see Bent Juel-Jensen (ed.), *Two Poems by the Countess of Pembroke* (Oxford: Oxford University Press, 1962) and G. F. Waller (ed.), *"The Triumph of Death" and Other Unpublished and Uncollected Poems by Mary Sidney, Countess of Pembroke*, Elizabethan and Renaissance Studies (Salzburg: Institut für Englische Sprache und Literatur, 1977).

[38] Francis Osborne, *Memoirs on the Reign of King James* (London: J. Grismond, 1658), Wing O 515, 335–36, 408. Three of the Countess of Pembroke's letters are included in Sir Tobie Matthew, *A Collection of Letters*, ed. John Donne (London: Henry Herringman, 1660), Wing M 1319.

[39] British Library Addit. MS 15232, reprinted in Frances B. Young, *Mary Sidney, Countess of Pembroke* (London: David Nutt, 1912), 54.

[40] *Conversations with Drummond*, in Herford and Simpson (eds.), *Works of Ben Jonson*, I, 143.

whom he described in glowing terms as "most aequall with virtue and her blood: The Grace, and Glory of women." It is significant that of the plays reprinted in Jonson's first folio, only this one is dedicated to a woman. In his collection of epigrams (ciii), Jonson further called attention to her family heritage as a Sidney and affirmed that she lived up to the name. In a second, longer epigram (cv), he insisted on Lady Mary's role as a model woman who served as "Natures Index" and noted that when "drest in shepheards tyre, who would not say: / You were the bright *Oenone, Flora,* or *May?*" (ll. 9–10). Possibly this is a more topical reference to her role in Jonson's pastoral, but the author presented Lady Mary as the epitome of all mythological women, a composite of Diana's virtue, Athena's wisdom, and Juno's majesty. In "To Sir Robert Wroth" (*Forest,* iii) Jonson commended "thy noblest spouse" (l. 55) and called attention to the evening entertainments at her home, in which "*Apollo's* harp and *Hermes'* lyre resound, / Nor are the *Muses* strangers found" (ll. 51–52). More specifically, he praised Lady Mary's poetry in his sonnet of tribute (*Underwood,* xxviii).

There has been some speculation concerning the nature of Jonson's relationship with Lady Mary Wroth. On the basis of meager evidence, the nineteenth-century critic Frederick Fleay asserted that the Celia of Jonson's poems was really Lady Mary. His only support is given as follows:

> The allusion to Jonson's having been "a lover" in this sonnet, his exscribing the lady's MS sonnets, the juxtaposition of the Celia and Wroth poems, with many other little indications too numerous to give here, induce me to think that Lady Mary was Celia, and that Jonson met her at Penshurst in 1604. Her husband may have been jealous of the translations from Catullus, etc. made for her, and interpreted them as expressions of Jonson's own feelings. But certainly Jonson intended no unlawful suit in this instance.[41]

Curiously, Jonson included in the *Underwood* an "Ode" (xxvii) in which he referred to Celia as if she were a real person. After mentioning Petrarch's Laura and Sidney's Stella, the poet questioned, "And shall not I my *Celia* bring, / Where men may see whom I doe sing?" (ll. 31–32). But within the poems written to Celia (*Forest,* v, vi, and ix), it is extremely difficult to find proof that might link them to Lady Mary; in fact, all three lack any individualizing portrayal of the woman and closely follow the classical models of Catullus and Philostratus.[42]

[41] Frederick G. Fleay, *A Biographical Chronicle of the English Drama, 1559–1642* (2 vols.; London: Reeves and Turner, 1891), I, 327–28.

[42] For sources of the Celia poems, see Commentary, Herford and Simpson (eds.), *Works of Ben*

Jonson included several specific place names in one of the Celia poems: "all the grasse that *Rumney* yeelds, / Or the sands in *Chelsey* fields, / Or the drops in silver *Thames*" (*Forest*, vi, ll. 13–15). Although Romney is located on the east coast of Kent, near Penshurst, and the Chelsea fields could refer to the home of the Dudleys, these lines do not provide accurate identification. They may indeed point to another of the Sidney women, Elizabeth, Countess of Rutland, the daughter of Sir Philip Sidney. Jonson wrote three poems in her honor and according to the *Conversations with Drummond*, he regarded the countess as "nothing inferior to her Father" in poetry.[43] The *Conversations* also suggest that Jonson's visits to the countess aroused the anger of her husband, Roger Manners, fifth Earl of Rutland: "Ben one day being at table with my Lady Rutland, her husband comming in, accused her that she kept table to poets, of which she wrott a letter to him which he answered. My Lord intercepted the letter, but never challenged him." By contrast, the *Conversations* contain little information concerning Jonson's relationship with Lady Mary, except the cryptic statement, "my Lady wroth is unworthily maried on a Jealous husband."[44] Jonson thus seems to have taken an interest in extending courtly compliment to both of these women, perhaps in an effort to strengthen his relationship to the Sidney-Herbert family and to his chief patron, William Herbert, third Earl of Pembroke.

Lady Mary's poetry also received commendation from Jonson's friend, the Scottish writer William Drummond. Among the Hawthornden manuscripts, now at the National Library of Scotland, there are two poems, an ode and a sonnet, both dedicated to Lady Mary Wroth.[45] Although Drummond confessed in the ode that he had never met her, he described his enthusiastic response to her poetry: "Your spacious thoughts with choice inventiones free, / Show passiones power, affectiones severall straines" (ll. 5–6). Following Jonson, Drummond also used Lady Mary's favorite form, the sonnet, to pay tribute not simply to her beauty, but to her power of mind (l. 13). With the familiar pun on worth and Wroth, Drummond commended especially her "worth accomplisht."

In an introductory poem to his 1611 translation of Homer, George Chap-

---

Jonson, XI, 37–43; A. D. Fitton-Brown examined Jonson's debt to Philostratus in *MLR*, LIV, 554–57.

[43] Herford and Simpson (eds.), *Works of Ben Jonson*, I, 138. For an opposing opinion, see May N. Paulissen, "The Love Sonnets of Lady Mary Wroth: A Critical Introduction" (Ph.D. dissertation, University of Houston, 1976), 22. Paulissen uses the place names to argue for a positive identification.

[44] Herford and Simpson, *Works of Ben Jonson*, I, 142.

[45] L. E. Kastner (ed.), *The Poetical Works of William Drummond of Hawthornden* (2 vols.; Manchester: Manchester University Press, 1913), II, 271, 277.

man praised Lady Mary as "the comfort of learning, sphere of all vertues" and used the imagery of her uncle's *Astrophil and Stella* to describe her as "the Happy Starre discovered in our Sydneian Asterisme."[46] In the same year John Davies of Hereford published a commendatory sonnet on the subject of celestial music:

> To the Lady Wroth.
> In the deserved praise of heavenly Musick: resembling it
> to God Himselfe.
>
> The Motion which the nine-fold sacred quire
> Of angells make; the blisse of all the blest,
> Which (next the Highest) most fils the high'st desire
> And moves but soules that move in Pleasures rest.
> 5   The heavenly charme that lullabies our woes,
> And recollects the mind that cares distract;
> The lively death of joyfull Thoughts o'rethrowes:
> And brings rare joyes but thought on, into act,
> Which (like the soule of all the world) doth move.
> 10 The universall nature of this All;
> The life of life and soule of joy and love;
> High Raptures heaven; the That I cannot call
>   (Like God) by reall name: And what is this?
> But musick (next the Highst) the highest blisse.[47]

George Wither in his *Abuses Stript and Whipt* also praised her,

> But *Arts sweet Lover*; (unto whom I know
> There is no happie *Muse* this day remaines;
> That doth not for your *Worth* and bounty owe,
> Even himselfe, his best and sweetest straines.)[48]

Although Wither did not specifically mention her poetry, he referred to "Those *Muses* unto whom you are enclinde" (l. 15).

At the beginning of the funeral elegy *Lachrimae Lachrimarum*, published in 1613 to commemorate Sir William Sidney, Joshua Sylvester alluded to Lady Mary Wroth through the anagram of *AL-WORTH*, as indicated in the margin of the text:

> Although I knowe None, but a *Sidney's* Muse
> Worthy to sing a *Sidney's* Worthyness:

[46] George Chapman, *The Iliads of Homer* (London: N. Butler, 1611), STC 13634, sig. Gg₄ᵛ.

[47] Grosart (ed.), *Complete Works of John Davies*, II, 56. See also Davies' epigram to Lady Mary Wroth, II, 63; William Gamage's epigram 25 to Lady Mary Wroth is very similar in content: Gamage, *Linsi-Woolsie*, STC 11544, sig. D₃ᵛ.

[48] George Wither, *Abuses Stript, and Whipt* (London: F. Burton, 1613), STC 25891, sig. V₂.

None but Your Owne *AL-WORTH Sidnëides   Anagram, *La. Wroth
In whom, her *Uncle's* noble Veine renewes (ll. 1–4)[49]

The reference is an important one, because it suggests that she was writing poetry by 1613, long before the publication of her work in 1621. Indication that her poems were read in manuscript prior to publication is provided by Jonson's reference in *Underwood*, xxviii to "exscribing" her sonnets and by the existence of the Folger manuscript, which contains earlier versions of her published poetry.

Several anonymous poems in manuscript give further testimony to Lady Mary's literary activities. In the Muniment Room of the Duke of Rutland at Belvoir Castle (Letters and Papers, XXIV, f. 54) is an unsigned acrostic sonnet, beautifully embellished in gold leaf, which lauds her patronage:

> To the Honorable Lady the Lady Mary Wroth.
>
> L   ove, Birth, State, Bounty and a Noble mynde
> a   ssume in you a happie residence
> d   isposinge all your Actions to their kinde
> y   nspir'd to you by Vertues influence
>
> 5   M   arvell not Lady then that Men distrest
> a   nd such whom fortune and the world doth scorne
> r   epayre to You, since in your Noble brest
> y   mpressions of a Poor mans cares are borne
>
> W   ith you ther is a happines of fate
> 10 r   eaching att that to which Your hope aspires
> o   ver Your life guidinge your Honor'd state
> t   o tyme, to fortune and Your high desires
> h   ow Nobly then sitts Vertue in your brest
>   Richer adorn'd then is by mee exprest.

The presence of this poem among the Rutland papers is not surprising because Lady Mary and Elizabeth, Countess of Rutland, were first cousins and exchanged frequent visits.[50]

A second anonymous tribute to Lady Mary Wroth's patronage appears in a manuscript miscellany containing verses by Thomas Carew, Aurelian Townsend, Francis Beaumont, and other seventeenth-century poets, as well as the prose *Paradoxes and Problems* of John Donne. In the Wyburd manuscript at the

---

[49] Joshua Sylvester, *Lachrimae Lachrimarum* (London: H. Lownes, 1613), STC 23578, sig. H₂.

[50] *HMC*, Rutland, I, 418. Elizabeth, Countess of Rutland, visited Lady Wroth at Loughton and Durrance: *HMC*, De L'Isle, IV, 234, 236, 243, 245. The Countess of Rutland died in 1612.

Bodleian Library, the poem addressed to her is undated and contains no initials or other clues to authorship.[51] The writer, however, claims to have left the court, which he calls "the bright deceiver," to live in an Arcadian setting where he may devote his efforts to verse and meditation:

Ode: To the Lady Ma[ry] wrath

Ladie, when I from you returne
(Which be donne never by my will)
Something does from my heart distill
Soe heavy, it were not to bee borne
5   Save that new hopes the place fulfill
Of being happie in returne.

How slowe progress my Joyes have made
In our late planetary Course
Witness my self from ill to worse
10   Whose poore designement art Convey'd
My reason finding noe discourse
That should forbidd Mee to be sad.

Whether unto the Shadowes bent
I sought retyrement under trees
15   Or to the flame which each eye sees
To warme my hopes had small intent
Which way soever I turn'd myne eyes
The summe was but my discontent.

Then I resolv'd for further ease
20   For ease of my unquiett spiritt
(In which the Court could see noe Meritt)
With safest feare not to displease
To retyre home, and not deferr itt
Where I might welcome bee and please

25   Or els look out uppon the Earth
Some humble yet Convenient Cell
Whereof my self might dwell
And pass my daies in happie Mirth
Till nature pleasd to reappeale

---

[51] The Wyburd manuscript (Bodleian MS. Don. b. 9) has been described by W. Carew Hazlitt for his edition of *Poems of Thomas Carew* (London: Roxburghe Library, 1870), xv–xvi, and by Rhodes Dunlap (ed.), *Poems of Thomas Carew* (Oxford: Clarendon Press, 1949), lxix. The unsigned "Ode: To the Lady Ma[ry] wrath" is found on ff. 35ᵛ–37; neither Hazlitt nor Dunlap believed Carew to be the author. I have regularized u/v and i/j and have capitalized the first letter of each line.

30   The deed shee gave mee in my birth

With this my thoughts beganne t'aspire
To brave low-things, yet safe as truth
That ere myne age, which hard pursueth
Before myne owne perpetuall fire
35   I should discerne a Troupe of youth
All parts of my deceaseing fire.

In which deare pleadges of the love
Betweene a virtuous wife and Mee
(Which as one Flesh, one Soule should bee)
40   My happines might equall prove,
And with my hopes soe well agree
That death might change itt, not remove.

Heere I foresayde, new love to wage
With my neglected Muse forever
45   And to forsake her Service never
But spend the relique of myne age
Farre from the Court, the bright deceiver
In such a gladd Apprentissage.

Where I might bee my self and free
50   And knowe noe more Comaunds but Ten
Wide of the frownes of our great Men
And of the fained smiles I see
Aparted soe, I might againe
Retrive divine Philosophye

55   Which had to my soe great regrett
Ly'en unsaluted all too long
Whilst I was pressing in the thronge
To bee the least among the greate
But there I did advise my song
60   Should to a gentler key be sett

Security knowne but to fewe
That in the Tents of Kings doe dwell
Should bee my Study and to doe well
With greatest zeale and make least shewe
65   Or in my Solitarie Cell
With prayers to give heaven his due

My innocent delights to bee
Some grove neere to a liveing Spring
Heareing those Birds their passions Sing

70 That sleepe in May with open eye[52]
    Or under some broad leafie tree
    Enquire the Cause of every thing.

    The different motion of the heav'en
    That turnes about with speedie flight
75 The laboures of that Changeing light
    That is the lowest of the Seav'en
    What power to hearbes prescribd aright
    And what unto the Starrs is given

    Thus Ladie I resolv'd and gave
80 My rest of life to bee employd
    Never too sadd, nor yet ore joyd
    Wishing what I with ease might have
    Till with disease of age annoyde
    Mine eyes did anchor in the grave

85 After which sadd and latest Cloze
    Of Soules divided from theire stay
    Have meditations as they saye
    Myne shall her whole discourse compose
    In her soe vast, yet winged way
90 Of the best things yo'are one of those.

Although her name thus appears frequently in dedications to books and in manuscript poems, it is difficult to determine the actual extent of her role as a patron. Her reputation as a member of the Sidney family was doubtless responsible for many of the compliments addressed to her. Yet a statistical study of the role of female patrons in Renaissance England shows that she was honored in an exceptionally large number of works. Of the twenty-two women who received dedications in at least six books, all belonged to royalty or the highest aristocracy, with the two notable exceptions of Ladies Anne Bacon and Mary Wroth.[53]

Despite her fame as a patron, her literary endeavors could easily have met the same fate as much of the Countess of Pembroke's poetry, had not certain circumstances led to the publication of her work. Lady Mary's husband died on March 14, 1614, and was buried at Enfield Church, near his favorite estate of Durrance. In his will, written March 2, 1614, Sir Robert Wroth indicated

---

[52] The unknown author echoes Chaucer's famous lines from the General Prologue of *Canterbury Tales*: "And smale foules maken melodye / That slepen al the nyght with open ye" (ll. 8–9).

[53] Franklin B. Williams, "The Literary Patronesses of Renaissance England," *N&Q*, CCVII, 364–66. See also Franklin B. Williams, *Index of Dedications and Commendatory Verses in English Books Before 1614* (London: Bibliographical Society, 1962).

that he rested finally on good terms with his wife: "And I hartelie desire my sayed deere and loving wife that she will accept hereof as a testimony of my entire love and affection towards her, albeyet her sincere love, loyaltie, virtuous conversation, and behavioure towards me, have deserved a farre better recompense, yf the care of satisfying of my debts and supporting my house would have permitted the same."[54] Wroth's will also specifically entitled her to "all her books and furniture of her studdye and closett." He was eulogized in a poem by Richard Niccols, who repeated the traditional pun on his name: "In *Wroth* did place the O before the R, / And made it Worth, which since is made a star."[55]

Lady Mary's first child had been born only a month before the death of her husband. John Chamberlain wrote to Alice Carleton explaining that "Sir Robert Wroths lady after long longing hath brought him a sonne."[56] The child, named James in honor of the king, was christened with the following sponsors: the king (by his deputy, the Earl of Pembroke), the lord chamberlain to the king (the Earl of Suffolk), and Barbara Gamage.[57] But Lady Mary's situation was radically altered by her husband's death, as Chamberlain observed: she was left "a younge widow with £1,200 joynter, and a younge sonne not a moneth old: and his estate charged with £23,000 debt."[58] Although her financial problems were enormous, she insisted on handling them herself. In a letter to her father, Lady Mary related the details of her settlement with the executors of the estate over the wardship of her son, James (*HMC*, De L'Isle, V, 149–50). Her financial predicament, however, was worsened by the death of young James at Loughton on July 5, 1616.[59] As an unfortunate result, much of the estate fell to the father's uncle, John Wroth, and Lady Mary was left with mounting debts.

Despite the losses, she continued to play an active part in court and figured

[54] Nichols, *Progresses of James I*, II, 756. The will appears in Administrations of the Prerogative Court of Canterbury, 60 Lawe, and is reprinted in W. C. Waller, *Loughton, Essex* (Epping: Alfred Davis, 1900), 23–25.

[55] Richard Niccols, *Vertues Encomium, or The Image of Honour* (London: William Stansby, 1614), STC 18521, sig. E (Epigram 30, ll. 9–10).

[56] Norman E. McClure (ed.), *Letters of John Chamberlain* (2 vols; Philadelphia: American Philosophical Society, 1939), I, 512.

[57] Nichols (ed.), *Progresses of James I*, II, 756.

[58] McClure (ed.), *Letters of John Chamberlain*, I, 519.

[59] Nichols (ed.), *Progresses of James I*, II, 756. Philip Gawdy informed his cousin, "Lady Wroth's sonne and Heir dyed on Satterday last, by which meanes there is an uncle come to a great estate" (*HMC*, 7th Report, 529b). Her son, James, was buried at Enfield Church, where a coffin plate is attached to the wall of what was once the Wroth chapel. It reads: "Heere lyeth the boddey of James Wrothe the onlye sone of Sir Robert Wroth Knight and of the Lady Mary Sidne his wife eldest daughter of the Lord Vicount Lysle who dyed the 5 of July 1616 aged 2 years and 5 moneths."

in the gossip of the period. Her first cousin was William Herbert, third Earl of Pembroke, who led a distinguished career as a patron of poetry—he was the joint dedicatee of Shakespeare's first folio, as well as the patron of Jonson. He often shared his London home, Baynard's Castle, with the household of Sir Robert Sidney, who took an active interest in his training as a courtier. According to Rowland Whyte, he was a "melancholy young Man," who seemed indifferent to the quest for advancement in the queen's favor (Collins, II, 122). Yet Pembroke remained intensely loyal to his family, and when Sir Robert Sidney experienced financial difficulties in raising money for the dowry to be given to Wroth, he found that Pembroke was willing to furnish a thousand pounds (*HMC*, De L'Isle, III, 127)—a gift that was to prove highly ironical in the light of future events.

As a young man, Pembroke attracted notoriety because of his illicit affair with the courtier Mary Fitton, who bore his child. Although admitting paternity, he refused to marry her and at the queen's command was imprisoned in March, 1601. Upon his release a month later, he was banished from court and returned only after the accession of James I. He subsequently wedded Lady Mary Talbot, eldest daughter and co-heir of Gilbert Talbot, Earl of Shrewsbury, but his biographer Clarendon believed that the alliance was financially motivated, "for he paid much too dear for his wife's fortune, by taking her person into the bargain." Despite his marriage in 1604, Pembroke was linked romantically with several female courtiers, including Lady Mary Wroth. According to Clarendon, he was fascinated not so much by physical beauty as by "those advantages of the mind, as manifested an extraordinary wit, and spirit, and knowledge, and administered great pleasure in the conversation."[60]

But Pembroke and Lady Mary spent their time together enjoying more than just the advantages of the mind. A manuscript history of the Herbert-Pembroke family at the Cardiff Central Library, entitled *Herbertorum Prosapia*, states that Lady Mary Wroth bore two illegitimate children by Pembroke: "He had two naturall children by the Lady Mary Wroth the Earle of Leicesters Daughter, William who was a Captain under Sir Hen Herbert, Collonell under Grave Maurice, and dyed unmarried and Catherine the wife of Mr. Lovel neare Oxford."[61] This genealogical manuscript was compiled by Sir Thomas Herbert of Tintern, who was a cousin and acquaintance of William Herbert,

[60] Edward Hyde, first Earl of Clarendon, *History of the Rebellion*, ed. W. Dunn Macray (6 vols; Oxford: Oxford University Press, 1888), I, 73.

[61] Cardiff Central Library, Phillipps MS 5.7, p. 92. "Grave" is a foreign title, the equivalent of count. A brief reference to Lady Mary Wroth's illegitimate children occurs in Phillipps MS 3.10, f.54. M. A. Beese called attention to these records in "A Critical Edition of Poems Printed by John Donne the Younger in 1660, as Written by William Herbert, Earl of Pembroke" (B. Litt thesis, Oxford University, 1935), 98–99.

Earl of Pembroke. Through Pembroke's influence, Thomas Herbert sought advancement at court and eventually succeeded in becoming a gentleman-in-waiting to Charles I. In the years after the execution of the king, he turned to antiquarian interests, including the writing of the history of the Herbert lineage in 1681–1685. A second manuscript, also at Cardiff, refers to Lady Mary Wroth's two children by Pembroke, but mentions only their names.

The existence of the illegitimate children may help to explain a discrepancy found in earlier historical accounts, which disagree over whether Lady Mary had one or two sons.[62] As might be expected, there is very little documentary information concerning her second son, William Herbert. A possible reference to him occurs in the Sidney papers, in which Lady Mary's father wrote to his wife in 1615: "You have don very well in putting Wil away, for it had bin to greate a shame he should have stayde in the hous" (HMC, De L'Isle, V, 305). Sidney offered no further identification of "Wil." In 1640 one of Lady Mary Wroth's friends, John Leeke, mentioned her surviving son in a letter to his brother-in-law, Sir Edmund Verney: "I receved latly a curtuos and kinde letter from my owld mistres The Lady Mary Wrothe, in requitall whereof I have returned my thankfullnes in this letter wch I praye send to hir or rather send this my messenger to hir for she will wright back againe. She wrights me word that by my Lord of Pembroke's good mediation the Kinge hath given hir sonn a brave livinge in Ireland. She would send hir younge mann over to me to advise him the best I cann which I will doe" (HMC, 7th Report, 434b–435). Because the third Earl of Pembroke died in 1630, John Leeke is referring to Philip Herbert, Earl of Montgomery, who had succeeded to his brother's title. Although it is possible that the son mentioned could be a godson or adopted child, the letter suggests the active interest of the Pembroke family on behalf of the young man. The *Herbertorum Prosapia* indicates that William Herbert pursued a career as a military officer, serving first under Sir Henry Herbert and later under Prince Maurice, son of Frederick V and nephew to Charles I, one of the leaders of the royalist forces in the civil war. There are also references to a Colonel William Herbert who served under Sir Thomas Fairfax in 1645.[63] Unfortunately, Lady Mary's daughter is not mentioned in any other surviving family papers.

[62] The following accounts attribute a second son to Lady Mary Wroth: Daniel Lysons, *Environs of London* (4 vols.; London: T. Cadell and W. Davies, 1792–96), II, 317; William Robinson, *History and Antiquities of Enfield* (London: John Nichols, 1823), 148. These works mention only one son: Collins, II, 305; Philip Morant, *The History and Antiquities of the County of Essex* (2 vols.; London: T. Osborne, 1768), I, 164; *The Visitations of Essex*, Harleian Society, XIII, 330. Collins erroneously identifies the name of Lady Mary's son by Sir Robert Wroth as Robert, rather than James.

[63] *HMC*, Portland, I, 222 (May 14, 1645); I, 348 (Feb. 6, 1645/6).

Even in the licentious atmosphere of the Jacobean age, the scandal of illegitimate children would be likely to affect Lady Mary Wroth's standing as a leading court figure. In the years after her husband's death, beset with continual financial worries, she seems to have suffered a serious decline in social status. She was no longer a member of Queen Anne's intimate circle of ladies, nor was she invited to appear in masques or entertainments. A possible allusion to one of the children occurs in a poem written to Lady Mary by Edward, Lord Herbert of Cherbury:

A Merry Rime
Sent to Lady Mary Wroth upon the birth
of my Lord of Pembroke's Child.
Born in the spring.

Madam, though I'm one of those,
That every spring use to compose,
That is, add feet unto round prose.
Yet you a further art disclose,
5 You can, as everybody knows,
Add to those feet fine dainty toes,
Satyrs add nails, but they are shrews,
My muse therefore no further goes
But for her feet craves shoes and hose,
10 Let a fair season add a Rose
While thus attir'd we'll oppose,
The tragic buskins of our foes.[64]

In addition to acknowledging Lady Mary's skill as an artist, the poem strongly suggests that she has acquired enemies and lost favor.

Determined not to be a reclusive widow, Lady Mary Wroth began a close companionship with Dudley Carleton, as revealed by two letters she wrote to him in 1619 while he served as ambassador to the Hague. In these letters she mentioned his recent presence at Loughton, referred to some "rude lines" which she had given him, and thanked him profusely for a gift: "this latter favor and delicate present is such as I knowe nott whether I may bee glad of itt beeing soe rare and wellcome a juell to mee as by the estimation my injoyment is the greatest that may bee imagined for such a creaturs gaine, which shalbee cherisht with all care, and love by mee as yours and mine."[65] There was also

---

[64] G. C. Moore Smith (ed.), *Poems English and Latin of Edward, Lord Herbert of Cherbury* (Oxford: Clarendon Press, 1923), 42. Moore Smith postulated that the author may have wished to pay a compliment to Lady Mary Wroth by asking her to polish his verses; he suggested that the child may have been a son of Philip Herbert, rather than William Herbert (p. 154).

[65] *CSP, Domestic* (1619–23), 40.

some speculation that Lady Mary Wroth might marry Henry de Vere, the eighteenth Earl of Oxford (1593–1625), but he instead eventually wedded Diana Cecil.[66]

In this difficult period after her husband's death, Lady Mary continued to maintain ties to her old circle of friends. Anne Clifford recorded in her diary that she traveled to Penshurst, where she found Lady Dorothy Sidney, Lady Manners, and Lady Norris. "There was Lady Wroth who told me a great deal of news from beyond sea."[67] When Queen Anne died in 1619, Lady Mary participated as a member of the official procession at the state funeral, and she received a nominal mark of royal concern when James issued a warrant in 1621 to the Earl of Salisbury to provide her with deer from the king's forest.[68]

As both a participant and observer in the Jacobean court, Lady Mary knew the dangers of intrigue there. The Earl of Worcester, in speaking of the queen's ladies, declared: "the plotting and malice amongst them is such, that I think envy hath tied an invisible snake about most of their necks to sting one another to death."[69] In the years after Lady Mary lost her place among Anne's intimate circle of friends, she seems to have turned to the composition of a long prose romance, *The Countesse of Montgomery's Urania*. She chose to name the work in honor of a close friend and neighbor, Susan de Vere, the first wife of Sir Philip Herbert, Earl of Montgomery, brother of William Herbert. The two women had known each other as early as 1605, when they participated together in *The Masque of Blackness*, and evidence of their friendship appears in the Sidney correspondence, where frequent visits are mentioned.[70] Susan de Vere's sister, Lady Bridget Norris, and her brother, Henry, eighteenth Earl of Oxford, were also Lady Mary's close friends. The Countess of Montgomery was renowned as a great beauty, and on her wedding day, as Dudley Carleton records, the king announced fondly that "if he were unmarried, he would not give her, but keep her himself."[71]

The countess was well known for her activities as a patron, especially to John Donne, who wrote her a cordial letter enclosing a sermon she had requested.[72] Another clergyman, Robert Newton, dedicated to her in 1620

---

[66] Nichols (ed.), *Progresses of James I*, III, 547.

[67] V. Sackville-West (ed.), *The Diary of Lady Anne Clifford* (London: Heinneman, 1924), 76–77.

[68] Nichols (ed.), *Progresses of James I*, III, 541; *CSP, Domestic* (1619–23), 278.

[69] Lodge, *Illustrations*, III, 88.

[70] *HMC, De L'Isle*, III, 412, 421; IV, 45, 276, 282.

[71] Winwood, *Memorials*, II, 43; Lucy Aiken, *Memoirs of the Court of James I* (2 vols.; London: Longman, 1882), I, 205.

[72] R. C. Bald, *John Donne: A Life* (New York: Oxford University Press, 1970), 341. The letter to the Countess of Montgomery appears in John Donne, *Letters to Several Persons of Honour* (London: J. Flesher, 1651), 24–26.

The Countesse of Mountgomeries Eusebeia (STC 18509), a religious tract whose title resembles that of the *Urania*. When the countess died in 1629 from smallpox, the poet William Browne of Tavistock composed in her honor an epitaph of classic simplicity:

> Though we trust the earth with thee,
> We will not with thy memory;
> Mines of brass or marble shall
> Speak nought of thy funeral;
> 5   They are verier dust than we,
> And do beg a history:
> In thy name there is a tomb,
> If the world can give it room;
>   For a Vere and Herbert's wife
> 10   Outspeaks all tombs, outlives all life.[73]

ONE of the most significant developments in seventeenth-century prose fiction was the growth in popularity of the romance containing allusions to actual persons and places. The Scottish author John Barclay dedicated the first part of his Latin romance *Euphormionis Lusinini Satyricon* to James I in 1605, and this work has been regarded as the first satirical *roman à clef*. His later work, *Argenis*, published posthumously in 1621, greatly pleased the king, who commanded that it be translated into English. This romance became extremely popular in the Jacobean court, and Chamberlain described it as "the most delightfull fable that ever I met with."[74] Copies of *Argenis* circulated with manuscript keys to help the reader identify the actual persons represented by the fictitious characters. At the end of the English translation, the printer included a *clavis*, or key, "for the satisfaction of the Reader, and helping him to understand what persons were by the Author intended, under the faigned Names imposed by him upon them."

Like Barclay's two romances, Lady Mary Wroth's work employs some elements of the *roman à clef*, but the *Urania* also contains many purely imaginary adventures and miraculous incidents. Although all of the known surviving copies of the *Urania* have been searched for a key, comparable to the one belonging to *Argenis*, so far none has been found. One copy of the *Urania*, in the private collection of Dr. Bent Juel-Jensen, does contain annotations by an

---

[73] Gordon Goodwin (ed.), *The Poems of William Browne of Tavistock* (2 vols.; New York: Charles Scribner's, 1894), II, 294–95.

[74] McClure (ed), *Letters of John Chamberlain*, II, 428. David Fleming, "Barclay's *Satyricon*: The First Satirical *Roman à Clef*," *Modern Philology*, LXV, 95–102. See also Fleming's translation of the *Satyricon* (Nieuwkoop, Netherlands: B. de Graaf, 1973).

early seventeenth-century reader, William Davenporte. Unfortunately, these annotations make no reference to actual persons, but they are interesting as a record of one contemporary reader's response to the work. Davenporte's marginal comments contain frequent praise for Lady Mary Wroth's ability as a storyteller; for example, he notes, "Leandrus heere relates an excellent and pretye storye, Urania in the first joye off Love" (I. i. p. 34).

An important reference to the *Urania* as a *roman à clef* occurs in a letter from George Manners, seventh Earl of Rutland, dated May 31, 1640, in which he refers to a manuscript he had examined at Baynard's Castle in London (see his letter in the Appendix). Although the recipient is not specifically identified in the original letter, it is addressed to "noble cosin" and refers to "your Urania"; hence, Lady Mary seems to be the most likely correspondent: "Callinge to remembrance the favor you once did me in the sight of a Manuscrip you shewed me in your study att Banerds Castell And heere meetinge with your Urania I make bold to send this enclosed and begg a favor from you that I may read with more delight. If you please to interpret unto me the names as heere I have begunn them, wherein you shall much oblige me." It is unclear whether he is referring to a manuscript of the published *Urania*, the unpublished portion, or possibly both, but the Earl of Rutland clearly interpreted the pastoral romance as a *roman à clef*.

Because of the absence of an authorial key, it is necessary to exercise caution in identifying those passages that may refer to actual persons. One of the first critics of *Urania*, W. C. Waller, found frequent autobiographical references in the work, particularly whenever Lady Mary Wroth mentioned any noble knight and lady living together in a forest. One of the passages he cites simply does not contain enough detail to be identified as a self-reference, and another refers to the husband "as third son to an Earl," which would not apply to Sir Robert Wroth.[75] Waller also cites the very generalized story of Belizia, who is married to a Forrest Lord and lives a life of "cold despaire" because of disappointment in love (I. iv. p. 551). More recently, the story of Detareus and Bellamira has been suggested as possibly autobiographical because it describes the lives of a father and his eldest daughter, whose difference in age is twenty-four years (Sir Robert Sidney was born in 1563, and Lady Mary was probably born in 1587.[76] The story, told in three separate segments, describes Bellamira as a widow, whose only son dies, but she is betrayed by another man she loves and chooses to live in exile. Although this account may describe Lady

[75] W. C. Waller, "Wroth of Loughton Hall," 164, 172–74, refers to the following passages of *Urania* as autobiographical: I. ii. pp. 297–98; I. iv. p. 534; I. iv. p. 551.
[76] Witten-Hannah, "Lady Mary Wroth's *Urania*," 64. Bellamira's story appears in the following sections of *Urania*: I. ii. pp. 148–51; I. iii. pp. 326–37; I. iii. pp. 407–408.

Mary Wroth's own later life, the narrative of Detareus' adventures is highly sensational, involving a murder and suicide; it seems unlikely that the author would have wished to cast aspersions on the reputation of her own father, but it is extremely difficult to separate the accounts of actual events from those that are purely fictitious.

Of the many possible autobiographical references, there is one that contains a far greater concentration of detail and bears a very consistent agreement with the known facts of Lady Mary Wroth's life. Pamphilia, the central character of *Urania*, relates the account, "faigning it to be written in a Frensh story" (I. iii. p. 423). At the end of the narrative, the reader is told that it was "more exactly related then a fixion" (I. iii. p. 429). Both references tend to alert the audience to the presence of factual as opposed to imaginary events. Pamphilia begins by relating the life history of Bersindor, whose name appears to be an anagram for Robert Sidney. He is described as a "second sonne to a famous Nobleman, and one who had great imployment under the King," for Robert was the second son of Sir Henry Sidney. Bersindor's marriage "to a great Heyre in little Brittany, of rich possessions" (Barbara Gamage) is arranged through the agency of a "brother in Law" (Henry Herbert, second Earl of Pembroke). Then follows a brief account of the events leading up to the marriage, including the death of the lady's father and the hurried courtship by Bersindor. All of these details agree with the factual events described in the Stradling correspondence.

Bersindor's eldest daughter Lindamira (Lady Mary) grows up to become an active participant in court life, for she is described, immodestly perhaps, as "a Lady of great spirit, excellent qualities and beautifull enough to make many in love with her" (I. iii. p. 424). She is portrayed as a very faithful servant to the queen (Anne), but she suffers disgrace when a malicious rumor damages her reputation. Lady Mary's account of this reversal in fortune is especially moving:

> Lindamira remaining like one in a gay Masque, the night pass'd, they are in their old clothes againe, and no appearance of what was; she yet was grieved to the heart because she truly lov'd her mistris, as her disgrace went further then only discontent for the losse, or the note the world might take of it, which must like their reports be wiped away, or washed like linnen, which would bee as white againe as ever. But these pierced her heart, and she was inly afflicted, at all times she neverthelesse attended, never failing her duty, yet desirous to know the cause of this her misfortune. (I. ii. p. 424)

Lindamira fails in her effort to become reconciled to the queen, and she is obliged to retire from court to live with her husband. Although she is visited by her friends, she must endure "an unquiet life, & miserable crosses from her husband possessed with like, or more furious madnes in jealousie, her honor not touched, but cast downe, and laid open to all mens toungs and eares, to be used as they pleas'd" (I. ii. p. 425). The description of an unhappy marriage agrees with contemporary accounts of Lady Mary's alliance with Sir Robert Wroth. At the end of the narrative, Lindamira laments again the fact that the queen had withdrawn favor from her after "fourteen years unchang'd affection."

Lady Mary's description of Lindamira's downfall is valuable as an eyewitness account of the turbulent Jacobean court, but it is even more suggestive as an intimate view of the author's own career. It offers at least one possible explanation of why Lady Mary would embark on the writing of her vast prose romance, the *Urania*. Removed from the center of court life, she might wish to describe the competitive quest for royal favor, which could entail the use of any means, even slander or betrayal, to gain advancement. In addressing her romance to one of her closest friends, Susan, Countess of Montgomery, she could present a vast panorama of the world both women knew well. The result was an enormous book; there are nearly 350,000 words in the first part of the published *Urania*, and about 240,000 words in the unpublished second part. Although it is difficult to determine exactly when Lady Mary began composing her prose romance, it is likely that she did much of the writing in the years 1618–1620, when her involvement in court activities had diminished.

Shortly after the publication of the first part of the *Urania* in 1621, a violent quarrel erupted between Edward Denny, Baron of Waltham, and Lady Mary Wroth. Denny charged that he and his family had been maliciously slandered in the work and that his personal affairs had been thinly disguised in the episode of Seralius and his father-in-law.[77] Although Lady Mary claimed her innocence in satirizing Denny, she had presented an account that closely followed the known facts of his life.

Lord Denny's only daughter, Honora, was married in 1607 to James Hay, Viscount Doncaster, later created first Earl of Carlisle, a Scottish courtier who held the favor of King James. As Lady Mary records, the marriage was celebrated at the king's palace, "where great tryumphs were, Masques, and banquets, and such Court delights" (IV. iv. p. 438); Campion's Masque for Lord

[77] John J. O'Connor, "James Hay and the *Countess of Montgomery's Urania*," *N&Q*, CC, 150–52. See also Paul Salzman, "Contemporary References in Mary Wroth's *Urania*," *RES*, XXIX, 178–81.

Hay's marriage has in fact survived.[78] Lord Hay had a reputation for extravagance and proud display, as Osborne notes: he was famous for entertaining guests with an "ante-supper," in which the table was covered with rich dishes that were then thrown away before the actual meal was served.[79] Lady Mary describes the subsequent trials of Lord Hay's marriage, including his wife's adultery and the intervention of his father-in-law, Lord Denny, who threatened the life of his only daughter. Later she died, and Lord Hay became engaged to Lucy Percy, the younger daughter of the Earl of Northumberland. As contemporary letters show, the Percy family opposed the marriage, but the ceremony eventually took place in 1617.[80]

In retelling the episodes, Lady Mary spares no pains in exposing the violent behavior of both Lord Denny and James Hay. She omits mention, however, of another instance of Denny's brutality: he once tried to evict a petitioner and his family by besieging their home with twenty armed men in order to starve them into submission. His son-in-law, Lord Hay, was also frequently involved in violent disagreements and nearly fought a duel in 1613.[81] Lord Hay later quarreled with Lady Mary Wroth's younger brother, Robert, and their dispute resulted in an undignified brawl. Among the Sidney papers is a long, first-person account of the quarrel, in which Robert explains that despite his efforts, he was never able to discover the cause of Hay's rage (Collins, I, 121–27). Perhaps this final episode in 1620 had some influence on Lady Mary's decision to expose the volatile characters of Hay and his father-in-law in her book.

In two heated letters addressed to her, Lord Denny attacked the work and wrote a bitter poem in revenge. Once presumed lost, his verses are here reproduced from a contemporary manuscript:[82]

To Pamphilia from the father-in-law of Seralius

Hermophradite in show, in deed a monster
   As by thy words and works all men may conster
Thy wrathfull spite conceived an Idell book
   Brought forth a foole which like the damme doth look

---

[78] Nichols (ed.), *Progresses of James I*, II, 105–21.

[79] Osborne, *Memoirs*, 533. See also G. P. V. Akrigg, *Jacobean Pageant* (Cambridge: Harvard University Press, 1962), 163.

[80] McClure (ed.), *Letters of John Chamberlain*, II, 58, 114.

[81] *HMC*, Salisbury (Cecil), XXIII (Addenda, 1562–1605), 210; Akrigg, *Jacobean Pageant*, 255.

[82] *HMC*, Series 55, pt. 7: Manuscripts of Sir Hervey Juckes Lloyd Bruce, Preserved at Clifton Hall, Nottingham (1914), item 124. These manuscripts are now on deposit at the University of Nottingham Library, item Cl LM 85/1–5. See Josephine A. Roberts, "An Unpublished Literary Quarrel Concerning the Suppression of Mary Wroth's *Urania* (1621)," *N&Q*, CCXXII, 532–35. I wish to thank Margaret A. Witten-Hannah for offering several corrections in the transcription of the manuscripts.

5   Wherein thou strikes at some mans noble blood
      Of kinne to thine if thine be counted good
    Whose vaine comparison for want of witt
      Takes up the oystershell to play with it
    Yet common oysters such as thine gape wide
10   And take in pearles or worse at every tide
    Both frind and foe to thee are even alike
      Thy witt runns madd not caring who it strike
    These slanderous flying f[l]ames rise from the pott
      For potted witts inflamd are raging hott
15   How easy wer't to pay thee with thine owne
      Returning that which thou thy self hast throwne
    And write a thousand lies of thee at least
      And by thy lines describe a drunken beast
    This were no more to thee then thou hast donne
20   A Thrid but of thine owne which thou hast spunn
    By which thou plainly seest in thine owne glass
      How easy tis to bring a ly to pass
    Thus hast thou made thy self a lying wonder
      Fooles and their Bables seldome part asunder
25   Work o th' Workes leave idle bookes alone
      For wise and worthyer women have writte none.

Two additional copies of Lord Denny's poem, bearing a different title, "To the Lady Mary Wroth for writeing the Countes of Montgomeryes Urania," appear in seventeenth-century commonplace books.[83] Lord Denny's stinging rebuke outraged at least one later woman writer, Margaret Cavendish, Duchess of

[83] The Huntington MS HM 198 consists of two manuscripts bound in one volume with consecutively numbered leaves. Sir Edward Denny's poem to Lady Mary Wroth appears on f. 164. Lord Denny's poem is also included in British Library Addit. 22603, ff. 64ᵛ–65. The following substantive variants are found in these copies:

    l. 4 doth] did HM
    l. 5 strikes] kick'st HM,BL some mans] some mens HM; sometimes BL
    l. 6 thine] the HM, BL
    l. 7 whose] where HM,BL   comparison] comparisons HM, BL
    l. 8 the] an HM, BL
    l. 10 in] up HM, BL
    l. 12 not caring who] and cares not whom HM, BL
    l. 13 fames] flames HM, BL
    l. 17 lies] lines HM, BL
    l. 20 thine] thy BL
    l. 21 thine] thy BL
    l. 25 Work o th' Workes leave] Worke Lady woorke, lett HM, BL
    l. 26 For wise and worthyer women have writte] for wisest woomen sure have written HM, BL
        Signed: by the L:D HM; By the Ld Denny BL

Newcastle, who scornfully quoted the final couplet in her 1664 preface to *Sociable Letters*.[84]

At the end of one of his bitter messages to Lady Mary Wroth, Denny insisted that she should "repent of so many ill spent years of so vain a book" and pompously recommended that she should "redeem the time with writing as large a volume of heavenly lays and holy love as you have of lascivious tales and amorous toys; that at the last you may follow the example of your virtuous and learned aunt," the Countess of Pembroke.[85] Yet Lady Mary Wroth was not intimidated by Denny's power, influence, or insults. She responded by turning the verses back against him, and her rhymes match his, word for word:

Railing Rimes Returned upon the Author
by Mistress Mary Wrothe

Hirmophradite in sense in Art a monster
    As by your railing rimes the world may conster
Your spitefull words against a harmless booke
    Shows that an ass much like the sire doth looke
5   Men truly noble fear no touch of blood
    Nor question make of others much more good
Can such comparisons seme the want of witt
    When oysters have enflamd your blood with it
But it appeares your guiltiness gapt wide
10 And filld with Dirty doubt your brains swolne tide
Both frind and foe in deed you use alike
    And your mad witt in sherry aequall strike
These slaunderous flying flames raisd from the pott
    You know are false and raging makes you hott
15 How easily now do you receave your owne
    Turnd on your self from whence the squibb was throwne
When these few lines not thousands writt at least
    Mainly thus prove your self the drunken beast
This is far less to you then you have donne
20 A T{h}rid but of your owne all wordes worse spunn
By which you lively see in your owne glasse
    How hard it is for you to ly and pass
Thus you have made your self a lying wonder
    Fooles and their pastimes should not part asunder

[84] Margaret Cavendish, *Sociable Letters* (Menston: Scolar Press, 1969), sig. b: "It may be said to me, as one said to a Lady, *Work Lady*, Work let writing Books alone, for surely Wiser Women n'er writ one."

[85] *HMC*, Salisbury (Cecil), XXII, 161. The closing couplet of Denny's poem echoes his claim that Lady Mary should devote herself to works of biblical inspiration, rather than secular controversy.

25   Take this then now lett railing rimes alone
      For wise and worthier men have written none

Despite Lady Mary Wroth's show of courage, she was obliged to send letters to her friends for help. She wrote to William Feilding, first Earl of Denbigh, enclosing copies of the correspondence with Denny and the poems, in hopes that through his influence with James I he "might make all well with his Majesty" (*HMC*, Denbigh, V, 3).

Lady Mary even wrote to the Duke of Buckingham, the powerful friend of James I, to assure him that she never meant her book to offend and that she had already stopped the sale of it. Despite Lady Mary Wroth's request for "the king's warrant" to retrieve the copies of the *Urania*, there is no evidence in the records of the Stationers' Company that any official action was ever taken concerning the controversial volume. Her letter to Buckingham is especially interesting because she states that the books "were solde against my minde I never purposing to have had them published" (see the full text of the letter in the Appendix). An earlier critic of the *Urania*, Bridget MacCarthy, has suggested that Lady Mary composed the romance in an effort to raise money to pay her substantial debts, but in the early seventeenth century an author could expect very little financial return from publication: Milton, for example, was initially paid only £5 for *Paradise Lost*.[86] In fact, the letter to Buckingham suggests that Lady Mary was willing to suffer further financial setbacks to purchase the copies of the book, rather than allow them to remain in circulation where they might cause further embarrassment.

Although she protested to Buckingham that her purpose in writing the *Urania* was in "no way bent to give cause of offence," she chose to deal with extremely sensitive court intrigues. Indeed, her romance touched briefly on one of the most explosive incidents of James' reign, the Overbury affair. Lady Mary presented a very thinly disguised account of an unnamed gentlewoman, who described in first-person the early career of Frances Howard, Countess of Essex, and how she fell passionately in love with "this King of ungratefulness and cruelty," Robert Carr, the Earl of Somerset.[87] Despite her marriage to another lord, Robert Devereux, third Earl of Essex, she claimed, "A wife I lived, and yet a maid, my husband sometimes chafing, sometimes telling me, he thought I kept that Iuell for another: many suspicions this bred in him and

---

[86]Bridget G. MacCarthy claimed "this literary venture was a financial speculation"; *Women Writers: Their Contribution to the English Novel, 1621–1744* (Dublin: Cork University Press, 1946), 55. For a discussion of the financial rewards of Renaissance authors and the example of Milton, see Philip Gaskell, *A New Introduction to Bibliography* (New York: Oxford University Press, 1972), 183.

[87]Edward Le Comte called attention to the *Urania*'s portrayal of Frances Howard: *The*

furnished as many crosses for me" (I. iv. p. 478). At the end of a period of three years, the character relates how she renewed her relationship with "the King" (Carr), who revealed their affair to a gentleman friend (Sir Thomas Overbury). According to the *Urania*, the noblewoman was so outraged to learn that her lover would confide the secret of their relationship to another that she vowed revenge against anyone who would cruelly use her.

The account in the *Urania* thus stopped short of the actual murder of Sir Thomas Overbury in 1613, but Lady Mary Wroth provided sufficient indication of Frances Howard's emotional nature and her ruthless desperation. According to the author's contemporary view of the incident, the countess was in love with Robert Carr *before* she married Essex, and during the three-year period she remained faithful to Carr. It is interesting that Lady Mary thus attempted to view the Countess of Essex sympathetically by portraying her as the victim of passion and betrayal. When the *Urania* was published, contemporary interest in the Overbury incident remained at a high level, for the countess and her husband were pardoned and released from prison in January, 1622.[88]

Not surprisingly, Lady Mary's contemporaries acknowledged that the *Urania* contained allusions to court scandals. In a letter to Carleton, John Chamberlain reported that many people at court believed that the author "takes great libertie or rather licence to traduce whom she please, and thincks she daunces in a net."[89] Sir Aston Cokayne in his poem "A Remedy for Love" agreed, "The Lady *Wrothe's Urania* is repleat / With elegancies, but too full of heat."[90]

Although the published *Urania* unleashed a storm of criticism, it is significant that Lady Mary also wrote an unpublished manuscript, *The Secound Part of the Countesse of Montgomerys Urania*, now at the Newberry Library. The existence of this manuscript helps interpret the enigmatic conclusion of the printed *Urania*, which had described the reunion of the two central characters but had broken off in mid-sentence with the words, "Amphilanthus joying worthily in her; And" (I. iv. 558). After repeating the catch word "And," the second part of the *Urania* completes the rest of the sentence by recounting the new adventures of Pamphilia and Amphilanthus as they embarked for Italy. At the end of the second volume of the Newberry manuscript, Lady Mary Wroth

---

Notorious Lady Essex (New York: Dial, 1969), 213.

[88] William McElwee, *The Murder of Sir Thomas Overbury* (New York: Oxford University Press, 1952), 265.

[89] McClure (ed.), *Letters of John Chamberlain*, II, 427.

[90] *Poems of Sir Aston Cokayne* (London: P. Stephens, 1622), Wing C4897, 20.

left the narrative again in mid-sentence. It is unclear whether the author stopped working on the manuscript once the published first part of *Urania* was attacked, or whether she may have completed the project in a copy that has not survived. Unfortunately, the second part of the romance is not mentioned in any of the author's own correspondence.

ONE of the reasons Lady Mary favored the genre of pastoral is its mediation between the ideal realm of retreat and the actual world of court life. Lady Mary explored the genre by writing not only pastoral poetry and prose fiction, but also by composing a pastoral play in five acts, *Love's Victorie*. Her drama describes four pairs of lovers who are subject to the manipulations of Cupid and Venus. In an effort to demonstrate his powers, Cupid vows that he will bring all the lovers to confusion, but he assures his mother: "Then take noe care *loves victory* shall shine / When as your honor shall be raisd by mine" (Huntington MS HM 600, f.5; italics added). There are several other dramas with the same name: James Shirley's play *Rosania* or *Love's Victory* was licensed in 1640 and later published under the title *The Doubtful Heir* in 1652, and William Chamberlaine also issued a *Love's Victory* in 1658.[91] Neither work shows the influence of Lady Mary Wroth's play, which was written much earlier and remained unpublished.

One of the two holograph manuscripts of *Love's Victorie* originally belonged to Sir Edward Dering, who was known for his interest in amateur theatricals. Particularly in the 1620s Dering was a frequent theatergoer and an active buyer of playbooks. After the death of his first wife in 1622, Dering courted Anne Ashburnham, whose family was related to that of the powerful George Villiers, Duke of Buckingham. Throughout Dering's second marriage his interest in theatrical performances seems to have been intense. Lady Mary Wroth may have become acquainted with Dering by means of several different family ties, especially through his close friendship with her brother-in-law, Sir John Hobart (who was the husband of Lady Philip Sidney); one of Dering's account books records their visit to a London theater together. In addition, Dering's sister Margaret married Sir Peter Wroth of Blenden-Hall in Bexley, a cousin to Sir Robert Wroth.[92]

[91] Gerald E. Bentley, *The Jacobean and Caroline Stage* (7 vols.; Oxford: Oxford University Press, 1956), V, 1368.

[92] Dering's "Book of Expences" is now on deposit at the Kent County Record Office: Cat U350/ E4; the visit to the theatre with Sir John Hobart is transcribed in T. N. S. Lennam, "Sir Edward Dering's Collection of Playbooks, 1619–1624," *Shakespeare Quarterly*, XVI, 150; John Bruce, Preface to *Proceedings Principally in the County of Kent*, ed. L. B. Larking (London: Camden Society, 1862), xxv.

Some of the best evidence of the relationship between the two families may be found in a letterbook belonging to Dering at the British Library.[93] The autograph book contains three letters of invitation to members of Lady Mary's family to visit Surrenden, Dering's home. One is addressed to Sir John Hobart, who is asked to deliver a second invitation to Sir Robert Sidney, second Earl of Leicester, for August 19, 1629. An additional letter is addressed to Viscount Strangford, who was the husband of Barbara, Lady Mary's sister. There is no reference to the performance of theatricals, but such a large gathering of the two families would be an appropriate occasion.

Beginning with the earliest pastoral tragicomedy, Tasso's *Aminta*, this dramatic genre often contained personal allusions. In her play Lady Mary followed the convention by including two characters, Philisses and his sister Simena, whose names appear to be anagrams for Sir Philip Sidney and his sister, Mary Sidney, Countess of Pembroke. In *Love's Victorie* both characters are depicted as poets who give demonstrations of their art. A third character is Musella, Philisses' beloved, whose name may combine an association with the allegorical Muse of poetry and an allusion to the figure of Stella in Sidney's sonnet sequence.

Several of the characters in *Love's Victorie* also appear in the Newberry manuscript of the second part of the *Urania*. At the beginning of the second book Lady Mary describes a group of eight lovers led by a distinguished brother and sister who excel in writing poetry (II. ii. f. 5ᵛ). These two are described in detail, including a birth mark consisting of a heart, with a dart shot through it (II. ii. f. 7), probably a reference to the Sidney pheon. The basic plot of this story in the *Urania* closely parallels that of *Love's Victorie*, for the young lovers suffer as a result of Cupid's revenge. Appearing in both works are the disguised shepherds Arcas, who sings doleful ballads, and Rustick, a comic buffoon who falls in love with Magdaline; in the play her name is abbreviated to Dalina, but her fickle, aggressive character remains unchanged. The similarities between this episode of *Urania* and *Love's Victorie* may point to a close proximity in composition of the works. In spite of the difficulty of determining the play's actual date of composition, it is likely to belong to the 1620s when Lady Mary was working on the unfinished *Urania*.

In the years after the publication of her prose romance the author participated little in the court's activities and entertainments: she is recorded only in connection with the problems of settling her enormous debts. In an attempt to forestall the creditors, Lady Mary wrote to Sir Edward Conway, one of the principal secretaries of state under James I and Charles I, for a warrant of

---

[93] British Library MS 52798, ff. 27ᵛ–28ᵛ.

protection for a year. Although granted a warrant on March 11, 1623, Lady Mary Wroth was faced with the suit of Ellis Rothwell, a member of King James's household, who insisted on immediate payment. To add to Lady Mary's humiliation, Secretary Conway wrote to her father asking him to pressure his daughter for the funds and expressing the king's displeasure. In quick reply, Sir Robert Sidney insisted that his daughter had handled her own affairs since widowhood and that she would not have requested protection except in the hope of discharging all her debts.[94]

In the following years, Lady Mary was forced to repeat the degrading process of requesting warrants for protection. By January, 1624, she had paid half of her debts, but Secretary Conway insisted that a Mr. Harding must receive compensation. Lady Mary was granted a new protection in February, 1624, but she had to obtain an additional one in April, 1627, and then another in March, 1628. To help relieve Lady Mary Wroth's financial troubles, her friends entered a proposal at court to grant her a penny tax on salt produced in the towns between the Tees and the Tweed, but the index to the Patent rolls contains no entry to show that the duty was ever granted.[95]

During her later years, Lady Mary's place of residence is often difficult to determine. In April, 1621, the Sidney papers record that she was planning to move to a new house, but she apparently had difficulty paying the rent, as indicated in her pleas for protection. Her letters to Conway in 1623 and 1624 are dated from Loughton, and her father visited her there. Although very few documents concerning her later life have survived, there is mention in 1630 of Lady Wroth in residence at Loughton. Later, in a letter to his brother-in-law, Sir Edmund Verney, John Leeke referred to her in 1640, but he did not indicate where she was living.[96] Three years afterwards she was residing in Woodford, where she was preparing to profit from a transfer of Luxborough for the term of her life. The purchase money for this estate and some lands in Enfield was set at £10,000.[97] In 1643 her name appears as "Dame Mary Wrothe of Woodford" in connection with the sale of additional lands, and the Parish Book of Woodford lists her tax payments for the years 1646 and 1648. She also apparently continued to own some further holdings, for her name appears in a 1645 list of the "owners' yearly revenue and personal estates of the

[94] *CSP, Domestic* (1619–23), 596, 599.

[95] *CSP, Domestic* (1623–25), 155, 473; (1628), 136; (1628–29), 44; (1635–36), 43.

[96] *HMC*, De L'Isle, V, 423; Chancery Forest Roll, no. 153, dated Sept. 21, 1630: Item: "We finde that Sir Robte Wroth, K⁺ᵉ, deceased about sixteene yeares past did build some parte of the howse called Loughton Hall upon an old ffoundacion, nowe in the occupaccion of the Lady Wroth." *HMC*, 7th Report, 434b–435.

[97] Close Roll, Ind. inr. 19 Car. I, vii (PRO C54/3313); first cited by W. C. Waller, "Wroth of Loughton Hall," 180.

parishioners of East Wickham."[98] The only extant reference to Lady Mary Wroth's death occurs in a Chancery Deposition of 1668, in which the event is said to have occurred either in 1651 or 1653.[99]

From beneath the sparce documentary records of her life, the clear outlines of Lady Mary's forceful personality emerge. As a child, reared both at tranquil Penshurst and in the war-torn Netherlands, she was instilled with a fierce pride in the Sidney heritage. Indeed, her closest associates constantly encouraged her to sustain the family tradition by serving as a poet and a patron. To fulfill these ambitions, she faced many obstacles, including a disappointing marriage that resulted in massive debts and a lifelong struggle to settle them. But she trusted in an ability to make her own decisions, even when these might lead to greater misfortune. Her independent spirit is shown by her alliance with Pembroke and her willingness to flaunt convention by bearing his children. Although she lost her privileged position in Queen Anne's circle, she relied upon the satirical vision of her prose fiction to expose the court for its underlying corruption and hypocrisy. In her poetry, she turned to examine a more deeply personal goal which in her own life seemed to remain elusively beyond her grasp: the possibility of ever attaining an enduring human relationship in love.

[98] Conveyance Acc 454 D/DGn, June 14, 1643; Parish Book of Woodford D/p 167/1/1, April 26, 1646 and January 8, 1647/8, Essex County Record Office, Chelmsford; CSP, Domestic (Addenda, 1625–49), 675.

[99] Chancery Proceedings Before 1714: 110, Whittington (PRO C10; 110/89); first noted by W. C. Waller, "Wroth of Loughton Hall," 180.

II

THE NATURE OF THE POETRY

PAMPHILIA TO AMPHILANTHUS

LADY Mary Wroth's contemporaries recognized that her verse belonged to the Petrarchan tradition and strongly identified her as Sir Philip Sidney's successor, "In whom, her *Uncle's* noble Veine renewes."[1] Despite the early seventeenth-century fashion of "hard lines" and metaphysical wit, Lady Mary chose to reach back to a much older poetic model. Although her sonnet collection uses the voice of a female persona, the sequence contains many Elizabethan elements, especially in its structure, diction, and imagery. Yet the distinctive tone of her poems is much closer to that of Donne's lyrics, with a harsh, occasionally cynical attitude toward earthly constancy.

Lady Mary's preference for the older Petrarchan forms may be best understood in the context of a seventeenth-century critical essay on poetry, which was addressed to her: Dudley, third Baron North's "Preludium to the first Verses," which appeared as the introduction to his collection of poems.[2] In this essay North attacks the metaphysical poets who "like ill-ranging Spaniels . . . spring figures, and ravished with their extravagant fancies, pursue them in long excursions, neglecting their true gain and pretended affection." He prefers instead poetry that is clear and easily understood; "good sense and matter elegantly delivered," he argues, should be favored over "extravagancy of fancy and conceit." North eloquently defends the plain style, in which much of Lady Mary's own poetry was written. At one point, North refers directly to her: "I wish your Ladiships authority would so abate the price that our poorer abilities might hold trade without straining." By referring to her "authority," North may be alluding either to Lady Mary's role as a patron or, more likely, as a fellow poet dedicated to the style of plain eloquence. He seems

---

[1] Joshua Sylvester, *Lachrimae Lachrimarum* (London: H. Lownes, 1613), STC 23578, sig. H₂.

[2] Although Lady Mary Wroth's name is not explicitly mentioned, the essay refers to "your unimitable Uncles extant works" and includes a marginal annotation to Sir Philip Sidney. Earlier studies have suggested that the "Preludium" was addressed to Lady Mary Wroth: Lester Beaurline, "Dudley North's Criticism of Metaphysical Poetry," *HLQ*, XXV, 304; Margaret Crum, "Poetical Manuscripts of Dudley Third Baron North," *Bodleian Library Record*, X, 103.

to have composed the "Preludium" before the death of Prince Henry in 1612, when he was preparing many of his own manuscript poems.[3]

Like North's poems, Lady Mary's sonnet collection, *Pamphilia to Amphilanthus*, first circulated in manuscript among her friends. Her sequence exists in at least two distinct versions: the first, now at the Folger Library, is a fair copy in the author's hand, containing many corrections and revisions; the second text appears in a separately numbered section following the prose romance, *The Countesse of Montgomery's Urania* (1621). The two versions include many of the same sonnets, but they differ most significantly in the selection and order of the individual poems.

In identifying the central figure in her collection, Lady Mary Wroth followed Sidney's *Astrophil and Stella* by choosing a name of Greek derivation. In both versions of the sequence, the protagonist is Pamphilia, whose name means "all-loving." To emphasize that she is the speaker of the collection, Lady Mary signed the name Pamphilia in the Folger manuscript after the first group of poems (P1–55) and after the farewell sonnet (P103). Her beloved is appropriately called Amphilanthus, whose name signifies "the lover of two;" as explained in the prose text of the *Urania*, where he is shown to be unfaithful to Pamphilia (I. ii. p. 250). The prose romance supplies many additional details concerning both characters: for example, Pamphilia is described as an unusually learned woman, "being excellent in writing" (I. i. p. 51).[4]

Lady Mary may also have wished to identify her protagonist with one of the most famous women writers of antiquity—Pamphila, who lived under the reign of Nero. She was described by Edward Phillips in his *Theatrum Poetarum Anglicanorum* as a poet: "Epidaurian, the Daughter of Soteridas, of whose writing several works as well in Verse as Prose, are reckon'd up by Suidas, in all which so great was her Repute, that her statue is said to have been erected by Cephisodorus."[5] Regrettably, none of Pamphila's poetry has survived, but a small fragment of her voluminous history, written in Greek, remains. According to Suidas, Pamphila divided her history into thirty-three books, and it was

---

[3] Dudley North, *A Forest of Varieties* (London: R. Cotes, 1645), Wing N 1283. A later revised version of North's work is *A Forest Promiscuous of Several Seasons Productions* (London: D. Pakeman, 1659), Wing N 1284. A manuscript copy of Dudley North's "Preludium" appears among the North papers at the Bodleian Library: MS North e. 41.

[4] It is possible that Pamphilia's name is also intended to recall the two major heroines of Sidney's *Arcadia*, Pamela and Philoclea, who similarly express their amatory sufferings in poetry.

[5] Edward Phillips, *Theatrum Poetarum Anglicanorum* (London: Charles Smith, 1675), Wing N 2075, 245. She is also mentioned in Jacques du Bosc, *The Compleat Woman*, trans. N. N. (London: T. Harper: 1639), STC 7266, 28: "Pamphila wrote some thirty Books of History, which all her age esteemed."

well known to later writers, such as Aulus Gellius, who quoted from it. Al though there is little biographical information concerning Pamphila, she describes herself as a married woman who wrote down the conversations of her learned guests and other material gleaned from her reading in the form of an extensive commentary.[6] Like her distinguished namesake, Pamphilia is portrayed as a dedicated and prolific writer, and for obvious reasons Lady Mary Wroth's contemporaries regarded the fictional character as autobiographical. When Sir Edward Denny launched his attack against the prose romance *Urania*, he openly identified the author as Pamphilia in his verse poem. Once involved in the quarrel with Denny, Lady Mary denied the connection, but she still used the name as her own in the taunting verse reply to him.

It is far more difficult, however, to establish any real life figure behind the character of Amphilanthus. He is described only in very general terms, and surely some seventeenth-century readers of the sequence must have delighted in speculating over his identity. Lady Mary's husband, Sir Robert Wroth, would probably be excluded on the grounds that the relationship portrayed in the sequence is extramarital. Other possible candidates, previously mentioned in the account of the author's life, include Sir Dudley Carleton; Henry Vere, Earl of Oxford; and William Herbert, Earl of Pembroke. Although a case could be made for any of these men, Lady Mary Wroth provides a significant clue in the *Urania*, when she indicates that Pamphilia and Amphilanthus are first cousins (see the charts of characters on p. 147). Only William Herbert would meet this qualification, but it is important to note that Lady Mary provides few explicit indicators within the poems, in contrast to Sidney in the "Rich" sonnets of *Astrophil and Stella*.[7]

Unfortunately, only the barest circumstantial evidence exists to support the identification of the Earl of Pembroke as Amphilanthus. Early in his life, because of the scandal with Mary Fitton, Pembroke had acquired a reputation as a rake: in fact, his biographer Clarendon believed that the central flaw of his character was that "he was immoderately given up to women."[8] In addition to unfaithfulness, a second characteristic attributed to Amphilanthus is his skill

[6] The surviving fragment of Pamphila's history may be found in C. Müller (ed.), *Fragmenta Historicorum Graecorum* (Paris: Didot, 1860–61), III, 520–22. *The Attic Nights of Aulus Gellius*, trans. John C. Rolfe (3 vols; London: William Heinemann, 1927), III, 101, 113.

[7] For a more detailed discussion of the identity of Amphilanthus, see Josephine A. Roberts, "The Biographical Problem of *Pamphilia to Amphilanthus*," *Tulsa Studies in Women's Literature*, I, 43–53.

[8] Edward Hyde, first Earl of Clarendon, *History of the Rebellion*, ed. W. Dunn Macray (6 vols.; Oxford: Oxford University Press, 1888), I, 73. For an account of the Fitton scandal, see J. Dover Wilson (ed.), *An Introduction to the Sonnets of Shakespeare* (New York: Cambridge University Press, 1964), 83–87.

in composing love poetry. Although Pembroke's lyric poems were not published until thirty years after his death, his verse may be found scattered throughout a number of early seventeenth-century commonplace books. Within the second part of the *Urania* Lady Mary Wroth has the character Amphilanthus recite a poem that she claims was written by him: "Had I loved butt att that rate" (N2). The same poem appears in four different manuscripts at the British Library, where it is specifically attributed to Pembroke in three of the copies.[9] Such an ascription may be simply a coincidence, but the evidence strongly suggests that Lady Mary Wroth was paying tribute to Pembroke's artistic gifts by including his poem in the *Urania*.

As early as 1613, Lady Mary's poems were being read in manuscript by her friends. The Folger copy of *Pamphilia to Amphilanthus* consists of 110 poems plus a group of seven miscellaneous pieces that appear after the farewell sonnet, P103. Whereas the Folger manuscript contains numerous authorial corrections, which were later incorporated in the printed text, it is clear that the sonnet sequence underwent a much more substantial revision when Lady Mary began composing the *Urania* in the period of 1618–1620. The structure of the sequence was tightened by reducing the number of poems: some pieces were eliminated entirely, and others were transferred, in revised form, to the text of the prose romance. The result was a final group of eighty-three sonnets and twenty songs, which were carefully arranged in four distinct, yet interrelated, sections.[10]

The sequence opens with Pamphilia's dream vision, in which she witnesses the triumph of Venus and Cupid over her heart. As a helpless victim of love, she is powerless to overcome the troubling fears and hopes that beset her mind. The first section of fifty-five poems is designed to show Pamphilia's conflicting emotions as she attempts to resolve the struggle between passionate surrender and self-affirmation. Rather than offering a steady progression of attitudes, Lady Mary chooses to dramatize the mental processes through which Pamphilia seeks to discover the truth of her own feelings.[11] The first section ends with the persona's determination to love as an individual choice, rather than as an edict imposed by the gods (P55).

[9] Harley MS 6917, ff. 33ᵛ–34; British Library Addit. MS 25303, f. 130ᵛ; Addit. MS 21433, ff. 119ᵛ–20ᵛ; Addit. MS 10309, ff. 125–25ᵛ.

[10] Other critics have viewed the structure of the collection differently: Margaret A. Witten-Hannah described the manuscript as divided into two sections, the first entitled *Pamphilia to Amphilanthus* and the second *A Crowne of Sonnets*: "Lady Mary Wroth's *Urania*: The Work and the Tradition" (Ph.D. dissertation, University of Auckland, 1978), 143. May N. Paulissen described *Pamphilia to Amphilanthus* as containing four sequences: "The Love Sonnets of Lady Mary Wroth: A Critical Introduction" (Ph.D. dissertation, University of Houston, 1976), 191.

[11] See the editor's discussion, "Lady Mary Wroth's Sonnets: A Labyrinth of the Mind," *Journal of Women's Studies in Literature*, 1, 319–29.

Following an interlude of songs, the second section explores a darker side of passion: the lover's susceptibility to doubt, jealousy, and despair. Within the second section (P63–72) Lady Mary made the most significant revisions in the replacement of five of the original ten poems. She inserted sonnets stressing the capricious activities of Cupid, who is portrayed as a tiny, mischievous boy. This Anacreontic Cupid amuses himself by trifling with human emotions; in one sonnet he is compared to a skillful juggler, who captivates his audience: "Butt if hee play, his gaine is our lost will: / Yett childlike, wee can nott his sports refuse" (P64.13–14). Pamphilia expresses her frustration in love by denigrating Cupid as the representative of infantile, self-centered feelings: "Indeed I lov'd butt wanton boy nott hee" (P72.14). As part of the internal debate, Pamphilia's mockery produces a sudden guilty reaction, for she abruptly repents of treason against the god of love and vows to reward him with a "Crowne" of praise (P76.12).

In contrast to the Anacreontic figure of the second section, Pamphilia turns to regard Cupid as a mature, esteemed king, whose behavior is just and reasonable. The treatment of Cupid as a monarch, found in the accounts of the medieval Courts of Love, is especially stressed in the third section (P77–90).[12] Quite literally, this group of fourteen sonnets forms a circular crown, for it imitates the Italian verse form, the *corona*, in which the last line of the first sonnet serves as the first line of the next. Pamphilia begins by acknowledging the tremendous power exercised by the ruler in his Court of Love, but she soon finds it impossible to sustain her glorification of Cupid. By the end of the third series of sonnets, she admits that ambivalent feelings still disturb her: "Curst jealousie doth all her forces bend / To my undoing; thus my harmes I see" (P90.11–12). Once more, Pamphilia's skepticism returns, and she admits that in her own mind she finds no single, all-powerful monarch. An interlude of songs follows in which she continues to debate which representation of Cupid comes closest to the truth. Surprisingly, one of the few nineteenth-century critics of Lady Mary's poetry, Frederick Rowton, failed to notice the significance of this debate. After reading two of the opposing poems, he attacked what he believed were the author's inconsistencies: "The reader will not fail to notice the remarkably contradictory sentiments which these two poems present upon that important subject. . . . which doctrine are we to believe?"[13] Rowton failed to see that Lady Mary's purpose was not merely to present a doctrine, but rather to show the mind of a woman in the process of evaluating the varied interpretations of the essence of love.

[12] W. A. Neilson, *The Origins and Sources of the Court of Love* (1899; rpt. New York: Russell and Russell, 1967), 24–70.

[13] Frederick Rowton (ed.), *The Female Poets of Great Britain* (London: Longman, 1848), 29.

Finl section

Following her failed attempt to idealize passion, Pamphilia gradually begins in the final section of the sequence to accept pain as a necessary complement to joy in love and to recognize the unpredictability of human emotions. Many of the sonnets in the last group (P95–103) are extremely melancholy in tone, and the predominant imagery is that of the winter world of clouds, shadows, and darkness. In the last two sonnets, however, a fragile hope emerges, for Pamphilia's sufferings have taught her to prize a type of love finer than she once accepted. She vows to surmount her inner conflicts and to focus attention on heavenly love, "which shall eternall goodnes prove" (P103.6).

This final version of Lady Mary Wroth's sonnet sequence, with its careful charting of the ebb and flow of human emotions, owes much to the model of Sidney's *Astrophil and Stella*. Like Astrophil, Pamphilia engages in an internal struggle between rebellion and submission to love. Yet whereas Sidney's protagonist regards Stella as the epitome of virtue and beauty, Pamphilia shares no delusions about Amphilanthus: she recognizes his inconstancy, and many of the sonnets deal with the theme of betrayal. In fact, the bitter tone of Lady Mary's sequence more closely resembles the final section of *Astrophil*, in which the lover is estranged from his beloved. Thus in her collection Lady Mary eliminates much of the playful humor associated with the depiction of Sidney's frustrated suitor (for example, in the poems to Stella's lap dog or her bird). She does follow Sidney by including a number of sonnets that deal with the adventures of the Anacreontic Cupid, who had become a very popular figure in English poetry as a result of the overwhelming success of *Astrophil and Stella*.[14] Although the tracing of specific sources in Lady Mary Wroth's poems is often impossible because of traditional imagery and *topoi* shared by many of the later Elizabethan sonneteers, the notes to her poems list a number of likely borrowings from her uncle's collection.

Lady Mary also adopted several of Sidney's technical innovations in her sonnets. One distinctive mark of her style is the use of the compound epithet, which Sidney had made famous.[15] Her compounds range from the simplest, such as "my woe-kil'd heart" (P13.4) to the most complex, as in "theyr love-burnt-harts desires" (P29.10). She also followed Sidney in the use of a great variety of stanzaic and metrical patterns in her verse. In the first section of *Pamphilia to Amphilanthus*, she alternated groups of sonnets according to the Italian and English modes: Italian, P1–6, 15–20, 29–34; English, 8–13, 22–27 (25 excepted), 36–41. Departing from Sidney's marked preference for one major sonnet form (*abbaabba cdcdee*), which his brother, Sir Robert Sidney,

---

[14] See Lisle C. John, *Elizabethan Sonnet Sequences: Studies in Conventional Conceits* (New York: Columbia University Press, 1938), 67–77.

[15] Ringler, liii.

also adopted, Lady Mary favored a rhyme scheme using a slightly different sestet (*abba abba ccdeed*). She included a total of twenty-one variations in the rhyme scheme, far more than in *Astrophil*.[16]

Another important source of influence for Lady Mary's poetry was her father's verse, which has been only recently discovered in a unique manuscript. It is likely that many of these poems were written while Sir Robert Sidney was stationed in Flushing, and they reflect his wartime experience: the anguish of separation from loved ones, the horrors of death, and the depths of personal despair. Despite the fact that half of Sir Robert Sidney's poems are sonnets, he uses a far different tone and imagery than is found in *Astrophil*. Many of the poems contain vivid references to excruciating physical pain: one sonnet describes a galley slave who is beaten continually, "whoe on the oare doth stretch / his lims all day, all night his wounds doth binde" (Sonnet 19, 11.7–8). Even though he wrote love poems addressed to a lady named Charys, these are marked as well by a dark, brooding hopelessness. He rarely includes the lighter poems on Cupid found in the sequences composed either by his brother or by Lady Mary Wroth.[17]

Few of Sir Robert Sidney's intimate circle of family and friends seem to have been acquainted with his verse. It is not known exactly when Lady Mary gained access to her father's writings, but her knowledge of them can be seen in her imitations of several specific poems.[18] The most important is her "Crowne of Sonnets," probably based on Sir Robert Sidney's incomplete *corona*, which consists of only four poems and a quatrain of a fifth. At the bottom of the

---

[16] Lady Mary Wroth wrote a total of 105 sonnets: 83 in *Pamphilia to Amphilanthus*, 19 in the published *Urania*, and 3 in the Newberry manuscript. She tended to use highly compressed schemes; out of a total of 28 patterns, the five most popular ones include:

abba abba ccdeed	—32 sonnets
abab baba cdcdee	—18 sonnets
abba abba cddcee	—12 sonnets
abab baba ccdeed	— 8 sonnets
abba abba cdcdee	— 5 sonnets

For a comparison with Sidney's variations in the sonnet form, see Ringler, 448.

[17] Peter J. Croft announced his discovery of Sir Robert Sidney's poems in *Autograph Poetry in the English Language* (2 vols.; London: Cassell, 1973), I, 22. He described the manuscript in the *Catalogue of Valuable Printed Books* . . ., [Monday, 18 November; Tuesday, 19 November 1974] (London: Sotheby, 1974), Lot 390, 95–101.

[18] Hilton Kelliher and Katherine Duncan-Jones call attention to Lady Mary Wroth's imitations of three of her father's poems, "A Manuscript of Poems by Robert Sidney: Some Early Impressions," *British Library Journal*, I, 114–15: Robert Sidney's Song 3 (P7), Song 11 (P42), Song 20 (U30). See also Deborah K. Wright, "The Poetry of Robert Sidney: A Critical Study of his Autograph Manuscript" (Ph.D. dissertation, Miami University, 1980) and Katherine Duncan-Jones, "'Rosis and Lysa': Selections from the Poems of Sir Robert Sidney," *ELR*, IX, 240–63, along with the same author's modernized transcription of the entire manuscript, "The Poems of Sir Robert Sidney," *English*, XXX, 3–72.

[handwritten margin note: 17 sonnets in his "corona"?]

manuscript is Sir Robert Sidney's own handwritten comment that "the rest of the 13 sonnets doth want" (f. 15). Perhaps this unfinished "Crowne" served as a challenge to his daughter's poetic talents, for she attempted an even more complex version—a chain of fourteen sonnets. Rather than writing her *corona* to Charys or any other individual, she deliberately chose to dedicate it to the most idealistic concept of love. Yet as we have seen, the persona of her "Crowne of Sonnets" learns that it is impossible to sustain a perfect vision and returns at the end to her awareness of the human weaknesses that undermine love. One of the greatest similarities between the verse of father and daughter may be seen in this attitude of somber introspection. Appropriately, Sir Robert Sidney pointed to the dominant tone of both collections when in the final couplet to Song 19 he wrote, "But greef and angwish are the measure / that do immortalize our loves."

Apart from the influence of the Sidneys, it is more difficult to determine the other sources of Lady Mary's poetry. Much of her mythological imagery derives from Ovid, who was one of her favorite authors. She pays tribute to him in the *Urania* when the character Antissia meets a scholar, "one who had bin mad in studying how to make a piece of poetrie to excell Ovid, and to bee more admired then hee is" (II. i. f. 13). She was also an avid reader of Spenser's *Faerie Queene*, as shown in her borrowings (see U47). It is possible that she had read Shakespeare's sonnets, but the evidence is not conclusive.[19] Of the other lyrical poets available to her, Samuel Daniel, Fulke Greville, Ben Jonson, and William Herbert may have served as influences, although specific borrowings from these writers are more doubtful.

Lady Mary Wroth was thus unlikely to proclaim that she was "no pickpurse of another's wit" (*AS* 74), but she did offer a number of important innovations to the sonnet sequence. Through the creation of a female persona, she was the first English writer to reverse the sexual roles within a complete sonnet collection. Regardless of the traditional apostrophes to night, sleep, hope, absence, and despair contained in many of her poems, she introduced a significant change in the focus of the sequence. Unlike the male sonneteers who often lavished praise (or mock dispraise) upon the woman's physical attributes, Lady Mary's collection deliberately subordinates the role of the beloved. Because the rhetoric of wooing or courtship is largely absent from her collection, the poet places far greater emphasis on the persona's internal struggles, as she comes to recognize the potential dangers inherent in romantic love.

For Pamphilia, constancy is a cardinal virtue, and she is in fact renowned as the "true paterne of excellent affection and affections truth" (I. iii. p. 315).

---

[19] Waller, 9.

But faced with Amphilanthus' betrayal, she must begin to re-examine her own self-deceptive misconceptions of love, both in the guise of the infantile and the idealized versions of Cupid. By the end of the sequence, the persona prepares to abandon faith in any lasting human relationship and to redirect her constancy toward divine love.[20] The final sonnet is ultimately reminiscent of Sir Philip Sidney's famous farewell to physical passion, "Leave me ô Love, which reachest but to dust" (CS 32).

Ironically, Lady Mary Wroth's prose fiction demonstrates that Pamphilia is unable to sustain such ethereal constancy. Within the *Urania* the internal debate concerning love becomes even more explicit than in the revised version of the sonnet sequence, for the fiction shows how Pamphilia confronts the fundamental inequity of the double standard, in which women are expected to remain constant whereas men are not. She wittily observes the difference: "being a man, it was necessary for him to exceede a woman in all things, so much as inconstancie was found fit for him to excell her in" (I. ii. p. 264). Although Pamphilia decides to remain a virgin monarch and dedicate her life to the service of her country, in imitation of the historical Queen Elizabeth, she eventually relinquishes her vows. She comes to recognize the impossibility of maintaining perfect constancy in a world of human frailty: "butt itt is a strange, and rare thing in reason that all men showld bee borne under that fatall rule of inconstancy, for when did any one see a man constant from his birthe to his end, therfor women must think itt a desperate destinie for them to bee constant to inconstancy, butt alas this is woemens fortunes" (II. i. f. 8ᵛ). In the Newberry manuscript of the second part of the *Urania*, which is characterized by an atmosphere of profound disillusionment, both Pamphilia and Amphilanthus betray their pledges of constancy to marry other partners.

The URANIA

The intense, ambivalent passion of Pamphilia for Amphilanthus thus furnished the nucleus for Lady Mary's immense work of prose fiction, the *Urania*. In both the published and unpublished parts of the romance the unhappy relationship of these two characters serves as the central focus of an intricately woven plot in which Pamphilia's vow of constancy in love is tested by a series of trials, separations, and deceptions, involving an enormous cast of additional

[20] Two studies that stress Pamphilia's ascent to divine love include Elaine V. Beilin, "'The Onely Perfect Vertue': Constancy in Mary Wroth's *Pamphilia to Amphilanthus*," *Spenser Studies*, II, 229–45, and May N. Paulissen, "Forgotten Love Sonnets of the Court of King James: The Sonnets of Lady Mary Wroth," *Publications of the Missouri Philological Association*, III, 24–31.

characters. In accordance with the genre of pastoral romance, the *Urania* features a variety of narrators whose tales mirror the changing moods and problems of the central heroine. Lady Mary Wroth organized her cast of characters as members of an imaginary royal family, descending from the kings of Morea and Naples (see the genealogical chart on p. 147, which identifies all the major figures). In the unpublished part of the *Urania* the same family relationships exist, but the author established a second generation of characters.

In constructing her romance, Lady Mary drew freely upon Sir Philip Sidney's pastoral fiction for inspiration. Her opening scene echoes the beginning of the *New Arcadia*, in which the shepherds Strephon and Klaius lament the disappearance of a mysterious shepherdess, Urania, who is described as both a simple country girl and a great goddess, the Venus Urania, dividing "her heavenly beautie, betweene the Earth and the Sea."[21] Lady Mary extends the fiction by describing the quest Urania undertakes to learn her true identity; through amorous adventures, she is led to recognize her royal parentage, and in one of the climactic moments of the romance she recovers a book describing her life history (I. iii. p. 388). The closest friend of Pamphilia, Urania functions as a confidante and as a source of sound advice concerning human relationships.

Although Lady Mary used the *Arcadia* as a point of departure for her romance, she excluded many of the distinctive elements found in Sidney's work. Most of her characters belong to the highest aristocratic class, and there are thus few base-born figures, such as Dametas or Mopsa, who provided burlesque humor in the *Arcadia*. In addition to restricting the tone of the work, Lady Mary devoted little attention to the political issues that fascinated Sidney: the nature of kingship, the administration of justice and mercy, the question of rebellion. She also severely limited the accounts of battles and heroic deeds, in order to focus major attention on the topic of love.

Throughout the text of the *Urania*, Lady Mary inserted poems to emphasize key moments of crisis and discovery. She included nineteen sonnets, many of which were appropriately assigned to Pamphilia, who confesses, "I seldome write any but sonnets" (I. iii. p. 392). The remaining thirty-seven poems consist of a wide variety of forms—madrigals, dialogues, ballads. The longest poem (U52) is a well-paced pastoral narrative which ends in an Ovidian metamorphosis of the grief-stricken lover. Lady Mary experimented with quantitative verse in at least one poem (U49), in which she imitated sapphics. As in the *Old Arcadia*, where eclogues appear at the conclusion of each book,

[21] Sidney, *Works*, I, 6.

she placed at the end of the first book of *Urania* a group of three songs (U13–15), which answer each other.

When Lady Mary introduced previously written poems into the text of the *Urania*, she often heavily revised the verse to adapt to the speaker and the situation. An excellent example is U24, which was changed to fit the character of Antissia, an impulsive, high-strung woman who is in love with Amphilanthus. Lady Mary revised the poem to emphasize Antissia's extreme feelings as she begins to recognize that her affection can never be requited. By substituting highly explosive language, the poet reveals Antissia's childish, self-centered attitude toward love and her refusal to accept responsibility for her actions. Antissia's final comparison of herself to a salamander, which according to Renaissance mythographers can take its nourishment from flames, expresses the obsessive nature of her feelings; later in the *Urania* when she plots to murder Amphilanthus, she fulfills her vow emphatically expressed in the final version of the poem: "soe shall those flames my being give" (U24.26). The early copies of U17 and U18 (in the Folger manuscript) and U9 (in the British Library manuscript) also may be compared with the later versions to show Lady Mary's process of revising the poetry to suit the context of the fiction.

The speakers of the poems in the *Urania* include a wide variety of human types, ranging from saintly lovers to gigolos. Because the romance often provides significant information concerning the speakers, I have included in the notes a brief account of the background of each poem. In many cases, the prose text also directs the critical interpretation of a poem, as shown in U35, where the forsaken lover Dorolina delivers a catalogue of famous women deceived by men. Although the speaker herself confesses that "the Verses are long and teadious" (I. iii. p. 418), her admission reinforces the despairing mood of the poem. A very different speaker is the Florentine knight (U53), whose poetry reflects his humorous inability to stop talking: he "talked on, and regarded, or not, said Verses, spake Prose, and Rime againe, no more heeding answers" (I. iv. p. 538).

The second part of the *Urania*, found in the Newberry manuscript, contains far less poetry. Although Lady Mary Wroth continued to use a mixture of speakers, the poems tend to be mainly songs, with only a few sonnets (N1, N3, N17). The verse shows her interest in exploring the mind under states of extreme pressure, as in N6 and N7, which are assigned to Antissia, who has now been driven insane. Yet the second volume of the Newberry text contains only one poem, which suggests that the prose narrative was occupying a greater degree of Lady Mary's attention. In the second part of the *Urania*, which was left unfinished, one of the characters alluded to the difficulty of continuing to write poetry in a hostile environment: "wee have some [poets] that dare venture in thes troublesom times, for itt [is] dangerous, butt noe danger can make dauntless spiritts stoope" (II. ii. f. 5ᵛ). Partly because of the controversy that arose over the first part of the *Urania*, the second part did not appear in print, and it is significant that the manuscript contains several blanks for poems which were never included.

Despite Lady Mary's willingness to remove copies of the published *Urania* from sale, the controversy surrounding the book did not deter seventeenth-century readers. Henry Peacham, for example, claimed in 1622 that the "late-published *Urania*" had shown the author to be the "inheritrix of the Divine Wit of her Immortle Vncle." In a catalogue of women writers, Thomas Heywood described her as "the ingenious Ladie, the late composer of our extant *Urania*," and Edward Phillips mentioned her under the section, "Women Among the Moderns Eminent for Poetry," where he referred to the author as "an Emulatress perhaps of Philip Sidney's *Arcadia*." In *The Ladies Dictionary*, the *Urania* was also described in comparison with Sidney's work: "a Poetical History, much of the same Nature, being a very curious piece, tho not meeting with the like general reception." [22]

It is possible that the *Urania* furnished a contemporary dramatist, James Shirley, with plot material for his play, *The Politician* (1655). Gerard Langbaine in his *Account of the English Dramatick Poets* (1691) first observed a similarity between the play and one of the stories contained in the romance: "A story resembling this, I have read in the first book of the Countess of *Montgomery's Urania*, concerning the King of *Romania*, the Prince *Antissius*, and his Mother-in-law." [23] Langbaine referred to the tale of the treacherous second wife of the king of Romania, who cleverly turned the king against his faithful son Antissius and attempted to seize the throne through a conspiracy with one of his servants. [24] Shirley's basic plot is very similar, for the king of Norway was deceived by his second wife, Marpisa, who slandered the young prince and

---

[22] Henry Peacham, *The Compleat Gentleman* (London: F. Constable, 1622), STC 19502, 161; Thomas Heywood, *Gynaikeion: or Nine Bookes of Various History, Concerninge Women* (London: A. Islip, 1624), STC 13326, 398; Phillips, *Theatrum Poetarum Anglicanorum* (London: Charles Smith, 1675), 260; N. H., *The Ladies Dictionary: Being a General Entertainment for the Fair-Sex: A Work Never Attempted in English* (London: John Dunton, 1694), Wing N99, 418.

[23] Gerard Langbaine the Younger, *An Account of the English Dramatick Poets* (Oxford: G. West and H. Clements, 1691), Wing L373, 481.

[24] Lady Mary Wroth's tale of the king of Romania appeared in I, i, pp. 24–27, 42–48, 58–61. Edward Huberman examined Shirley's use of the plot material from *Urania* in his edition of *The Politician* (Ph.D. dissertation, Duke University, 1934), 2–15. He suggests that Lady Mary's account of the Romanian king and Shirley's play may also draw upon a common source—the episode of Plangus and his stepmother in Sidney's *New Arcadia*. See also Robert S. Forsythe, *The Relation of Shirley's Plays to the Elizabethan Drama* (New York: Columbia University Press, 1914), 271–79.

plotted to have him killed as part of her effort to usurp the throne with the assistance of the politician, Gotharus. Shirley's court, like that of *Urania*, is rife with corruption and villainy, yet despite the shift in setting to Norway, the play contains close parallels to Lady Mary's principal characters. The major difference is that the dramatist devotes greater attention to Gotharus and the double betrayal of Marpisa and her co-conspirator. In creating his plays, Shirley frequently borrowed plot material from prose romances, and a dramatic version of *Arcadia* is often attributed to him.[25]

The *Urania* was little known to readers in succeeding generations, but the literary historian Sir Egerton Brydges printed some extracts from Lady Mary Wroth's work in 1815, with the following judgment on the merits of the poetry, as compared with the prose: "It will be more to the purpose of modern literature to give copious extracts from its numerous, intermingled poetry; as specimens of Lady Mary Wrothe's talents never occur in modern revivals of forgotten genius."[26]

LOVE'S VICTORIE

It is not surprising that Lady Mary would undertake the writing of a play as a result of her active interest and participation in dramatic entertainments. She had performed in masques and probably in amateur theatricals, and she also attended plays, as suggested by her references to the theater in the *Urania*: "yet he unmoveable, was no further wrought, then if he had seene a delicate play-boy acte a loving womans part, and knowing him a Boy, lik'd onely his action" (I. i. p. 60). In writing her own play, *Love's Victorie*, Lady Mary followed many of the established conventions of one of the most popular forms of early seventeenth-century drama, the pastoral tragicomedy, yet it is clear that no single play served as a dominant source.[27] Rather, she seems to have drawn upon a broad range of literary predecessors.

Lady Mary carefully designed her play to provide two internal commentators on the action—the characters Venus and Cupid, who observe and direct the behavior of ten young people. When Venus notices that some of the

[25] Alfred B. Harbage questioned the attribution: "The Authorship of the Dramatic *Arcadia*," *Modern Philology*, XXXV, 233–37.

[26] Sir Egerton Brydges, *Restituta, or Titles, Extracts, and Characters of Old Books in English Literature Revived* (4 vols.; London: T. Bensley, 1815), II, 264.

[27] For the development of the pastoral tragicomedy as a distinctive genre, see Homer Smith, "Pastoral Influence in the English Drama," *PMLA*, XII, 355–460; Josephine Laidler, "A History of Pastoral Drama in England Until 1700," *Englische Studien*, XXXV, 193–259; W. W. Greg, *Pastoral Poetry and Pastoral Drama* (1905; rpt. New York: Russell and Russell, 1959); Marvin T. Herrick, *Tragicomedy* (Urbana: University of Illinois Press, 1955), 125–71.

humans disdain the power of Cupid, she urges her son to show that "Love can in all spiritts raine" (f. 5). Once her son agrees to make each of the young lovers suffer, he uses his arrows of "jealousie, malice, feare, and mistrust" (f. 5) to throw the mortals into confusion. Lady Mary creates dramatic irony by showing that though the young lovers cry out to the gods, they are largely unaware of their presence on stage as manipulators of the plot. The mythological characters also advise the audience of the progress of the tragicomedy and reassure us that "sweetest is that love obtaind with paine" (f. 20^v).

Lady Mary's use of the mythological figures is reminiscent of a device found in the earliest model of pastoral tragicomedy, Tasso's *Aminta*.[28] Tasso included a prologue to his play in which a belligerent Cupid announces his determination to prove his power. Venus does not appear, but Tasso's Cupid explains that she has given him instructions. Although the mythological figure occurs only at the beginning of the *Aminta*, this device was copied by a number of successive playwrights. Samuel Daniel, for example, introduced his pastoral tragicomedy, *Hymen's Triumph* (1614) with the mythological figure of Hymen, who struggles with the forces of envy, avarice, and jealousy. Indeed, the use of the mythological commentators was so popular that Jonson mocked the device in the induction to *Cynthia's Revels* (1600): "Take anie of our play-bookes without a CUPID, or a MERCURY in it, and burne it for a heretique in Poetrie."[29] Of course, Jonson himself used Cupid as a commentator in this play and in a series of entertainments: *The Christmas Masque* (1616), *Love Freed from Ignorance and Folly* (1616), and *A Challenge at Tilt* (1616). He included both Venus and Cupid as participants in the Haddington Masque, or *The Hue and Cry After Cupid* (1608), a masque Lady Mary may have attended. Because of her friendship with Jonson, there is a strong possibility that she was influenced by the dramatist's use of the internal commentators, particularly since in plays like *Cynthia's Revels* they recur throughout the action, rather than appearing only in the prologue.[30]

Just as the *Urania* offers an anatomy of amorous relationships, so Lady Mary Wroth's play presents four different couples who demonstrate that "love hath as many ways / to winn, as to destroy" (f. 3). She depicts Philisses and Musella as the virtuous lovers, whose union withstands a period of misunderstanding and a threat of external interference. The love of the second couple is disrupted

---

[28] Torquato Tasso, *Aminta*, ed. Ernest Grillo (London: J. M. Dent, 1924), 51.

[29] Herford and Simpson (eds.), *Works of Ben Jonson*, IV, 36 (ll. 47–49). Jonson also noted the popularity of Cupid as a presenter of masques: "his old task, / Turn the stale prologue to some painted mask" (*The Forest*, 10, ll. 19–20).

[30] Another possible influence on the design of *Love's Victorie*, with its intermingling of mortals and immortals, would be Shakespeare's *A Midsummer Night's Dream*, but there is no proof that Lady Mary had read or seen the play.

by baser emotions: Lissius first needs to overcome his scornful pride, and his beloved Simena must learn to control her jealousy. Lady Mary shows that self-doubt and mutual mistrust nearly bring the love of this second pair "to deaths river brink" (f. 18). The third couple, the Forester and Silvesta, are neoplatonic idealists who have chosen both love and chastity. Their comic counterparts are Rustick and Dalina, who frantically pursue earthly, physical lust. Lady Mary's use of the four contrasting couples reinforces her theme of the variety of human response in love and resembles the complex plotting of other pastoral tragicomedies, such as John Fletcher's *The Faithful Shepherdess* (1608).

One of the theoretical questions faced by the dramatists of pastoral was whether to include comic elements in their plays. Samuel Daniel argued in the prologue to *Hymen's Triumph* that the pastoral should deal with "tender passions, motions soft, and grave."[31] Jonson, however, took the opposite position and maintained, according to the *Conversations with Drummond*, that comedy belonged as an essential ingredient of the pastoral. On this issue Lady Mary clearly agreed with Jonson, for the gentle, playful humor found in *Love's Victorie* is one of the drama's most appealing features. The character Rustick, a country buffoon, supplies much of the comedy through his spirited, though misguided, wooing of Musella; he delivers songs of adoration comparing the redness of her cheeks to "okar spred / On a fatted sheeps back" (H4). Although the courtier-shepherds constantly outmatch him in contests of wit, Rustick is proud of his own "art to hold a plowe" (f. 19ᵛ). Humor is also provided by such female characters as the fickle Dalina and the over-eager lover, Climeana, whose pursuit of men ends in comic disappointment: "a woman woo, / the most unfittest, shamfullst thing to doo" (f. 14).

Lady Mary's character Rustick bears some similarity to Lorel, the rude swineherd in Jonson's *The Sad Shepherd*, but it is unlikely that this play served as a direct source.[32] Although critics disagree over the exact dating of Jonson's only surviving pastoral play, most believe that the dramatist was continuing to work on it in the years before his death in 1637. Yet, as W. W. Greg noted in his edition of *The Sad Shepherd*, some similarities exist between this late play and Jonson's earlier lost pastoral, *The May Lord*, which was described in the *Conversations with Drummond:* both works feature a country setting, the wise shepherd Alken, and an enchantress or witch.[33] Because the *Conversations* provide so little specific information concerning *The May Lord*, recent scholars

---

[31] Alexander B. Grosart (ed.), *The Complete Works in Verse and Prose of Samuel Daniel* (4 vols.; London: privately printed, 1885), III, 331.

[32] C. H. J. Maxwell (ed.), *"Love's Victorie"* (M.A. thesis, Stanford University, 1933), xx.

[33] W. W. Greg (ed.), *Ben Jonson's Sad Shepherd with Waldron's Continuation* (Louvain, Belgium: A. Uystpruyst, 1905), xiv–xix.

have debated whether the work was actually a pastoral play, a poem, or a narrative.[34] Drummond does, however, record that Jonson assigned a part to Lady Mary Wroth and that he deliberately chose to include comic elements, which are described in terms more appropriate to dramatic action: "Contrary to all other pastoralls, he bringeth the Clownes making Mirth and foolish Sports."[35] It is very possible that Jonson's earlier work, *The May Lord*, exerted strong influence over Lady Mary's pastoral, particularly in the use of comedy. Although she probably never saw *The Sad Shepherd*, Jonson reiterated the importance of humor when he wrote in the prologue, "But here's an heresy of late let fall, / That mirth by no means fits a pastoral" (ll. 31−32).

Like Jonson's pastoral play, *Love's Victorie* also features a series of inter-mingled songs which add variety to the drama. Composed in rhymed verse, the play contains some poems embedded within the actual text; for example, the Forester's speech, beginning "Did ever cruelty itt self thus showe?" forms a complete sonnet (ff. 2−2ᵛ). Rather than fragmenting the text of the play, I have included in this edition those songs of more than one stanza in length, which appear at intervals in the Huntington manuscript.

By the beginning of the seventeenth century, amateur theatricals had developed into a popular form of entertainment in the great country houses. Sir Philip Sidney's *The Lady of May*, performed at the Earl of Leicester's home, Wanstead, is one of the finest early examples of an English pastoral designed for a private audience. Because Sidney's entertainment is extremely short and lacks the five-act structure of a play, it did not serve as an actual model for *Love's Victorie*, but it does contain some similar features: the contrast between shep-herds and foresters, the use of comic characters, and the intermingling of songs. Unfortunately, the Huntington text of *Love's Victorie* provides little information concerning the actual performance of the play. No cast list is included, and there are few stage directions, with the exception of the depar-tures of characters from stage (identified by *ex.*). The manuscript is divided into acts, but not scenes.

Lady Mary Wroth was by no means the first Englishwoman to compose a play, for she had been preceded by Elizabeth Cary, Viscountess Falkland, whose *Tragedy of Mariam* was composed several years before it was first pub-lished in 1613.[36] Similarly, Lady Mary's aunt, the Countess of Pembroke, had shown a strong interest in classical drama through her verse translation of

[34] Raymond Urban, "Jonson's Pastoral Comedies," *Harvard Library Bulletin*, XXIII, 295−323. I. A. Shapiro challenged Urban's assumption that *The May Lord* was a play: "Jon-son's *The May Lord*," *Harvard Library Bulletin*, XXVIII, 258−63.

[35] Herford and Simpson (eds.), *Works of Ben Jonson*, I, 143.

[36] A. C. Dunstan and W. W. Greg (eds.), *The Tragedy of Mariam* (Oxford: printed for the Malone Society, 1914).

Robert Garnier's *Antonie* (1592). Both of these plays, however, were composed essentially as closet dramas, without concern for performance. In the later seventeenth century women dramatists increased in number, partly because Queen Henrietta Maria gave added impetus to the writing of plays by acting in a pastoral of her own composition at Somerset House in 1626.[37] Although performances by female royalty had been fairly common in the French court, Henrietta Maria's acting was unusual for the English. She helped set a new fashion, and moreover, she and her maids performed together in *The Shepherd's Paradise* (1633), an eight-hour pastoral composed by Walter Montague.[38] Shortly afterward, several other women dramatists began their careers, including the Duchess of Newcastle and her stepdaughters.

As in the case of Lady Mary Wroth's play, many writings by Renaissance women authors remained unpublished. John Davies of Hereford called attention to this phenomenon in a joint dedication to three of England's most famous literary women—Lucy, Countess of Bedford, Mary, Countess of Pembroke, and Elizabeth, Lady Cary—in which he observed, "You presse the *Presse* with little you have made."[39] In his 1612 preface to *Polyolbion*, Michael Drayton complained more generally of the reluctance of contemporary poets to publish their works: "Verses are wholly deduc't to Chambers, and nothing esteem'd in this lunatique Age, but what is kept in Cabinets, and must only passe by Transcription."[40] Although there were some exceptions, such as the publication of the Countess of Pembroke's translations, the same author's metrical versions of the Psalms remained in manuscript until 1823. As the textual introduction to the *Urania* will show, there is no conclusive evidence that Lady Mary actively sought to have her works published, and she even disclaimed such an intention in her letter to Buckingham. The strong social pressures against publication may be seen clearly in the reaction of Dorothy Osborne, when the Duchess of Newcastle's poetry was first printed: "she could never bee soe rediculous else as to venture at writeing book's and in verse too."[41]

Lady Mary Wroth was well aware that in the early seventeenth century relatively few other women were poets: in the *Urania*, Amphilanthus observes

[37] HMC, XVI, 47, Salvetti Correspondence, as recorded in Alfred Harbage, *Cavalier Drama* (1936; rpt. New York: Russell and Russell, 1964), 12.

[38] Harbage, *Cavalier Drama*, 18.

[39] Alexander B. Grosart (ed.), *The Muse's Sacrifice, or Divine Meditations, 1612,* in *The Complete Works of John Davies of Hereford* (2 vols.; London: Chertsey Worthies Library, 1878), Vol. II, Pt. I, p. 4.

[40] J. William Hebel (ed.), *The Works of Michael Drayton* (5 vols; Oxford: Basil Blackwell, 1933), IV, v.

[41] G. C. Moore Smith (ed.), *The Letters of Dorothy Osborne to William Temple* (Oxford: Clarendon, 1928), 37.

that "poetry is an art rare in women and yett I have seene some excellent things of their writings" (I. iii. p. 336). On the Continent, women poets had flourished much earlier, as seen in the achievements of the French writers Marguerite de Navarre, Pernette du Guillet, and Louise Labé, as well as of the Italians Veronica Gambara, Vittoria Colonna, and Gaspara Stampa. By contrast, until Lady Mary Wroth's time, the majority of English women poets had been primarily interested in religious, as opposed to secular writings.[42] Very few of these poets had composed sonnets; in addition to Queen Elizabeth, Lady Mary's other main predecessor may have been the Countess of Oxford, who is credited with four sonnets on the death of her son.[43] Lady Mary emerges alone among her contemporary women writers in creating a complete English sonnet sequence and in leaving behind a varied collection of lyric verse.

After the controversy surrounding the publication of some of her writing in 1621, Lady Mary Wroth's literary fame suffered partly because of the inaccessibility of her work. More than forty years later, the Duchess of Newcastle alluded to the public hostility Lady Mary had faced when the *Urania* was first printed, but by this time the number of secular women poets had increased to include such figures as Katherine Philips, Anne Bradstreet, and the duchess herself.[44] There were, however, very few critical evaluations of Lady Mary's poetry until the twentieth century. As part of his biographical article on Lady Mary Wroth in the *DNB*, Sir Sidney Lee claimed that her sonnets revealed a "lyric faculty and fluency." Later, R. Brimley Johnson called more specific attention to the "Crowne of Sonnets dedicated to love" in *Pamphilia to Amphilanthus*, which he believed "ensures her position among the lyrists of her age."[45]

In assessing literary reputation, there is admittedly a strong temptation for any editor to magnify the achievements of his subject. In the case of Lady Mary Wroth, the poems as a group vary widely in quality, from those that merely repeat the well-worn Elizabethan conceits to others that rise above the traditional imagery to present an intensely ambivalent response to love. Such

[42] See Charlotte Kohler, "The Elizabethan Woman of Letters: The Extent of Her Literary Activities" (Ph.D. dissertation, University of Virginia, 1936).

[43] The four sonnets attributed to the Countess of Oxford are included in John Soowthern, *Pandora* (London: T. Hackette, 1584), STC 22928, but Soowthern may have revised these poems. George B. Parks (ed.), *Pandora* (New York: Columbia University Press, 1938), 3. Elizabeth Cary, Viscountess Falkland, wrote a dedicatory sonnet, which precedes *The Tragedy of Mariam*. Although Isabella Whitney wrote secular love verse, she did not compose sonnets: *A Sweet Nosegay, or Pleasant Posye* (London: n.p., 1573), STC 25440.

[44] Preface to Margaret Cavendish, *Sociable Letters* (Menston: Scolar Press, 1969), sig. b.

[45] R. Brimley Johnson, *The Birth of Romance*, Vol. I of *The English Literature Library* (London: Bodley Head, 1928), 137.

sonnets as P8, P22, and P26 deserve to be included in twentieth-century anthologies of Renaissance verse because they vividly express the immediacy and urgency of the speaker's internal debate. Among some of Lady Mary's finest poems are the sonnets included in the "Crowne" (P77–90), where she skillfully conducts a labyrinthine journey through the persona's mind. Her songs, especially the pastoral eclogues U13 and U14, are fine examples of her plain style at its best: a union of delicate, unpretentious diction and careful craftsmanship.

Lady Mary may have chosen to adhere so closely to the well-defined Petrarchan mode in her poems because of a desire to perpetuate the Sidneian literary tradition in an age that was already turning to new fashions: in each of the three major genres of her work, she emulated the forms earlier used by her uncle—the sonnet sequence, pastoral romance, and pastoral drama. But in each of these forms, Lady Mary introduced original perspectives, as in her reversal of the roles of lover and beloved in the sonnets. Although she is undoubtedly a minor Renaissance poet, Lady Mary Wroth occupies a prominent position as a pioneering woman author, who was the first to write a full-length work of prose fiction, as well as a large body of secular love poetry.

Perhaps one of the best introductions to her poems is provided by Ben Jonson in his tribute to Lady Mary's verse. As the *Conversations with Drummond* suggest, Jonson believed that the sonnet form was too restrictive and inflexible: "he cursed petrarch for redacting Verses to Sonnets, which he said were like that Tirrants bed, where some who were too short were racked, others too long cut Short."[46] Although there are only five sonnets among Jonson's collected poems, he deliberately employed the form in this case as part of his compliment to Lady Mary. Jonson clearly distinguished his own poetic practice from hers in line 2, but he indicated his willingness to "exscribe," or copy out the poems by hand. The final image of *"Venus Ceston,"* the magical girdle that conferred beauty on the wearer and aroused love in the beholder, is Jonson's graceful praise of both the woman and the artist.[47]

A Sonnet,
to the noble Lady, the Lady
MARY WROTH

I that have beene a lover, and could shew it,
    Though not in these, in rithmes not wholly dumbe,

---

[46] Herford and Simpson, *Works of Ben Jonson,* I, 133–34.

[47] Venus' ceston, lent to Hera for the seduction of Zeus (*Iliad,* xiv, 214), is discussed by Jonson in his note to *Hymenaei,* 407: "Venus girdle . . . was fain'd to be variously wrought with the needle, and in it woven *Love, Desire, Sweetnesse, soft Parlee, Gracefulnesse, Perswasion,* and all the *Powers of Venus,*" Herford and Simpson, *Works of Ben Jonson,* VII, 224.

Since I exscribe your Sonnets, am become
A better lover, and much better Poet.
5 Nor is my Muse, or I asham'd to owe it
   To those true numerous Graces; wherof some,
   But charme the Senses, others over-come
Both braines and hearts; and mine now best doe know it:
For in your verse all *Cupids* Armorie,
10   His flames, his shafts, his Quiver, and his Bow,
   His very eyes are yours to overthrow.
But then his Mothers sweets you so apply,
Her joyes, her smiles, her loves, as readers take
For *Venus Ceston*, every line you make.

III

THE PRESENT TEXT AND CANON

The Manuscripts

LADY Mary Wroth's correspondence, transcribed from the original manu-
scripts and presented in the Appendix to this edition, provides invaluable
evidence for a study of the author's handwriting. In two of the eight signed
autograph letters, addressed to Queen Anne and George Villiers, Duke of
Buckingham, Lady Mary uses a formal italic hand, slightly inclined toward
the right and distinguished by numerous pen lifts. A sample of her formal
italic script may be seen in Figure 3, Lady Mary's letter to Buckingham. Here
with the exception of the paired consonants *ch*, *ct*, and *st*, she separates the
individual letters of whole words. In copying the consonants *b*, *d*, *f*, and *h*, the
author uses clubbed ascenders that resulted from exerting greater pressure on
the tip of the pen and became fashionable in the early seventeenth century.
Other prominent features include the capital letter *I*, consisting of a looped
hook and crossed curve, the capital letter *L*, with its elaborately flourished
descender, and the punctuation mark resembling a diagonally crossed *S*,
which appears following the salutation to Buckingham. These features of her
formal italic hand may also be seen in Figure 4, the Folger Library's autograph
manuscript of Lady Mary's sonnet sequence, *Pamphilia to Amphilanthus*. She
clearly reserved her meticulous italic script for the preparation of fair copies of
her poems and for correspondence with persons of high rank.

The remaining six autograph letters, written to personal friends or to
associates concerning financial matters, appear in a slightly different cursive
italic style. Although a comparison of the two hands reveals many similarities
in the formation of letters, the cursive script largely eliminates the use of
clubbed ascenders and frequent pen lifts; for example, the cursive *t* consists of a
downstroke and a looped bottom that crosses the stem in one continuous
motion. Figures 6 and 7 show that in her cursive hand Lady Mary simplified
the elaborate capital *I* by using a looped hook without a separate cross.
Similarly, the *r*, which in the formal italic consists of a downstroke and dot,
becomes a single uninterrupted stroke in the more informal style. Lady Mary
employs the cursive italic extensively in the rough drafts of her writing, as
revealed by the Newberry manuscript of the second part of the *Urania*, where

the text contains very frequent corrections and cancellations. Occasionally, the author includes a mixture of the formal and cursive italic styles, as in the case of Letter XII, addressed to Sir Edward Conway, where she switches from the cursive hand to the formal italic in the list of creditors and amounts copied at the end of the correspondence. All eight of the surviving autograph letters contain Lady Mary's same distinctive signature, beginning with an elaborately flourished capital letter *M* and a continuous stroke that links the last letter of her given name to the first letter of her surname (see Figure 3a).

ONE of the poet's most valuable literary manuscripts is the Folger text of *Pamphilia to Amphilanthus* (V. a. 104), which contains copies of each of the songs and sonnets in the sequence, with the exception of "Forbeare darke night, my joyes now budd againe" (P4). The manuscript also includes six poems that did not appear in Lady Mary's published work (F1–6), as well as copies of nine poems that were later interspersed throughout the text of the prose romance, the *Urania:* U12, U13, U14, U17, U18, U24, U32, U34, U52. A small quarto (19 x 14 cm) consisting of sixty-six leaves, the Folger text is written in the author's well-proportioned formal italic hand. Even though Lady Mary's name does not appear on this copy of her poems, the manuscript contains authorial corrections, which were later incorporated in the published versions of the poems. From Joshua Sylvester's reference to Lady Mary Wroth's poetry in 1613, it is clear that she was writing her poems and circulating them by hand long before the publication date of 1621. The watermark of the Folger copy is similar to that found in Briquet 2291 (1587) and Heawood 481 (1602), and this approximate dating also indicates that the holograph manuscript of her poems precedes that of the published version.[1]

The name of Isaac Reed, the Shakespearean editor and bibliophile (1747–1807), appears on the inside cover of the manuscript. In the catalog of his collection, it is listed as "Pamphilia to Amphilanthus. Songs, Sonnets, etc. Written in the Time of Q. Elizabeth, or James I (beautifully written and bound in morocco)."[2] The manuscript was sold in 1807 to Richard Heber, who sold it in 1836 to Thomas Thorpe. In the same year, Thorpe resold the manuscript to Sir Thomas Phillipps, whose name appears on f. 1 of the text. At the 1899 sale of Phillipps' manuscripts, it was purchased by Sotheran for H. C. Folger.[3]

---

[1] For assistance in photographing and identifying the watermark, I wish to thank Laetitia Yeandle, curator of manuscripts at the Folger Shakespeare Library. G. F. Waller provided a very brief description of the Folger manuscript in his edition of *Pamphilia to Amphilanthus*, 22–23.

[2] *Bibliotheca Reediana* (London: J. Barker, 1807), item 8684, 395.

[3] Heber (London, 1836, XI, n. 1110) to Thorpe (Cat. 1836, n. 1026), who sold it to

Because of the numerous dissimilarities between the autograph and the printed versions of Lady Mary Wroth's sonnet sequence, it is clear that the Folger manuscript was not used as the copy-text for the 1621 edition. In analyzing the relationship between the versions, the differences may be grouped according to three main categories, although these are by no means entirely exclusive. Grammatical corrections form one major type of change, which Lady Mary was conscientious in supplying. The Folger manuscript shows her care in altering verb and tense forms, and the printed version reveals even more examples of these adjustments. For instance, the manuscript's "no desart ever have a shade soe sadd," was altered in the 1621 version to "No Desart ever had a shade so sad" (P23.10). In addition to changes in subject-verb agreement, Lady Mary also made numerous pronoun revisions, such as my / mine and thy / thine, in which the second pronoun form was substituted before vowels: thus "thy Image" appears in the printed version as "thine Image" (P24.2). These changes are typically found elsewhere in Lady Mary Wroth's manuscripts and seem to reflect her meticulous approach to writing.

More significant are the stylistic alterations that were incorporated into the printed version. Several of the poems in the Folger text underwent improvements in the meter of the verse, as in the line "to looke on, losses now unjust prove my fare," in which the adjective "unjust" was altered to the single syllable "must" (P33.3). The reverse process occurs in the line, "Carrying him ∧ unto a Mirtle bowre" (P96.12), in which the word "safe" was inserted in the 1621 version. Lady Mary's revisions often produce a sharpening of diction, as in the substitution of "grace" for "force" (P47.8), or the alteration of the subject of the line, "Cupid would needs make mee a lover bee" (P72.1), to "Folly." The Folger manuscript gives evidence of Lady Mary Wroth's concern with word choice, as demonstrated by her description of the God of Love's trickery of human beings, who are deceived by "the image, and service of his tirannies" (P64.8). In the manuscript she altered the term "image" to read "maske," and she later changed the entire description to "the badge, and office of his tyrannies," a more concrete and vivid phrase.

Another important stylistic change involves her use of the second person pronouns, thou and you, which vary from one group of sonnets to the next to reflect Pamphilia's uncertain relationship with Amphilanthus. As in Shakespeare's sonnets, where the variations in personal pronouns reflect changing states of mind, so in Lady Mary Wroth's sequence the shifts are thematically significant. Occasionally, the poet altered a sonnet to intensify the shift from

---

Phillipps (n. 9283). From Phillipps (London, 1899, n. 991) to Sotheran for H. C. Folger; Catalogue of the Folger Library.

one pronoun used at the beginning of a poem to its opposite at the end: for example, the 1621 version reveals a substitution of the pronoun "thou" throughout the first three quatrains of a sonnet describing submission to love. This change provides greater contrast with the persona's cry of rebellion in the final couplet: "Yett this Sir God, your boyship I dispise" (P8.13).

The third major type of change is organizational, for Lady Mary reduced the number of poems included within the collection from 110 in the Folger manuscript to a printed total of eighty-three sonnets and twenty songs. The poems appear in the Folger manuscript in the following order:

> P1–3, F1, P5–16, P64, P68, P70, P20–24, P72, P26–29, P65,
> P31–39, P95, P97, P42–46, P96, P48–55, Blank, P56–57, U18,
> P58–61, U14, P62, U12, P63, P17, P30, P66–67, P18, P69, P19,
> P71, P25, P73, F2, P74–75, U13, P76, P77–90, Blank, F3,
> P91–93, U34, P94, P40, P47, P41, P98–103, U32, F4, F5, Blank,
> U52, F6, U17, U24.

In both the manuscript and printed editions, the first group of fifty-five poems is arranged so that a song follows each sub-group of six sonnets. When Lady Mary refashioned the structure of the collection for the 1621 version, she relegated several of the poems dealing with Cupid's capricious power to a position later in the sequence (P64, P70, P95). Following an interlude of songs, she made the most substantial revisions in the second series (P63–72), where she transferred five of the original ten poems and reassembled many of the sonnets concerned with the Anacreontic Cupid. Her revision heightened the sudden, climactic reversal in the persona's mind, as Pamphilia dramatically repents of mockery against the God of Love and vows to reward him with praise (P76.12). Immediately afterward, Lady Mary Wroth's *corona*, "A crowne of Sonetts dedicated to Love" (P 77–90) appears in the same order in both the manuscript and published versions. The farewell sonnet, or *commiato* poem, "My muse now happy lay thy self to rest" (P103), is identified in the Folger manuscript by markings, including the name of Pamphilia, to indicate the end of the sequence. After this farewell sonnet, the manuscript includes a group of miscellaneous poems, some of which were later distributed throughout the text of Lady Mary Wroth's prose romance.

The relationship between the Folger manuscript and the printed version may be summarized, with M representing the original draft of part one of the romance *Urania* and S1–3 the manuscript versions of *Pamphilia to Amphilanthus*, which circulated separately. Lady Mary Wroth clearly shared with her father, Sir Robert Sidney, an interest in the careful disposition of the sonnets within the sequence. Sidney's manuscript (British Library Addit. 58435)

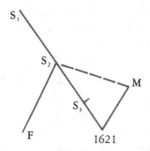

contains major revisions in arrangement and shows the artist's deliberate efforts to select and renumber the individual poems.

THE Newberry manuscript (Case Ms fY 1565.W 95) consists of Lady Mary Wroth's unpublished continuation, *The [first and] secound booke of the secound part of the Countess of Montgomerys Urania*. The manuscript is divided into two volumes (30 × 18 cm), in which the individual bifolio sheets have been folded and pasted into a modern binding with calf spine. The first volume consists of sixty-eight leaves, and the second volume of sixty-two leaves. The text is incomplete since there are many blank spaces for names and poems, which were never inserted (see II. i. f. 21, blank for one poem and II. i. f. 53, blanks for two poems). In the first volume, one bifolio sheet (two leaves) is missing after f. 19, and the second volume ends abruptly in mid-sentence. The manuscript is in Lady Mary's cursive italic hand, but the writing is more cramped and hurried than that of her formal italic hand in the Folger manuscript.[4] She appears to have worked on the second part of the *Urania* over a period of time, as revealed by the use of different ink and pens. Dating the manuscript is extremely difficult because the text contains no clues and the watermark is rarely visible; the watermark on the final bifolio sheet of the first volume is the common foolscap. The manuscript is of special interest because it reveals Lady Mary Wroth's artistic practice of writing the poetry separately from the romance and then inserting the verse at a later time into the prose narrative. Such a practice was also followed by her uncle Sir Philip Sidney, as revealed by the state of the unique manuscript of the revised *Arcadia*.[5]

The Newberry Library purchased the manuscript of the unpublished *Urania* in 1935 from Ifan K. Fletcher, who had recently established a book-

[4] Ernest Frederick Detterer (1888–1947), a former curator at the Newberry Library, believed that the manuscript was in one hand, rather than two, as the dealer had described. See 1936 Booklist, No. 13, at the Newberry Library.

[5] Cambridge University Library MS K k. I. 5 (2). The manuscript has been described by Ringler, 529–31.

shop in London as a branch of the antique business of his father, J. Kyrle Fletcher, of Newport in South Wales. According to Mrs. C. A. Fletcher, her late husband Ifan acquired many books and manuscripts from the library of the Morgan estate at Tredegar Park, close to Newport. On the inside cover of both volumes of the manuscript is the name Charles Morgan, possibly the autograph of Sir Charles Robinson Morgan, first Baron Tredegar. The signature of Charles Morgan is very similar to that found in the papers of the first Baron Tredegar (1792–1875), now deposited at the National Library of Wales. Other previous owners of the manuscript are unknown, but fortunately it did not remain in the library of Lady Mary Wroth's home, Loughton Hall, which was destroyed by fire in 1836.

The Newberry manuscript provides the text of eighteen unpublished poems, which are widely separated throughout the romance. Most of them appear in the first book of the continuation, for in the second book Lady Mary Wroth included only two versions of a single poem (N18). As in the published *Urania*, Lady Mary brought the central characters, Pamphilia and Amphilanthus, together at the end of the second part, but she broke off the manuscript with the promise of new adventures.

ONE of Lady Mary's poems, "Railing Rimes Returned upon the Author," appears in manuscript copy in the Clifton Collection at the University of Nottingham (MS Cl LM 85/1–5). This copy is not in Lady Mary's hand, but it represents the only version of the poem that has survived. Other copies of the quarrel poems exchanged between Edward Denny, Baron of Waltham, and Lady Mary were sent to interested court parties, such as William Feilding, first Earl of Denbigh, but no additional copies of Lady Mary's rebuttal to Lord Denny have been found.

A HOLOGRAPH manuscript of Lady Mary Wroth's pastoral play, *Love's Victorie*, is at the Henry E. Huntington Library (HM 600).[6] The manuscript is a folio (31.5 × 18.5 cm) containing twenty-one leaves. Lady Mary Wroth wrote most of the play in her formal italic hand (used in the Folger manuscript), but in copying the speeches of the mythological characters, Venus and Cupid, she employed her cursive italic hand, found in the Newberry manuscript.[7] Although the play was largely composed in decasyllabic couplets, it

[6]The Huntington manuscript was catalogued as anonymous, c. 1630. It is listed as anonymous in Gerald E. Bentley, *The Jacobean and Caroline Stage* (7 vols.; Oxford: Oxford University Press, 1956), V, 1368–69 and in Alfred Harbage, *Annals of English Drama*, 975–1700, rev. by Samuel Schoenbaum (London: Methuen, 1964), 146.

[7]The Huntington version of *Love's Victorie* has been edited by C. H. J. Maxwell (M.A.

contains a mixture of alternative rhyme and nine songs. The Huntington copy of *Love's Victorie* is incomplete, for the text begins in the midst of Act One and breaks off at the very beginning of Act Five.

There are frequent revisions in the manuscript, especially in the scenes involving the mythological characters. At the end of Act One, the conversation between Venus and Cupid appears to have been added to the text because it is written in Lady Mary's informal hand and does not fill the space allotted for it; a blank page (f. 5ᵛ) follows before the beginning of the second act. Similarly, the next exchange between Venus and Cupid appears to have been added on a half sheet inserted into the manuscript. At the end of Act Three the speech of Venus is left blank, and Cupid's lines are canceled at the conclusion of Act Four.

The irregular format of the manuscript also suggests that the Huntington text represents an intermediate, rather than a final state of composition: $iii + 1 + 2^4 + 3^4$ (imperfect, consisting of 3 sheets and 2 half sheets) $+ 4^4 + 5^6 + 6 + iii$. The watermark of the paper is similar to that found in Briquet 7211 (1589) and Heawood 1721A (1614).

Peter J. Croft, Librarian of King's College, Cambridge, has identified a second holograph manuscript of *Love's Victorie* containing a complete version of the text. This copy now exists in private hands in England, but plans are underway to prepare a critical edition of the play. Unlike the Huntington manuscript, this second version opens with an appearance of Venus and Cupid; it includes an interlude featuring the same characters at the end of Act Three, and it provides Act Five in its entirety, in which the four pairs of lovers are reconciled.

The play was first mentioned by James O. Halliwell-Phillipps in 1853, when he described an anonymous manuscript at the Public Library of Plymouth as a "play, copied from the original MS in the possession of Sir Edward Dering."[8] He listed the Plymouth copy of *Love's Victorie* as a quarto, but this transcript, no longer at the Public Library, is apparently lost. The "original MS" he mentioned may be tentatively identified as the holograph copy of the play, now at the Huntington. Halliwell-Phillipps had an opportunity to become familiar with the contents of Sir Edward Dering's library

---

thesis, Stanford University, 1933). Maxwell believed that the manuscript was written by two different copyists, and she was unable to identify the author of the play.

[8] James O. Halliwell-Phillipps, *A Brief Description of the Ancient and Modern Manuscripts Preserved in the Public Library, Plymouth* (London: C. & J. Adlard, 1853), 21. Halliwell-Phillipps later described *Love's Victorie* in his *Dictionary of Old English Plays* (London: John Russell Smith, 1860), 156: "A pastoral drama under this title exists in MS in private hands, and copious extracts from it were printed in 4to, 1853."

while he was preparing an edition of Dering's manuscript of the two parts of *Henry IV*, published by the Shakespeare Society in 1845. The manuscripts belonging to Dering, which Halliwell-Phillipps examined, were later dispersed in a succession of four sales of the Surrenden library.[9]

Sir Edward Dering (1598–1644) was a baronet distinguished by his interest in amateur theatricals. At his home in Surrenden, near Pluckley in Kent, he held performances of plays in which friends and members of his family participated. One important piece of evidence relating to these presentations is found in Dering's abridged manuscript of the two parts of Shakespeare's *Henry IV*, now located at the Folger Library.[10] Included in this manuscript is a small scrap of paper in Dering's hand which lists the names of characters from John Fletcher's *The Spanish Curate* and, for these parts, the corresponding names of relatives, friends, and neighbors. This incomplete cast list also provides a valuable clue to the dating of the Folger manuscript, for it was probably written between 1622, when *The Spanish Curate* was licensed to be played, and 1624, when Francis Manouch, whose name appeared on the cast list, moved from the region.[11] In his library at Surrenden Sir Edward Dering kept records of plays he had attended as a young man. His fascination with the theater in the 1620s and 1630s may also be seen in his family papers, which include an account book listing the purchase of nearly 250 playbooks for his library at Surrenden.[12]

The Huntington manuscript of *Love's Victorie* can be traced back to Quaritch's Catalogue of December 1899, where it is described as a small folio of twenty-one leaves; the catalogue briefly noted, "The play is full of musical lines and does not deserve to be lost."[13] The manuscript eventually passed into

---

[9] The catalogues of the London auctioneers Puttick and Simpson at the British Library record four major sales of the Surrenden library: June 8, 1858; July 10, 1861, Feb. 4, 1863, and July 13, 1865.

[10] George W. Williams, and G. B. Evans (eds.), *The History of King Henry the Fourth*, as revised by Sir Edward Dering, Bart (Washington, D.C.: Folger Facsimiles, 1973).

[11] S. B. Hemingway (ed.), *New Variorum of Henry IV, Part One* (Philadelphia: Lippincott, 1936), 496. A. R. Humphreys has suggested a slightly later date of 1623–24 in his introduction to the New Arden edition of *Henry IV, Part Two* (London: Methuen, 1966), lxxxiv.

[12] P. Gemesge described an account by Sir Edward Dering of five Latin plays presented at Cambridge in March, 1614: *Gentleman's Magazine*, XXVI, 223–25. T. N. S. Lennam, "Sir Edward Dering's Collection of Playbooks, 1619–1624," *Shakespeare Quarterly*, XVI, 145. G. Blakemore Evans has suggested that three Shakespearean prompt-books, now at the University Library of Padua, may once have belonged to Dering: *Shakespearean Prompt-Books of the Seventeenth Century* (6 vols.; Charlottesville: Bibliographical Society of the University of Virginia, 1960), I, 8–11. He later cast doubt on this attribution: "New Evidence on the Provenience of the Padua Prompt-Books," *Studies in Bibliography*, XX, 239–42.

[13] Bernard Quaritch's Catalogue, no. 194 (December, 1899), item no. 1116, 163.

the hands of the American collector, William Augustus White, whose name is written in pencil in the upper right hand corner of the manuscript, along with the date 6 March 1901. The Huntington Library acquired the manuscript from White's estate, probably in the 1920s, according to Mary Robertson, curator of manuscripts.

The 1621 Edition of THE COUNTESSE OF MONTGOMERY'S URANIA

The title page of the 1621 edition of *Urania* was engraved by the Dutch artist, Simon van de Passe, who also executed portraits of members of the Sidney-Herbert family: Sir Robert Sidney; Mary, Countess of Pembroke; William Herbert, third Earl of Pembroke; Philip Herbert, Earl of Montgomery; and Sir Henry Hobart (father of John Hobart, Lady Mary's brother-in-law.) [14] Van de Passe lived in England from 1612 to 1623, and during this time he completed portraits of James I and many other members of the court. The title page is an illustration of a central allegory in the *Urania*, the Throne of Love, which is described in detail early in the romance (I. i. 39–40). The first tower to the bottom left of the engraving, Cupid's Tower, or the Tower of Desire, is designed for false lovers, who are forced to endure torments and punishments. The second, belonging to Venus, is the Tower of Love, which may be entered by any suitor, provided that he is willing to face such threats as Jealousy, Despair, and Fear. The third tower is guarded by the figure of Constancy and cannot be entered until the previous obstacles have been surmounted. Constancy holds the keys to the Throne of Love, a palace that is open only to those few men and women who possess this cardinal virtue. As a symbol of love's supremacy, the palace is situated on a steep hill that overshadows the plains below. Not only is the Throne of Love a central point of reference for the prose romance, but also it serves as a source for much of the imagery of Lady Mary's poems.

No dedicatory epistles, poems, or prefatory material follow which is unusual in a book written by a noble author and dedicated to a prominent courtier, Susan Herbert, Countess of Montgomery. The text of the romance begins on signature B_1, suggesting, perhaps, that the printer expected some preliminary material he did not later receive. Although the 1621 *Urania* broke off abruptly in mid-sentence, this ending could have been designed as a

---

[14] A. M. Hind, *Engraving in England in the 16th and 17th Centuries* (3 vols.; Cambridge: Cambridge University Press, 1952–64), II, plates 153c, 155a, 157a, 157b. Crispin van de Passe, Simon's brother, executed a portrait of Sir Philip Sidney, II, plate 142.

stylistic similarity to Sir Philip Sidney's *New Arcadia*, which also concluded in mid-sentence.[15] The sonnet sequence, appearing at the end of the romance, was separately numbered.

It is unclear to what extent, if any, the author participated in the publication of her work, for in her letter to the Duke of Buckingham she claimed that the books of the *Urania* "were solde against my minde I never purposing to have had them published."[16] Yet she admitted having sent the Duke of Buckingham his own personal copy, and the illustration for the title page was chosen by someone well acquainted with the nature of her romance.

The publishers John Grismand and John Marriott entered the *Urania* in the Stationers' Register on July 13, 1621, but the actual printer of the volume was Augustine Mathewes. Although Mathewes' name does not appear on the title page, the editors of the revised STC identified him on the basis of the typographical ornaments.[17] Mathewes' reputation as a printer had been tarnished on several previous occasions; along with Grismand and Marriott, he had been fined for printing *Wither's Motto* (1621) without a license and in 1630 for printing a book by Sir Henry Wotton without entrance. For such offenses, he was accused in 1629 by the commissioners of the Stationers' Company of "dealing with offensive, prohibited, and unlicensed books."[18] It is quite possible, then, that the *Urania* may have been entered for publication without the author's permission. Unlike the example of Sir John Harington, who carefully supervised the printing of his translation of *Orlando Furioso*, there is no indication that Lady Mary Wroth ever read the proofs of her book. On the other hand, if her manuscript was entered without permission, she did not initiate any legal proceedings to stop the publication.

After the withdrawal from sale of Lady Mary Wroth's romance in December, 1621, the book was never reprinted. A slightly altered version of one of the poems, "All night I weepe, all day I cry, Ah mee" (P14) appeared anonymously in the collection *Wit's Recreations* (1645). Sir Egerton Brydges reprinted several pages from the beginning of *Urania* (I, 1–3) and sixteen of the poems in *Restituta*: U1, U2, U13, U14, U18, U26, U45, U46, U55, P28,

---

[15] A new edition of *The Countess of Pembroke's Arcadia* was published in 1621, so Lady Mary's *The Countesse of Montgomery's Urania* may have been considered a companion volume. See Graham Parry, "Lady Mary Wroth's *Urania*," *Proceedings of the Leeds Philosophical and Literary Society*, Literary and Historical section, XVI, 54.

[16] Bodleian Library MS Add. D. 111. ff. 173ʳ⁻ᵛ (December 15, 1621). When Lord Denny attacked the *Urania* for its allusions to his personal life, Lady Mary Wroth also disclaimed reference to any actual persons or events.

[17] Katharine F. Pantzer (ed.), *A Short-Title Catalogue of Books* (Rev. ed; London: Bibliographical Society, 1976), II, 479.

[18] William A. Jackson (ed.), *Records of the Court of the Stationers' Company, 1602–1640* (London: Bibliographical Society, 1957), 135, 224, 466, 478.

P60, P70, P74, P93, P96, and P103.[19] Two songs, "Who can blame mee if I love" (U14) and "Love a child is ever criing" (P74) have been reprinted by Alexander Dyce in *Specimens of British Poetesses*, by Alexander Rowton in *The Female Poets of Great Britain*, and by A. H. Bullen in *Poems, Chiefly Lyrical*. More recently, Ann Stanford has selected six of the poems for her anthology: U5, U33, U40, U49, U53, and P26.[20]

The engraved title page of *The Countesse of Montgomery's Urania* is reproduced on p. 76. The collation of the volume is as follows, 2°: [A]¹ B–3Y⁴ 3Z⁶ 4A–4F⁴, with Lady Mary's sonnet sequence occupying 4A–4F⁴. Despite the quarrel over the *Urania*, at least twenty-one copies have survived.[21] In the preparation of this edition of the poems, the following copies, signified by *STC* abbreviations, have been examined: L (2 copies), O; F (2 copies), HD, HN, LC, N, Y.

Collation of the poems in (1) Newberry Case Y 155.W94, (2) Folger STC 26051, copy 1, (3) Yale (Beinecke) In W946 + 621, (4) Huntington 60769 reveals a number of verbal variants and spelling differences:

			Corrected	Uncorrected
U9,	1.4	P3ᵛ	subject (2, 3, 4)	subjects (1)
	1.37	P3ᵛ	choicest (2, 3, 4)	choises (1)
	1.40	P3ᵛ	exelencie (1, 4)	exclencie (2, 3)
U15,	1.5	V4ᵛ	seemst not (1, 2, 4)	seemst not not (3)
U18,	1.7	2Aᵛ	their (4)	shew (1, 2, 3)
	1.20	2Aᵛ	let (4)	lest (1, 2, 3)
U19,	1.6	2Bᵛ	fore (4)	force (1, 2, 3)
	1.7	2Bᵛ	marres (4)	marrs (1, 2, 3)
U20,	1.1	2E2ᵛ	powers (1, 2, 3)	powres (4)
	1.3	2E2ᵛ	ruine (2, 3, 4)	ruiue (1)
U22,	1.12	2I	sting (1, 3)	string (2, 4)
	1.13	2I	desect (1, 3)	desist (2, 4)
	1.13	2I	vaines (1, 3)	daines (2, 4)
	1.14	2I	Hold (1, 3)	Holds (2, 4)

[19] Sir Egerton Brydges, *Restituta, or Titles, Extracts, and Characters of Old Books in English Literature Revised* (4 vols.; London: T. Bensley, 1815), II, 260–75.

[20] Alexander Dyce (ed.), *Specimens of British Poetesses* (London: T. Rodd, 1827), 40–41; Frederick Rowton (ed.), *The Female Poets of Great Britain* (London: Longman, 1848), 27–29; A. H. Bullen (ed.), *Poems, Chiefly Lyrical, from Romances and Prose Tracts of the Elizabethan Age* (London: J. C. Nimmo, 1890), 80–82; Ann Stanford (ed.), *The Women Poets in English* (New York: McGraw-Hill, 1972), 37–40. Betty Travitsky reprints the concluding paragraph of the 1621 prose *Urania*, along with five of the "Crowne" sonnets: *The Paradise of Women: Writings by Englishwomen of the Renaissance* (Westport, Conn.: Greenwood Press, 1981), 135–39.

[21] I wish to thank Katharine Pantzer, director of the *STC* revision, who has kindly furnished information concerning the location of copies: L (2 copies). L4. C4. DUL. LEEDS. M² (imp.). O. Juel-Jensen; Skretkowicz; CHI. F (2 copies). HD. HN. LC. N. WTL. Y. Robert Taylor; Witten-Hannah.

1.17	2I	anotamise (1, 3)	annottomise (2, 4)
U23, 1.16	2K	slew (1, 2, 4)	shew (3)
1.34	$2K^v$	ere (1, 3, 4)	e're (2)
U25, 1.10	$2N2^v$	rise (1)	ries (2, 3, 4)
U28, 1.10	$2R2^v$	'Twas (4)	Twas (1, 2, 3)
U31, 1.6	$3C2^v$	see (4)	fee (1, 2, 3)
U52, 1.138	$3V^v$	to (1, 2, 3)	too (4)
P18, 1.6	4B	likenesse of (1)	likenesse of of
P40, 1.2	$4C^v$	birth (1, 3)	blrth (2, 4)
1.13	$4C^v$	Hope (1, 3)	Hode (2, 4)
P45, 1.10	4C3	is, wordes (3)	is $\wedge$ wordes (1, 2, 4)
P47, 1.2	$4C3^v$	makes (1, 3, 4)	make (2)
1.10	$4C3^v$	fix't, (1, 3, 4)	fix't $\wedge$ (2)
1.13	$4C3^v$	eyes (1, 3, 4)	eye (2)
P48, 1.10	$4C3^v$	eyes, (1, 3, 4)	eyes $\wedge$ (2)
1.11	$4C3^v$	show'd; (1, 3, 4)	show'd. (2)
P53, 1.14	4D	truely (2, 3, 4)	trurly (1)
P61, 1.10	$4D2^v$	me, (2)	me $\wedge$ (1, 3, 4)
P62, 1.14	4D3	your (2)	you (1, 3, 4)

The Newberry Library's *Urania* has been used as the copy-text for those poems that do not appear in the holograph manuscripts, but readings of the corrected variants listed above have been substituted for the uncorrected ones.[22]

The Newberry copy is distinctive because of the printer's correction of its final page, in which the word FINIS is removed and an ornament, consisting of two winged putti supporting a shield, appears in its place. The same printer's ornament appeared at the end of Book Three of the *Urania* (I, iii, p. 429). Because the romance breaks off abruptly in mid-sentence, the word FINIS was inappropriate, and the printer may have chosen the ornament as a substitute; only one other copy, thus far examined, contains this change.[23] The Newberry copy was owned by Robert Dormer, Baron of Wyng, who was reared as a ward to Philip Herbert, Earl of Montgomery, after the death of his father in 1616.

[22] For further bibliographical information, see William Carew Hazlitt, *Handbook to the Popular, Poetical, and Dramatic Literature of Great Britain* (London: J. R. Smith, 1867), 680; William Thomas Lowndes, *The Bibliographer's Manual of English Literature* (4 vols.; London: Henry G. Bohn, 1857–64), IV, 3004; S. Austin Allibone, *A Critical Dictionary of English Literature and British and American Authors* (3 vols.; Philadelphia: J. B. Lippincott, 1859–71), III, 2869.

[23] Margaret Witten-Hannah records that a copy of the *Urania* at the Alexander Turnbull Library in Wellington, New Zealand also contains the ornament of the two winged putti and shield: "Lady Mary Wroth's *Urania*: The Work and the Tradition" (Ph.D. dissertation, University of Auckland, 1978), 102–103.

IV

THE EDITORIAL PROCEDURE

IT IS clear that *both* versions of *Pamphilia to Amphilanthus*—the poet's auto-graph manuscript and the printed text—provide a modern editor with extremely valuable information. As I have argued, the 1621 text represents a later version of the sonnet sequence, containing authorial changes. Although it would be possible simply to edit the published text, as Gary Waller has done, a major disadvantage is that this copy contains the printer's accidentals rather than the poet's own orthography, punctuation, capitalization, verse arrangement, and word division.[1] The printed text tends to modernize spell-ing (although it is often inconsistent in the treatment of silent *e*'s), and to substitute more conventional forms for the poet's own. In the Folger manu-script, for instance, Lady Mary Wroth writes, "Nor I chang from his love, / Butt still increase as th'eith of all my bliss" (P47.11–12). Here the author drops the initial (and probably unsounded) letter *h* of height, and this characteristic spelling is found elsewhere in the poet's autograph manuscripts. By contrast, the printed version states, "But still increase as th'earth of all my blisse," which seems to represent the printer's misreading of the author's original spelling. Also, in some instances the disposition of the verse on the printed page differs from the poet's ordinary practice, such as in the printer's division of quatrains in some of the sonnets.

Yet the most significant area in which the accidentals depart from the author's own is that of punctuation. Unlike Lady Mary Wroth's very light pointing of her autograph manuscripts, including the Folger copy of the sonnet sequence, the punctuation in the 1621 text is extremely heavy. Nearly every line has some type of strong punctuation, such as the period or semi-colon. Often the heavy pointing in the 1621 text violates the enjambement of the poet's lines, as in this case in the printed version: "The hellish spirit, Absence, doth arest. / All my poore senses to his cruell might" (P52.12–13); the manuscript contains no end punctuation after the first line. A further distinctive characteristic of Lady Mary Wroth's sonnets is the use of enjambe-ment between stanzas, and here also the printed text tends to disrupt the flow

[1] See my review of Waller's edition of *Pamphilia to Amphilanthus: Seventeenth-Century News*, XXXVI, 59–60.

of the verse: the 1621 version describes how love fills "no eye with wonder more then hopes still bee. / Bred in my breast, when fires of Love are free" (P55.4–5), where the final period after "bee" interrupts the meaning of the lines.

In this edition, the holograph manuscript of *Pamphilia to Amphilanthus* at the Folger Library has been selected as the copy-text for the songs and sonnets because it provides a fair copy of the poems in the author's hand and gives evidence of Lady Mary's own capitalization, punctuation, orthography, and word division. The Folger text also shows Lady Mary's corrections, which were included in the printed edition of 1621. In the present text, I have expanded manuscript abbreviations, capitalized the first letter of each line of verse, and regularized the use of i/j, ∫ / s, and u / v. I have tried to follow Lady Mary's punctuation whenever possible. In several instances she used the reversed semicolon, a mark of punctuation indicating an emphatic pause. In the text the reversed semicolon is printed as a modern semicolon, but the textual notes record her use of this distinctive symbol.[2] In the Folger manuscript she occasionally used the semicolon followed by the virgule as final punctuation to the poem (; /). This practice is also adopted in some of the poems contained in the Newberry manuscript, and in each case I have substituted a period as end punctuation. Wherever punctuation is missing at the conclusion of a poem, I have silently supplied the period.

I have followed the orthography of the manuscript despite the occasional variations in the spelling of a single word. The manuscript contains some misleading spellings, such as the number two ("tow"), the adverb too ("to"), and the adverb off ("of"). In these three cases where Lady Mary Wroth's orthography may create serious confusion for a modern reader, I have included the corrected spelling from the 1621 text, but have indicated the change in a textual note.

Although the original manuscript of the first part of the prose romance *Urania* has not survived, in preparing the text Lady Mary inserted poems at various points throughout the romance and reordered the final sonnet sequence, *Pamphilia to Amphilanthus*. The revised order of poems seen in the 1621 edition is clearly not the kind of change likely to have been made independently by a compositor or typesetter. For this reason, the 1621 arrangement has been adopted, since it appears to represent the author's final intentions regarding the order of the poems. The numbering of the sequence in the 1621 edition has been recorded, but for greater convenience the poems

---

[2] Hilary Jenkinson, "Notes on the Study of Punctuation of the Sixteenth Century," *RES*, II, 153.

also have been renumbered in brackets. Substantive variants from the 1621 edition have been incorporated in the text in the author's spelling, except in those cases where the variants appear to be the result of typographical or printer's error. Doubtful cases are discussed in the textual notes. The 1621 edition altered Lady Mary Wroth's spelling and punctuation and italicized all of the songs in the sonnet sequence; these changes have not been incorporated into the present text, since it is unlikely that they are authorial. Variants in accidentals have not been recorded, unless they affect the meaning of the lines.

Although nearly three-fourths of all of Lady Mary's poems appear in autograph copies, the 1621 edition of *Urania* provided the text of forty-seven poems not included in her manuscripts. For those works, I have used the 1621 edition and indicated this fact in a note to the individual texts. Because the present edition is based on both manuscript and published sources, there are some differences in appearance among the poems included from the *Urania*, but the underlying principle has been to retain as many features of Lady Mary Wroth's own style as possible: in the words of W. W. Greg, "so long as there is any chance of an edition preserving some trace, however faint, of an author's individuality, the critic will wish to follow it."[3] The poems interspersed throughout the prose of the *Urania* were not originally numbered, but in present text they have been identified by the initial U and numbered in brackets according to the order in which they appear in the romance.

The same editorial procedure described above has been followed in the transcription of poems contained in the Newberry and Huntington manuscripts.

[3] W. W. Greg, *The Editorial Problem in Shakespeare* (Oxford: Clarendon Press, 1942), li.

The
Countesse
of Mountgomeries
URANIA.
Written by the right honorable the Lady
MARY WROATH.
Daughter to the right Noble Robert
Earle of Leicester.
And Neece to the ever famous, and re-
nowned S.r Phillips Sidney knight. And to
y.e most excel.t Lady Mary Countesse of
Pembroke late deceased.

LONDON
Printed for IOH MARRIOTT
and IOHN GRISMAND. And
are to bee sould at their shop-
pes in S.t Dunstons Church
yard in Fleetstreet and in
Poules Ally at y.e signe of
the Gunn.

1621

Title-Page of *The Countesse of Montgomery's Urania* (1621). Reproduced by
permission of the Huntington Library, San Marino, California.

Holograph letter from Lady Mary Wroth to George Villiers, Duke of Buckingham (Bodleian MS Add. D. 111, ff. 173ʳ⁻ᵛ). Reproduced by permission of the Bodleian Library, Oxford.

A crowne of Sonetts.
dedicated to loue

In this strang labourinth how shall I turne?
wayes are on all sids while the wayes I miss:
if to the right hand, ther, in loue I burne;
lett mee goe forward, therin danger is;

If to the left, suspition hinders bliss,
lett mee turne back, shame cries I ought returne
nor faint though crosses wth my fortunes kiss;
stand still is harder, allthough sure to mourne;

Thus lett mee take the right, or left hand way;
goe forward, or stand still, or back retire;
I must thes doubts indure wthout allay
or help, butt traueile find for my best hire;

yett that wch most my troubled sence doth moue
is to leaue all, and take the thread of loue

Is to leaue all and take the thread of loue
whose line straite leads vnto the soules content
wher choyce delights wth pleasures wings doe moue,
and idle phantsie neuer roome had lent,

When chaste thoughts guide vs then our minds ar bent
to take that good wth ills from vs remoue,
light of true loue, brings fruite wth none repent
butt constant louers seeke and wish to proue;

Loue is the shining starr of blessings light;
the feruent fire of zeale, the roote of peace,
the lasting lampe fed wt the oyle of right;
Image of fayth, and wombe for ioyes increase

loue

Holograph manuscript of *Pamphilia to Amphilanthus* (Folger MS V.a.104,
f. 43). Reproduced by permission of the Folger Shakespeare Library,
Washington, D.C.

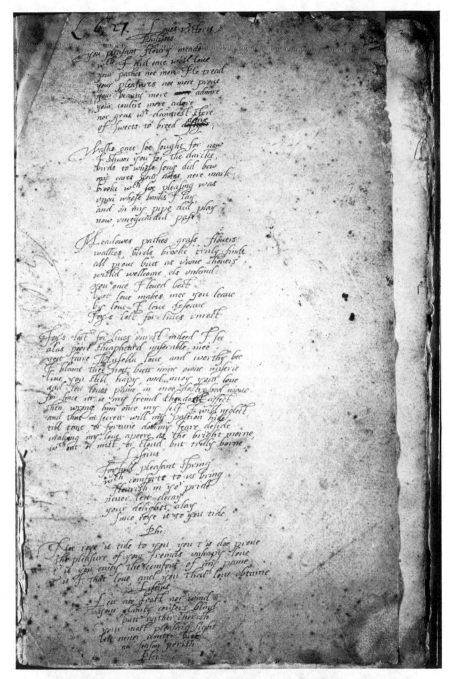

Holograph manuscript of *Love's Victorie*; Lady Mary Wroth's formal hand
(Huntington MS HM 600, f. 1). Reproduced by permission of the
Huntington Library, San Marino, California.

let them alas, and let them selues beguile
they shall haue torments when they shrinke to smile
they are nott yett in pride of all theyr scorne
~~but~~ ere they haue theyr pleasures haulfway worne
they shall both cry, and waile, and weepe
and for our mercy shall most humbly creepe
loue hath more glory when as greatest sprites
hee downeward throwe vnto his owne delights
then take noe care loues victory shall shine
when as your honor shall bee raisd by mine

             Venus
Thanks Cupid if thou doe performe thy ashe
and nede you must for ~~gods~~ must vain noe troshe
lest mortalls neuer shrink itt od or vaine
       heere
so ~~tender~~ thas soule can in all spiritts raine
prinses as nott exempsed from our mighs
~~and much~~
~~strike~~ les should sheapheards scorne vs and our righs
though they as well can loue and like affects
they must nott therfor our commands reiect

             Cu:
~~Yf~~ Nor shall, and mark butt what my vengeanes is
He miss my force or they shall vans theyr blis
and arrows heere I haue of purpose framd
Ch as they qualities for are they namd
                 leaue
Loue, iealousie, malice ~~hate~~ and mistrust
yett all thes shall att last incounter iust
harme shall bee non, yett shall they harme indure
for som small season then at ioy bee sure
like you this mother, ve: Sume I like this well
and faile nott nor in least part at this spell;

                               8

Holograph manuscript of *Love's Victorie*; Lady Mary Wroth's informal hand (Huntington MS HM 600, f. 5). Reproduced by permission of the Huntington Library, San Marino, California.

Holograph manuscript of *The Secound Part of the Countesse of Montgomery's Urania* (Newberry Case MS fY 1565.W95, Vol. I, f. 1). Reproduced by permission of the Newberry Library, Chicago.

LADY MARY WROTH'S POEMS

Pamphilia to Amphilanthus
A SONNET SEQUENCE

I.

[P1] When nights black mantle could most darknes prove,
      And sleepe deaths Image did my senceses hiere
    [From] knowledg of my self, then thoughts did move
      Swifter then those most swiftnes need require:

5 In sleepe, a Chariot drawne by wing'd desire
      I sawe: wher sate bright Venus Queene of love,
      And att her feete her sonne, still adding fire
      To burning hearts which she did hold above,

  Butt one hart flaming more then all the rest
10   The goddess held, and putt itt to my brest,
      Deare sonne, now shutt sayd she: thus must wee winn;

  Hee her obay'd, and martir'd my poore hart,
      I, waking hop'd as dreames itt would depart
      Yett since: O mee: a lover I have binn.

1-4. The dream-vision of Venus and Cupid recalls the opening of Petrarch's *Trionfe d'Amore*, in which the narrator experiences a vision of love's conquest. See Ernest Hatch Wilkins (trans.), *The Triumphs of Petrarch* (Chicago: University of Chicago Press, 1962), 5-6. On the popularity of Petrarch's *Trionfi*, see Frances A. Yates, *Astraea: The Imperial Theme in the Sixteenth Century* (London: Routledge and Kegan Paul, 1975), 112-20.

    2. senceses: "senses" in the 1621 text   hiere: hire

    5. Venus was traditionally represented as drawn in a chariot by doves: Ovid, *Metamorphoses*, XIV, 597. See also *AS* 79.4: "Which, coupling Doves, guides *Venus*' chariot right."

    8-9. Lady Mary Wroth also describes Venus holding a flaming heart in the symbolic episode (I. i. p. 39) illustrated on the title page of the *Urania*.

    12. The murder of the heart, a traditional conceit of the sonneteers, was used by Desportes, *Diane*, I, 6; Drayton, *Idea*, 2; and Sir Philip Sidney, *AS* 20.

2.

[P2] Deare eyes how well (indeed) you doe adorne
      That blessed sphaere, which gazing soules hold deere:
      The loved place of sought for triumphs neere:
      The court of glory, wher Loves force was borne:

5 How may they terme you Aprills sweetest morne
When pleasing looks from those bright lights apeere:
A sun-shine day; from clouds, and mists still cleere
Kind nursing fires for wishes yett unborne!

Two starrs of Heaven, sent downe to grace the Earthe,
10 Plac'd in that throne which gives all joyes theyr birthe;
Shining, and burning; pleasing yett theyr charmes;

Which wounding, even in hurts are deem'd delights,
Soe pleasant is ther force! Soe great theyr mights
As, happy, they can triumph in theyr harmes.

4. The imagery of the Court of Love, introduced in this sonnet, will reappear throughout the sequence: P3, 12, 76, 77–90, 92, 95, 98, 101. For literary background, see W. A. Neilson, *The Origins and Sources of the Court of Love* (1899; New York: Russell and Russell, 1967) and E. B. Fowler, *Spenser and the System of Courtly Love* (1935; New York: Phaeton Press, 1968).

9. Despite the traditional character of the eyes-stars comparison, it held special interest for Lady Mary because of her uncle's sonnet sequence. Note also that Sir Robert Sidney frequently includes the same imagery in his collection of poems (British Library Addit. MS 58435), Song 1.1–3: "O eyes, o lights devine / Which in unmatched face / Like twoe fayre suns, in cleerest heaven do shine." In transcribing excerpts from Sir Robert Sidney's poems, I have expanded abbreviations and capitalized the initial letter of each line of verse, but (with the exception of i and j, u and v), I have retained the original spelling and punctuation of the manuscript.

3.

[P3] Yett is ther hope: Then Love butt play thy part
✳ [Remember well thy self, and think on mee;]
Shine in those eyes which conquer'd have my hart;
And see if mine bee slack to answere thee:

5 Lodg in that brest, and pitty moving see
For flames which in mine burne in truest smart
Exiling thoughts that touch inconstancie,
Or those which waste nott in the constant art,

Watch butt my sleepe, if I take any rest
10 For thought of you, my spiritt soe distrest
As pale, and famish'd, I, for mercy cry;

Will you your servant leave? Think butt on this;
Who weares loves crowne, must nott doe soe amiss,
Butt seeke theyr good, who on thy force doe lye.

3. *AS* 12.1: "CUPID, because thou shin'st in *Stella's* eyes"
13. The reference to "loves crowne," a sign of Cupid's authority as absolute ruler, anticipates the later poems of the sequence: P76, 77–90, and 92. See *AS* First Song. 12: "Onely by you *Cupid* his crowne maintaineth."

4.

[handwritten: botanical image]

[handwritten: Night → dialectic between light & dark / nights & day]

{P4} Forbeare darke night, my joyes now budd againe,
     Lately growne dead, while cold aspects, did chill
     The roote at heart, and my chiefe hope quite kill,
     And thunders strooke me in my pleasures waine.

5 Then I alas with bitter sobs, and paine,
     Privately groan'd, my Fortunes present ill;
     All light of comfort dimb'd, woes in prides fill,
     With strange encrease of griefe, I griev'd in vaine,

  And most, when as a memory to good   *[handwritten: Memory: cf. 3.2]*
10 Molested me, which still as witnes stood,
     Of those best dayes, in former time I knew:

  Late gone as wonders past, like the great Snow, — *[handwritten: Seasonal]*
     Melted and wasted, with what, change must know:
     Now backe the life comes where as once it grew.

    4. waine: decline

    12. The reference to "the great Snow" is difficult to date with precision. In a letter to the Earl of Shrewsbury, Rowland Whyte described the effects of one of the coldest winters on the Sidney household: "The frost continues here in a very strange manner; the Thames so hardly frozen that it is made a beaten highway to all places of the city, but all bridges are in great danger upon a thaw. We at Baynard Castle watch and ward to preserve ours, that was but newly built." Quoted in Edmund Lodge, *Illustrations of British History, Biography and Manners* (3 vols.; 2nd ed.; London: John Chidley, 1838), III, 224 (January 26, 1607/8). The most famous seventeenth-century snow storms are described by Thomas Dekker in his pamphlets, *The Great Frost: Cold Doings in London* (1608) and *The Cold Year, 1614, a Deep Snow: in which Men and Cattell have Perished* (1615).

5.

[handwritten: Eyes]

{P5} Can pleasing sight, misfortune ever bring?
     Can firme desire a painefull torment try?
     Can winning eyes prove to the hart a sting?
     Or can sweet lips in treason hidden ly?

5 The Sun most pleasing blinds the strongest eye
     If too much look'd on, breaking the sights string;
     Desires still crost, must unto mischiefe hye,
     And as dispaire, a luckles chance may fling.

  Eyes, having wunn, rejecting proves a sting
10 Killing the bud beefor the tree doth spring; — *[handwritten: cf. 4.1]*
     Sweet lips nott loving doe as poyson prove:

  Desire, sight, Eyes, lips, seeke, see, prove, and find
     You love may winn, butt curses if unkind;
     Then show you harmes dislike, and joye in Love.

6. According to Renaissance scientists, the eyes emitted invisible shafts of light, which resulted in vision. See Donne's "The Extasie," 7–8: "Our eye-beames twisted, and did thred / Our eyes, upon one double string."

14. This poem uses the form of correlative verse (*carmen correlativum, vers rapportés*), which had become popular with neo-Latin and French vernacular poets in the later sixteenth century; see Ringler's note, 406. Sir Philip Sidney employed the form in AS 43, as did Sir Robert Sidney in Sonnet 31 and Pastoral 9.

6.

[P6] Ô strive nott still to heape disdaine on mee
      Nor pleasure take your cruelty to show
      On haples mee, on whom all sorrowes flow,
      And byding make: as given, and lost by thee,

5   Alas; ev'ne griefe is growne to pitty mee;
      Scorne cries out 'gainst itt self such ill to show,
      And would give place for joyes delights to flow;
      Yett wreched I, all torturs beare from thee,

    Long have I suffer'd, and esteem'd itt deere
10   Since such thy will; yett grew my paine more neere:
      Wish you my end? say soe, you shall itt have;

    For all the depth of my hart-held dispaire
      Is that for you I feele nott death for care;
      Butt now I'le seeke itt, since you will nott save.

Song. 1.

[P7] The spring now come att last
      To trees, fields, to flowers,
    And medowes makes to tast
      His pride, while sad showers
5   Which from mine eyes do flow
      Makes knowne with cruell paines
      Colde winter yett remaines
    Noe signe of spring wee know.

    The Sunn which to the Earth
10   Gives heate, light, and pleasure,
    Joyes in spring, hateth dearth,
      Plenty makes his treasure.
    His heat to mee is colde,
      His light all darknes is
15   Since I am bar'd of bliss
    I heate nor light beeholde.

A sheapherdess thus sayd
  Who was with griefe oprest
For truest love beetraid
20   Bard her from quiett rest
And weeping thus sayd she
  "My end aprocheth neere
  Now willow must I weare
My fortune soe will bee.

25 With branches of this tree
  I'le dress my haples head
Which shall my wittnes bee
  My hopes in love ar dead;
My clothes imbroder'd all
30   Shall bee with Gyrlands round
Some scater'd, others bound
Some ti'de, some like to fall.

The barck my booke shall bee
  Wher dayly I will wright
35 This tale of haples mee
  True slave to fortunes spight;
The roote shall bee my bed
  Wher nightly I will lye,
  Wayling inconstancy
40 Since all true love is dead.

And thes lines I will leave
  If some such lover come
Who may them right conseave,
  And place them on my tombe:
45 She who still constant lov'd
  Now dead with cruell care
  Kil'd with unkind dispaire,
And change, her end heere prov'd." Mutability!

17. This pastoral resembles Sir Robert Sidney's Song 3. 63–70:
Thus sayd a shepheard, once
With weights of change opprest
For hee had lost atonce
What ever hee lov'd best
And saw whyle he did mourn
The worldes fayre lookes renewed
Whyle hee a state past rewed
Which never would retourn.
Love not whoe have not lov'd
And whoe doe love, love nomore.

As Hilton Kelliher and Katherine Duncan-Jones note, Lady Mary Wroth omits the last two lines, which identify Sidney's poem as a variation on the Latin *Pervigilium Veneris*: "A Manuscript of Poems by Robert Sidney: Some Early Impressions," *British Library Journal*, I, 115. Her version is also distinctive because she reverses the situation of Sidney's poem by using a female shepherdess who laments the betrayal of her lover.

23. The willow is, of course, symbolic of disappointed love; compare *Othello*, IV. iii. 39.

7.

{P8}
    Love leave to urge, thou know'st thou hast the hand;
       'T'is cowardise, to strive wher none resist:
       Pray thee leave off, I yeeld unto thy band;
       Doe nott thus, still, in thine owne powre persist,

5   Beehold I yeeld: lett forces bee dismist;
       I ame thy subject, conquer'd, bound to stand,
       Never thy foe, butt did thy claime assist
       Seeking thy due of those who did withstand;

    Butt now, itt seemes, thou would'st I should thee love;
10   I doe confess, t'was thy will made mee chuse;
       And thy faire showes made mee a lover prove
       When I my freedome did, for paine refuse.

    Yett this Sir God, your boyship I dispise;
    Your charmes I obay, butt love nott want of eyes.

2. 'T'is: Ronald B. McKerrow notes that the spelling *'t'is* for *'tis* is "so common that it might almost be regarded as regular." *Prolegomena for the Oxford Shakespeare: A Study in Editorial Method* (Oxford: Clarendon, 1939), 25.

13–14. The mocking address to Cupid recalls the parody of courtly compliment in *AS* 53.7: "'What now sir foole,' said he, 'I would no lesse.'"

8.

{P9}
    Led by the powre of griefe, to waylings brought
       By faulce consiete of change fall'ne on my part,
       I seeke for some smale ease by lines, which bought
       Increase the paine; griefe is nott cur'd by art:

5   Ah! how unkindnes moves within the hart
       Which still is true, and free from changing thought:
       What unknowne woe itt breeds; what endles smart
       With ceasles teares which causelessly ar wrought.

    Itt makes mee now to shunn all shining light,
10   And seeke for blackest clouds mee light to give,

[handwritten: paradox: dark clouds shine?]

Which to all others, only darknes drive,
They on mee shine, for sunn disdaines my sight.

Yett though I darke do live I triumph may; *[handwritten: Builds upon the preceding paradox!]*
Unkindnes, nor this wrong shall love allay.

9.

[P10]   Bee you all pleas'd? your pleasures grieve nott mee:
Doe you delight? I envy nott your joy:
Have you content? contentment with you bee:
Hope you for bliss? hope still, and still injoye:

5   Lett sad misfortune, haples mee destroy,
Leave crosses to rule mee, and still rule free,
While all delights theyr contrairies imploy *[handwritten: Explains the paradox of 8.12-14]*
To keepe good back, and I butt torments see,

Joyes are beereav'd, harmes doe only tarry;
10   Dispaire takes place, disdaine hath gott the hand;
Yett firme love holds my sences in such band
As since dispis'ed, I with sorrow marry; *[handwritten: Autobiographical? or "I marry sorrow"?]*

Then if with griefe I now must coupled bee
Sorrow I'le wed: Dispaire thus governs mee.

14. See *AS* 100.14: "All mirth farewell, let me in sorrow live."

[handwritten: Excellent one to mull over with students!]

10.   *[handwritten: Who is the young traveller? her own heart?]*

[P11]   The weary traveller who tired sought
In places distant farr, yett found noe end
Of paine, or labour, nor his state to mend,
Att last with joy is to his home back brought; *[handwritten: Gilled]*

5   Finds nott more ease, though hee with joy bee fraught;
When past is feare, content like soules assend; *[handwritten: Neoplatonism?]*
Then I, on whom new pleasures doe dessend *[handwritten: embellished?]*
Which now as high as first borne bliss is wrought;

Hee tired with his paines, I, with my mind;
10   Hee all content receaves by ease of limms;
I, greatest hapines that I doe find
Beeleefe for fayth, while hope in pleasure swimms; *[handwritten: Fortunes of the lover have changed]*

Truth saith t'was wrong conseite bred my despite
Which once acknowledg'd, brings my harts delight.

91

1. The image of the weary traveller was a popular Renaissance *topos*: see John Lyly, *Euphues and His England*, eds. Morris Croll and Harry Clemons (London: George Rout-ledge, 1916), 221, and Rosalind's comment in *As You Like It*: "A traveller! By my faith, you have great reason to be sad. I fear you have sold your own lands to see other men's; then to have seen much, and to have nothing is to have rich eyes and poor hands" (IV. i. 21–25).

II.

[P12]   You endless torments that my rest opress
        How long will you delight in my sad paine?
        Will never love your favour more express?
        Shall I still live, and ever feele disdaine?

5   Alass now stay, and lett my griefe obtaine
        Some end; feede nott my hart with sharpe distress:
        Lett mee once see my cruell fortunes gaine
        Att least release, and long felt woes redress;

    Lett nott the blame of cruelty disgrace
10   The honor'd title of your Godhed, Love:
        Give nott just cause for mee to say a place
        Is found for rage alone on mee to move;

    O quickly end, and doe nott long debate
    My needfull ayde, least help do come too late.

12.

[P13]   Cloy'd with the torments of a tedious night
        I wish for day; which come, I hope for joy:
        When cross I finde new tortures to destroy
        My woe-kil'd hart, first hurt by mischiefs might,

5   Then cry for night, and once more day takes flight
        And brightnes gon; what rest should heere injoy
        Usurped is; hate will her force imploy;
        Night can nott griefe intombe though black as spite.

    My thoughts are sad; her face as sad doth seeme:
10   My paines are long; Her houers taedious are:
        My griefe is great, and endles is my care:
        Her face, her force, and all of woes esteeme:

    Then wellcome Night, and farwell flattring day
    Which all hopes breed, and yett our joyes delay.

1–5. The lover's alternative cries for the coming of night and day appear in *AS* 89;
Spenser, *Amoretti*, 86; and Sir Robert Sidney, Sonnet 19.1–4:

> When other creatures all in theyr kinde
> Comfort of light, quiet from darcknes featch
> Of wretched monsters, I most monstrous wreatch
> Nor day from paines, nor night with rest can finde.

9. her face: Night's

Song. 2.

[P14] All night I weepe, all day I cry, Ay mee;
I still doe wish though yett deny, Ay mee;
I sigh, I mourne, I say that still
I only ame the store for ill,   Ay mee;

5   In coldest hopes I freeze, yett burne Ay mee;   *Petrarch*
From flames I strive to fly, yett turne Ay mee;
From griefe I haste butt sorrowes hy,
And on my hart all woes doe ly Ay mee;

From contraries I seeke to runn Ay mee; *Contraries*
10   Butt contraries I can nott shunn Ay mee;
For they delight theyr force to try,
And to despaire my thoughts doe ty Ay mee;

Whether (alass) then shall I goe Ay mee;
When as dispaire all hopes outgoe Ay mee;
15   Iff to the Forest, Cupid hyes,
And my poore soule to his lawe ties Ay me;

To the Court? O no. Hee crys fy Ay mee;
Ther no true love you shall espy Ay mee;
Leave that place to faulscest lovers
20   Your true love all truth discovers Ay mee;

Then quiett rest, and noe more prove Ay mee;
All places ar alike to love Ay mee;
And constant bee in this beegunn
Yett say, till lyfe with love be dunn Ay mee.

1. A shortened, revised form of this poem appears anonymously in *Wit's Recreations*
(London: R. Cotes, 1645), Wing M1712, sig. V6:

> SIGHS
> All night I muse, all day I cry,
>   Ay me
> Yet still I wish, though still deny.
>   Ay me
> I sigh, I mourne, and say that still,

I onely live my joyes to kill.
    Ay me

I feed the pain that on me feeds,
    Ay me
My wound I stop not, though it bleeds;
    Ay me
Heart, be content, it must be so,
For springs were made to overflow.
    Ay me

Then sigh and weepe, and mourne thy fill,
    Ay me
Seek no redresse, but languish still,
    Ay me
Their griefes more willing they endure,
That know when they are past recure.
    Ay me

Norman Ault reprints a modernized text of this version in *Seventeenth Century Lyrics from Original Texts* (2nd ed.; New York: Sloane, 1950), 187.

13.

[P15] Deare fammish nott what you your self gave food;
            Destroy nott what your glory is to save;
            Kill nott that soule to which you spiritt gave;
            In pitty, nott disdaine your triumph stood;

5   An easy thing itt is to shed the blood
            Of one, who att your will, yeelds to the grave;
            Butt more you may true worthe by mercy crave
            When you preserve, nott spoyle, butt nurrish good;

        Your sight is all the food I doe desire;
10   Then sacrifies mee nott in hidden fire,
            Or stop the breath which did your prayses move:

        Think butt how easy t'is a sight to give;
            Nay ev'n deserte; since by itt I doe live,
            I butt Camaelion-like would live, and love.

14. The chameleon was formerly believed to live on air because of its inanimate appearance and its ability to exist for long periods without food: Pliny, *Natural History*, XXVIII, 8; Erasmus, *Similia*, ed. 1703, col. 607D; compare *Hamlet*: King. "How fares our cousin Hamlet?" Hamlet. "Excellent, i' faith, of the chameleon's dish: I eat the air, promise-cramm'd" (III. ii. 92–94).

14.

[P16] Am I thus conquer'd? have I lost the powers
            That to withstand, which joy's to ruin mee?

Must I bee still while itt my strength devowres
And captive leads mee prisoner, bound, unfree?

5 Love first shall leave mens phant'sies to them free,
Desire shall quench loves flames, spring hate sweet showres,
Love shall loose all his darts, have sight, and see
His shame, and wishings hinder happy howres;

Why should wee nott loves purblind charmes resist?
10 Must wee bee servile, doing what hee list?
Noe, seeke some hoste to harbour thee: I fly

Thy babish trickes, and freedome doe profess;
Butt Ô my hurt, makes my lost hart confess
I love, and must: So farwell liberty.

> 9. purblind: totally or quite blind
> 14. Loss of liberty was a favorite *topos* of the sonneteers from the time of Petrarch's
> *Rime* 97, "Ahi, bella liberta": Janet G. Scott, *Les Sonnets Elisabéthains* (Paris: Librairie
> Ancienne Honoré Champion, 1929), 305. See *AS* 2 and 47 (which also begins with a
> question and involves a sudden reversal in the concluding couplet).

15.

[P17] Truly poore Night thou wellcome art to mee:
I love thee better in this sad attire
Then that which raiseth some mens phant'sies higher
Like painted outsids which foule inward bee;

5 I love thy grave, and saddest lookes to see,
Which seems my soule, and dying hart intire,
Like to the ashes of some happy fire
That flam'd in joy, butt quench'd in miserie:

I love thy count'nance, and thy sober pace
10 Which evenly goes, and as of loving grace
To uss, and mee among the rest oprest

Gives quiet, peace to my poore self alone,
And freely grants day leave when thou art gone
To give cleere light to see all ill redrest.

16.

[P18] Sleepe fy possess mee nott, nor doe nott fright
Mee with thy heavy, and thy deathlike might
For counterfetting's vilder then deaths sight,
And such deluding more my thoughts doe spite.

5   Thou suff'rest faulsest shapes my soule t'affright
      Some times in liknes of a hopefull spright,
      And oft times like my love as in dispite
      Joying thou canst with mallice kill delight,

      When I (a poore foole made by thee) think joy
10   Doth flow, when thy fond shadows doe destroy
      My that while senceles self, left free to thee,

      Butt now doe well, lett mee for ever sleepe,
      And soe for ever that deare Image keepe,
      Or still wake, that my sences may bee free.

11. Apostrophe to Sleep: *AS* 39. See the depiction of the lover's nightmares in Sir
Robert Sidney's Sonnet 6.12–14:
    Repulses and the thowsand formed head
    Of scorn I see, while unjust night from me
    Her beauty hides, and shews her crueltee.

17.

[P19]   Sweet shades why doe you seeke to give delight
      To mee who deeme delight in this vilde place
      Butt torment, sorrow, and mine owne disgrace
      To taste of joy, or your vaine pleasing sight;

5   Show them your pleasures who saw never night
      Of griefe, wher joyings fauning, smiling face
      Appeers as day, wher griefe found never space
      Yett for a sigh, a grone, or envies spite;

      Butt O on mee a world of woes doe ly,
10   Or els on mee all harmes strive to rely,
      And to attend like servants bound to mee,

      Heat in desire, while frosts of care I prove,
      Wanting my love, yett surfett doe with love
      Burne, and yett freeze, better in hell to bee.

14. Sidney mocked this Petrarchan imagery in *AS* 6.1–4:
Some Lovers speake when they their Muses entertaine,
Of hopes begot by feare, of wot not what desires:
Of force of heav'nly beames, infusing hellish paine:
Of living deaths, deare wounds, faire stormes, and freesing fires:

18.

[P20]   Which should I better like of, day, or night
      Since all the day I live in bitter woe

    Injoying light more cleere my wrongs to know,
    And yett most sad, feeling in itt all spite;

5 In night, when darknes doth forbid all light
    Yett see I griefe aparant to the show
    Follow'd by jealousie whose fond tricks flow,
    And on unconstant waves of doubt allight,

    I can beehold rage cowardly to feede
10   Upon foule error which thes humours breed
    Shame, doubt, and feare, yett boldly will think ill,

    All those in both I feele, then which is best
    Darke to joy by day, light in night oprest
    Leave both, and end, thes butt each other spill.

   1. This poem continues the debate found earlier in P13.

Song. 3.

[P21] Stay, my thoughts, do nott aspire
    To vaine hopes of high desire:
    See you nott all meanes bereft
    To injoye? noe joye is left;
5   Yett still mee thinks my thoughts doe say
    Some hopes do live amid dismay;

    Hope, then once more hope for joy;
    Bury feare which joyes destroy;
    Thought hath yett some comfort giv'ne
10   Which dispaire hath from us drivn;
    Therfor deerly my thoughts cherish
    Never lett such thinking perish;

    'Tis an idle thing to plaine
    Odder farr to dy for paine,
15   Thinke, and see how thoughts do rise
    Winning wher ther noe hope lies:
    Which alone is lovers treasure
    For by thoughts wee love doe measure:

    Then kinde thought my phant'sie guide
20   Lett mee never haples slide;
    Still maintaine thy force in mee,
    Lett mee thinking still bee free:
    Nor leave thy might untill my death
    Butt lett mee thinking yeeld up breath.

19.

[P22] Come darkest night, beecoming sorrow best;
    Light; leave thy light; fitt for a lightsome soule;
    Darknes doth truly sute with mee oprest
    Whom absence power doth from mirthe controle:

5   The very trees with hanging heads condole
    Sweet sommers parting, and of leaves distrest
    In dying coulers make a griefe-full role;
    Soe much (alas) to sorrow are they prest.

Thus of dead leaves her farewell carpett's made:
10   Theyr fall, theyr branches, all theyr mournings prove;
    With leavles, naked bodies, whose huese vade
    From hopefull greene, to wither in theyr love,

If trees, and leaves for absence, mourners bee
Noe mervaile that I grieve, who like want see.

11. vade: to decay, fade, or wax weak, as a distinct word derived from the Latin *vadere*; compare Shakespeare, Sonnet 54.14

20.

[P23] The Sunn which glads, the earth att his bright sight
    When in the morne hee showes his golden face,
    And takes the place from taedious drowsy night
    Making the world still happy in his grace;

5   Shewes hapines remaines nott in one place,
    Nor may the heavens alone to us give light,
    Butt hide that cheerfull face, though noe long space,
    Yett long enough for triall of theyr might;

Butt never sunn-sett could bee soe obscure
10   No desart ever had a shade soe sadd,
    Nor could black darknes ever prove soe badd
    As paines which absence makes mee now indure;

The missing of the sunn awhile makes night
Butt absence of my joy sees never Light.

1. Lisle C. John offers a long catalogue of the sonneteers' use of the theme of absence: *The Elizabethan Sonnet Sequence: Studies in Conventional Conceits* (New York: Columbia University Press, 1938), 196. See especially *AS* 91.3–4: "And that faire you my Sunne, thus overspred / With absence' Vaile, I live in Sorowe's night." Sir Robert Sidney also uses a related image in Sonnet 30.1–2: "Absence, I cannot say thow hyd'st my light / Not darckned, but for ay sett is my Sunn."
10. desart: any uninhabited place, including forest terrain.

21.

[P24] When last I saw thee, I did nott thee see,
      Itt was thine Image, which in my thoughts lay
      Soe lively figur'd, as noe times delay
      Could suffer mee in hart to parted bee;

5   And sleepe soe favorable is to mee,
      As nott to lett thy lov'd remembrance stray,
      Least that I waking might have cause to say
      Ther was one minute found to forgett thee;

     Then since my faith is such, soe kind my sleepe
10   That gladly thee presents into my thought:
      And still true lover like thy face doth keepe
      Soe as some pleasure shadowe-like is wrought.

     Pitty my loving, nay of consience give
     Reward to mee in whom thy self doth live.

22.

[P25] Like to the Indians, scorched with the sunne,
      The sunn which they doe as theyr God adore
      Soe ame I us'd by love, for ever more
      I worship him, less favors have I wunn,

5   Better are they who thus to blacknes runn,
      And soe can only whitenes want deplore
      Then I who pale, and white ame with griefs store,
      Nor can have hope, butt to see hopes undunn;

     Beesids theyr sacrifies receavd's in sight
10   Of theyr chose sainte: Mine hid as worthles rite;
      Grant mee to see wher I my offrings give,

     Then lett mee weare the marke of Cupids might
     In hart as they in skin of Phoebus light
     Nott ceasing offrings to love while I Live.

5. The reference to the black Indian recalls Lady Mary's participation in Ben Jonson's *Masque of Blackness* (1606). See C. H. Herford and Percy Simpson (eds.), *The Works of Ben Jonson* (11 vols.; Oxford: Clarendon Press, 1925–52), VII, 161–202.
    9. receavd's: received is

23.

[P26] When every one to pleasing pastime hies
      Some hunt, some hauke, some play, while some delight

In sweet discourse, and musique showes joys might
[Yett I my thoughts doe farr above thes prise.]

5 The joy which I take, is that free from eyes
   I sitt, and wunder att this daylike night
   Soe to dispose [them-selves,] as voyd of right;
   And leave true pleasure for poore vanities;

When others hunt, my thoughts I have in chase;
10   If hauke, my minde att wished end doth fly,
   Discourse, I with my spiritt tauke, and cry
   While others, musique choose as greatest grace.

O God, say I, can thes fond pleasures move?
Or musique bee butt in sweet thoughts of love?

24.

{P27} Once did I heere an aged father say
   Unto his sonn who with attention hears
   What age, and wise experience ever clears
   From doubts of feare, or reason to betray,

5 "My Sonn" sayd hee, beehold thy father, gray,
   I once had as thou hast, fresh tender years,
   And like thee sported, destitude of feares
   Butt my young faults made mee too soone decay,

Love once I did, and like thee fear'd my love,
10   Led by the hatefull thread of Jelousy,
   Striving to keepe, I lost my liberty,
   And gain'd my griefe which still my sorrowes move,

In time shunn this; To love is noe offence
Butt doubt in youth, in age breeds penitence."

    1. This poem resembles Sir Philip Sidney's eclogue between old Geron and young Histor concerning the importance of constant love: *OA* 67.

Song. 4.

{P28} Sweetest love returne againe
   Make nott too long stay:
   Killing mirthe, and forceing paine
   Sorrow leading way:
5 Lett us nott thus parted bee
   Love, and absence ne're agree;

Butt since you must needs depart,
    And mee haples leave,
In your journey take my hart
10   Which will nott deseave
Yours itt is, to you itt flyes
Joying in those loved eyes,

Soe in part, wee shall nott part
    Though wee absent bee;
15   Time, nor place, nor greatest smart
    Shall my bands make free
Ty'de I ame, yett thinke itt gaine;
In such knotts I feele noe paine.

Butt can I live having lost
20   Chiefest part of mee
Hart is fled, and sight is crost
    These my fortunes bee
Yett deere hart goe, soone returne
As good there, as heere to burne.

1. In tone and content, this song is reminiscent of Donne's "Sweetest Love I Do Not Go."

25.

[P29] Poore eyes bee blind, the light behold noe more
    Since that is gon which is your deere delight
    Ravish'd from you by greater powre, and might
    Making your loss a gaine to others store,

5   Oreflowe, and drowne, till sight to you restore
    That blessed star, and as in hatefull spite
    Send forth your teares in flouds, to kill all sight,
    And looks, that lost, wherin you joy'd before.

Bury thes beames, which in some kindled fires,
10   And conquer'd have theyr love-burnt-harts desires
    Loosing, and yett noe gaine by you esteem'd,

Till that bright starr doe once againe apeere
    Brighter then Mars when hee doth shine most cleere
    See nott: then by his might bee you redeem'd.

7. flouds: obsolete form of floods
13. It is appropriate that the sonneteer compares her "star" with the masculine Mars, rather than the traditional feminine planet, Venus.

26.

[P30] Deare cherish this, and with itt my soules will,
    Nor for itt rann away doe itt abuse,
    Alas itt left poore mee your brest to chuse
    As the blest shrine wher itt would harbour still;

5 Then favor shew, and nott unkindly kill
    The hart which fled to you, butt doe excuse
    That which for better, did the wurse refuse,
    And pleas'd I'le bee, though hartles my lyfe spill,

Butt if you will bee kind, and just indeed,
10 Send mee your hart which in mines place shall feed
    On faithfull love to your devotion bound;

Ther shall itt see the sacrifises made
    Of pure, and spottles love which shall nott vade
    While soule, and body are together found.

    1. this: heart
    6. As Lisle John (*Elizabethan Sonnet Sequence*, 197) shows, the migration of the heart was a standard *topos* of the sonneteers. See especially *AS* Song 10.40–41: "We change eyes, and hart for hart, / Each to other do imparte."
    13. vade: fade; see P22.11

27.

[P31] Fy tedious Hope, why doe you still rebell?
    Is itt nott yett enough you flatterd mee?
    Butt cuningly you seeke to use a spell
    How to beetray, must thes your trophies bee?

5 I look'd from you farr sweeter fruite to see
    Butt blasted were your blossoms when they fell,
    And those delights expected from hands free
    Wither'd, and dead, and what seem'd bliss proves Hell.

Noe towne was wunn by a more plotted slight
10 Then I by you, who may my fortune write
    In embers of that fire which ruind mee,

Thus Hope, your faulshood calls you to bee tride
    You're loth I see the triall to abide;
    Prove true att last, and gaine your liberty.

    1. Sidney also addresses Hope with a question, *AS* 67.1: "HOPE, art thou true, or doest thou flatter me?"
    9. slight: sleight, deception

28.

[P32] Griefe, killing griefe: have nott my torments binn
      Allreddy great, and strong enough: butt still
      Thou dost increase, nay glory in mine ill,
      And woes new past affresh new woes beeginn!

5 Am I the only purchase thou canst winn?
      Was I ordain'd to give dispaire her fill
      Or fittest I should mounte misfortunes hill
      Who in the plaine of joy can-nott live in?

  If itt bee soe: Griefe come as wellcome ghest
10 Since I must suffer, for an others rest:
      Yett this good griefe, lett mee intreat of thee,

  Use still thy force, butt nott from those I love
      Lett mee all paines, and lasting torments prove
      Soe I miss thes, lay all thy waits on mee.

    1. The apostrophe to Grief closely follows the model of *AS* 94; both speakers rail
against grief, then suddenly turn to welcome the emotion.
    14. waits: obs. form of weights

29.

[P33] Fly hence O! joy noe longer heere abide
      Too great thy pleasures ar for my dispaire
      To looke on, losses now must prove my fare
      Who nott long since, on better foode relide;

5 Butt foole, how oft had I heavns changing spide
      Beefore of mine owne fate I could have care,
      Yett now past time, I can too late beeware
      When nothing's left butt sorrowes faster tyde;

  While I injoy'd that sunn whose sight did lend
10 Mee joy, I thought, that day, could have noe end
      Butt soone a night came cloth'd in absence darke,

  Absence more sad, more bitter then is gall
      Or death, when on true lovers itt doth fall
      Whose fires of love, disdaine rests poorer sparke.

30.

[P34] You blessed shades, which give mee silent rest,
      Wittnes butt this when death hath clos'd mine eyes,

And separated mee from earthly ties,
Beeing from hence to higher place adrest;

5   How oft in you I have laine heere oprest,
And have my miseries in woefull cries
Deliver'd forth, mounting up to the skies
Yett helples back returnd to wound my brest,

Which wounds did butt strive how, to breed more harme
10   To mee, who, can bee cur'de by noe one charme
Butt that of love, which yett may mee releeve;

If nott, lett death my former paines redeeme,
My trusty freinds, my faith untouch'd esteeme
And wittnes I could love, who soe could greeve.

12–14. The conclusion to this sonnet recalls the last stanza of Sir Robert Sidney's
Song 19.13–16:
> Mortal in love are joye and pleasure
> The fading frame, wherin love moves
> But greef and anguish are the measure
> That do immortalyze owr loves.

Song. 5.

[P35]   Time only cause of my unrest
By whom I hop'd once to bee blest
How cruell art thou turned?
That first gav'st lyfe unto my love,
5   And still a pleasure nott to move
Or change though ever burned;

Have I thee slack'd, or left undun
One loving rite, and soe have wunn
Thy rage or bitter changing?
10   That now noe minutes I shall see,
Wherin I may least happy bee
Thy favors soe estranging.

Blame thy self, and nott my folly,
Time gave time butt to bee holly;
15   True love such ends best loveth,
Unworthy love doth seeke for ends
A worthy love butt worth pretends
Nor other thoughts itt proveth:

Then stay thy swiftnes cruell time,
20   And lett mee once more blessed clime
To joy, that I may prayse thee:

Lett mee pleasure sweetly tasting
Joy in love, and faith nott wasting
   And on fames wings I'le rayse thee:
25 Never shall thy glory dying
Bee untill thine owne untying
   That time noe longer liveth;
T'is a gaine such tyme to lend:
Since soe thy fame shall never end
30   Butt joy for what she giveth.

31.

[P36] After long trouble in a taedious way
   Of loves unrest, lay'd downe to ease my paine
   Hopeing for rest, new torments I did gaine
   Possessing mee as if I ought t'obay:

5 When Fortune came, though blinded, yett did stay,
   And in her blesse'd armes did mee inchaine;
   I, colde with griefe, thought noe warmth to obtaine
   Or to dissolve that ice of joyes decay;

Till, 'rise sayd she, Reward to thee doth send
10   By mee the servante of true lovers, joy:
   Bannish all clowds of doubt, all feares destroy,
   And now on fortune, and on Love depend.

I, her obay'd, and rising felt that love
Indeed was best, when I did least itt move.

32.

[P37] How fast thou fliest, O Time, on loves swift wings
   To hopes of joy, that flatters our desire
   Which to a lover, still, contentment brings!
   Yett, when wee should injoy thou dost retire,

5 Thou stay'st thy pace faulse time from our desire,
   When to our ill thou hast'st with Eagles wings,
   Slowe, only to make us see thy retire
   Was for dispayre, and harme, which sorrowe brings;

O! slacke thy pase, and milder pass to love;
10   Bee like the Bee, whose wings she doth butt use
   To bring home profitt, masters good to prove
   Laden, and weary, yett againe pursues,

Soe lade thy self with honnye of sweet joye,
And doe nott mee the Hive of love destroy.

> 10–12. The image of the bee, which brings profit to others, was often used in illustrations of Sir Philip Sidney's motto: *sic vos non vobis*. See Emma M. Denkinger, "Some Renaissance References to *Sic Vos Non Vobis*," *Philological Quarterly*, x, 151–62.

33.

[P38] How many eyes poore Love hast thou to guard
     Thee, from thy most desired wish, and end?
     Is itt because some say thou'art blind, that bard
     From sight, thou should'st noe hapines attend?

5 Who blame thee soe, smale justice can pretend
     Since 'twixt thee, and the sunn noe question hard
     Can bee, his sight butt outward, thou canst bend
     The hart, and guide itt freely; thus unbard

Art thou, while wee both blind, and bold oft dare
10   Accuse thee of the harmes, our selves should find
     Who led with folly, and by rashnes blind
     Thy sacred powre, doe with a childs compare.

Yett Love this boldnes pardon: for admire
Thee sure wee must, or bee borne without fire.

> 9–10. See *AS* 5.5–6: "It is most true, what we call *Cupid's* dart / An image is, which for our selves we carve."

34.

[P39] Take heed mine eyes, how you your lookes doe cast
     Least they beetray my harts most secrett thought;
     Bee true unto your selves for nothings bought
     More deere then doubt which brings a lovers fast.

5 Catch you all waching eyes, ere they bee past,
     Or take yours fixt wher your best love hath sought
     The pride of your desires; lett them bee taught
     Theyr faults for shame, they could noe truer last;

Then looke, and looke with joye for conquest wunn
10   Of those that search'd your hurt in double kinde;
     Soe you kept safe, lett them themselves looke blinde
     Watch, gaze, and marke till they to madnes runn,

While you, mine eyes injoye full sight of love
Contented that such hapinesses move.

5–7. A similar depiction of the "all waching eyes" of jealousy is found in *AS*
78.12–13: "So manie eyes ay seeking their owne woe, / So ample eares as never good
newes know."

35.

{P40} Faulce hope which feeds butt to destroy, and spill
　　　　What itt first breeds; unaturall to the birth
　　　　Of thine owne wombe; conceaving butt to kill,
　　　　And plenty gives to make the greater dearth,

5　　Soe Tirants doe who faulsly ruling earth
　　　　Outwardly grace them, and with profitts fill
　　　　Advance those who appointed are to death
　　　　To make theyr greater falle to please theyr will.

　　　　Thus shadow they theyr wicked vile intent
10　　Coulering evill with a show of good
　　　　While in faire showes theyr malice soe is spent;
　　　　Hope kills the hart, and tirants shed the blood.

　　　　For hope deluding brings us to the pride
　　　　Of our desires the farder downe to slide.

2–3. The image of miscarriage aptly describes the deceptions of Hope, which "feeds
butt to destroy."

36.

{P41} How well poore hart thou wittnes canst I love,
　　　　How oft my griefe hath made thee shed for teares
　　　　Drops of thy deerest blood, and how oft feares
　　　　Borne testimony of the paines I prove,

5　　What torments hast thou sufferd while above
　　　　Joy, thou tortur'd wert with racks which longing beares
　　　　Pinch'd with desires which yett butt wishing reares
　　　　Firme in my faith, in constancy to move,

　　　　Yett is itt sayd that sure love can nott bee
10　　Wher soe small showe of passion is descrid,
　　　　When thy chiefe paine is that I must itt hide
　　　　From all save only one who showld itt see.

　　　　For know more passion in my hart doth move
　　　　Then in a million that make show of love.

Song. 6.

[P42]   You happy blessed eyes,
        Which in that ruling place
        Have force both to delight, and to disgrace,
        Whose light allures, and ties
5   All harts to your command
        O! looke on mee, who doe att mercy stand:

        T'is you that rule my lyfe
        T'is you my comforts give;
        Then lett nott scorne to mee my ending drive,
10   Nor lett the frownes of stryfe
        Have might to hurt those lights
        Which while they shine they are true loves delights;

        See butt, when Night appears,
        And Sunn hath lost his force
15   How his loss doth all joye from us divorce;
        And when hee shines, and cleares
        The heav'ns from clowds of night
        How happy then is made our gazing sight,

        Butt more then Sunns faire light
20   Your beames doe seeme to mee,
        Whose sweetest lookes doe tye and yett make free;
        Why should you then soe spite
        Poore mee as to destroy
        The only pleasure that I taste of joye?

25   Shine then, O deerest lights
        With favor, and with love,
        And lett noe cause, your cause of frownings move
        Butt as the soules delights
        Soe bless my then-bless'd eyes
30   Which unto you theyr true affection tyes.

        Then shall the Sunn give place
        As to your greater might,
        Yeelding that you doe show more parfect light,
        O, then, butt grant this grace
35   Unto your love-tied slave
        To shine on mee, who to you all fayth gave;

        And when you please to frowne
        Use your most killing eyes
        On them, who in untruth and faulcehood lyes;

40   Butt (deare) on mee cast downe
       Sweet lookes for true desire
       That bannish doe all thoughts of fayned fire.

> 7−12. A parallel is found in Sir Robert Sidney's Song 11.1−4:
> Thowghts unto me so deer
> As unto yow I live.
> Thowghts unto whome I give
> A mind from all els cleer.
> See Kelliher and Duncan-Jones, "A Manuscript of Poems by Robert Sidney," 114−15.

37.

[P43] Night, welcome art thou to my mind destrest
       Darke, heavy, sad, yett nott more sad then I
       Never could'st thou find fitter company
       For thine owne humor then I thus oprest.

5   If thou beest dark, my wrongs still unredrest
       Saw never light, nor smalest bliss can spy;
       If heavy, joy from mee too fast doth hy
       And care outgoes my hope of quiett rest,

    Then now in freindship joine with haples mee,
10   Who ame as sad, and dark as thou canst bee
       Hating all pleasure, or delight of lyfe;

    Silence, and griefe, with thee I best doe love
       And from you three, I know I can nott move,
       Then lett us live companions without strife.

> 9−14. The three companions, Night, Silence, and Grief, all appear in *AS* 96.1−5:
> THOUGHT with good cause thou likest so well the night,
>   Since kind or chance gives both one liverie,
>   Both sadly blacke, both blackly darkned be,
> Night bard from Sun, thou from thy owne sunne's light;
> Silence in both displaies his sullen might.

38.

[P44] What pleasure can a bannish'd creature have
       In all the pastimes that invented arr
       By witt or learning, absence making warr
       Against all peace that may a biding crave;

5   Can wee delight butt in a wellcome grave
       Wher wee may bury paines, and soe bee farr
       From lothed company who allways jarr
       Upon the string of mirthe that pastime gave;

The knowing part of joye is deem'd the hart;
10 If that bee gon, what joy can joy impart
  When senceless is the feeler of our mirthe;

Noe, I ame bannish'd, and no good shall find
  Butt all my fortunes must with mischief bind
  Who butt for miserie did gaine a birth.

 4. biding: shelter
 7–8. See *AS* 27.2, where Astrophil feels "most alone in greatest companie."

39.

[P45] Iff I were giv'n to mirthe 't'wowld bee more cross
  Thus to bee robbed of my chiefest joy;
  Butt silently I beare my greatest loss
  Who's us'd to sorrow, griefe will nott destroy;

5 Nor can I as those pleasant witts injoy
  My owne fram'd words, which I account the dross
  Of purer thoughts, or recken them as moss
  While they (witt sick) them selves to breath imploy,

Alas, think I, your plenty shewes your want,
10 For wher most feeling is, words are more scant,
  Yett pardon mee, Live, and your pleasure take,

Grudg nott, if I neglected, envy show
  'T'is nott to you that I dislike doe owe
  Butt crost my self, wish some like mee to make.

 5–7. Like Astrophil, the speaker regards her own writing with self-contempt: *AS* 50.7–8.

40.

[P46] Itt is nott love which you poore fooles do deeme
  That doth apeare by fond, and outward showes
  Of kissing, toying, or by swearings glose,
  O noe thes are farr off from loves esteeme;

5 Alas they ar nott such that can redeeme
  Love lost, or wining keepe those chosen blowes
  Though oft with face, and lookes love overthrowse
  Yett soe slight conquest doth nott him beeseeme,

'T'is nott a showe of sighes, or teares can prove
10 Who loves indeed which blasts of fained love
  Increase, or dy as favors from them slide;

Butt in the soule true love in safety lies
   Guarded by faith which to desart still hies,
   And yett kinde lookes doe many blessings hide.

   3. glose: veil with specious comments

41.

[P47] You blessed starrs which doe heavns glory show,
     And att your brightnes makes our eyes admire
     Yett envy nott though I on earth beelow
     Injoy a sight which moves in mee more fire;

5   I doe confess such beauty breeds desire,
     You shine, and cleerest light on us beestow,
     Yett doth a sight on earth more warmth inspire
     Into my loving soule, his grace to knowe;

Cleere, bright, and shining as you are, is this
10   Light of my joye, fixt stedfast nor will move
     His light from mee, nor I chang from his love,
     Butt still increase as th'eith of all my bliss.

His sight gives lyfe unto my love-rulde eyes
My love content beecause in his, love lies.

   12. th'eith: the height

42.

[P48] If ever love had force in humaine brest?
     If ever hee could move in pensive hart?
     Or if that hee such powre could butt impart
     To breed those flames whose heat brings joys unrest.

5   Then looke on mee; I ame to thes adrest,
     I, ame the soule that feeles the greatest smart;
     I, ame that hartles trunk of harts depart
     And I, that one, by love, and griefe oprest;

Non ever felt the truth of loves great miss
10   Of eyes, till I deprived was of bliss;
     For had hee seene, hee must have pitty show'd;

I should nott have bin made this stage of woe
Wher sad disasters have theyr open showe
O noe, more pitty hee had sure beestow'd.

12–14. For a similar image, see Fulke Greville's *Caelica*, 9.13: "For sorrow holds man's life to be her own, / His thoughts her stage, where tragedies she plays."

Song. 7.

[P49]   Sorrow, I yeeld, and greive that I did miss:
Will nott thy rage bee satisfied with this?
    As sad a Divell as thee,
    Made mee unhapy bee.

5   Wilt thou nott yett consent to leave, butt still
Strive how to showe thy cursed, devilsh skill;

I mourne, and dying am; what would you more?
My soule attends, to leave this cursed shore
    Wher harmes doe only flow
10   Which teach mee butt to know
The sadest howres of my lives unrest,
And tired minutes with griefs hand oprest:

Yett all this will nott pacefy thy spite;
No, nothing can bring ease butt my last night.
15   Then quickly lett itt bee
    While I unhappy see
That time, soe sparing to grant lovers bliss
Will see for time lost, ther shall noe grief miss,

Nor lett mee ever cease from lasting griefe,
20   Butt endless lett itt bee without reliefe:
    To winn againe of love,
    The favor I did prove;
And with my end please him; since dying I
Have him offended, yett unwillingly.

43.

[P50]   O dearest eyes the lights, and guids of love,
    The joyes of Cupid who himself borne blind
    To your bright shining doth his triumphs bind
    For in your seeing doth his glory move;

5   How happy are those places wher you prove
    Your heavnly beames which makes the sunn to find
    Envy, and grudging hee soe long hath shind
    For your cleer lights, to mach his beames above.

Butt now, Alas, your sight is heere forbid
10   And darknes must thes poore lost roomes possess

    Soe bee all blessed lights from henceforth hid
    That this black deed of darknes have excess,

For why showld heaven afford least light to those
Who for my misery such darcknes chose.

44.

<table>
<tr><td>[P51]</td><td>How fast thou hast'st (O spring) with sweetest speed</td></tr>
</table>

[P51] How fast thou hast'st (O spring) with sweetest speed
    To catch thy waters which befor are runn,
    And of the greater rivers wellcom wunn,
    'Ere thes thy new borne streames thes places feed,

5 Yett you doe well least staying heere might breed
    Dangerous fluds your sweetest banks t'orerunn,
    And yett much better my distress to shunn
    Which makes my teares your swiftest course succeed,

Butt best you doe when with soe hasty flight,
10   You fly my ills which now my self outgoe,
    Whose broken hart can testify such woe,
    That soe o'recharg'd my lyfe blood wasteth quite.

Sweet spring then keepe your way, bee never spent
And my ill days, or griefs assunder rent.

45.

[P52] Good now bee still, and doe nott mee torment
    With multituds of questions, bee att rest,
    And only lett mee quarrell with my brest
    Which still letts in new stormes my soule to rent;

5 Fy, will you still my mischiefs more augment?
    You say I answere cross, I that confest
    Long since, yett must I ever bee oprest
    With your toungue torture which will ne're bee spent?

Well then I see noe way butt this will fright
10   That Divell speach; Alas I ame possesst,
    And mad folks senceles ar of wisdomes right,

The hellish speritt absence doth arest
    All my poore sences to his cruell might,
    Spare mee then till I ame my self, and blest.

1. See Astrophil's two sonnets in answer to a friend, who chastises him for loving: *AS* 14 and 21.

46.

{P53} Love, thou hast all, for now thou hast mee made
      Soe thine, as if for thee I were ordain'd;
      Then take thy conquest, nor lett mee bee pain'd
      More in thy sunn, when I doe seeke thy shade,

5   Noe place for help have I left to invade,
      That show'de a face wher least ease might bee gain'd;
      Yett found I paine increase, and butt obtain'd
      That this noe way was to have love allayd,

When hott and thirsty to a well I came
10   Trusting by that to quench part of my flame,
      Butt ther I was by love afresh imbrac'd;

Drinke I could nott, butt in itt I did see
      My self a living glass as well as shee
      For love to see him self in truly plac'd.

47.

{P54} O stay mine eyes, shed nott thes fruitles teares
      Since hope is past to winn you back againe
      That treasure which beeing lost breeds all your paine,
      Cease from this poore betraying of your feares,

5   Think this too childish is, for wher griefe reares
      Soe high a powre, for such a wreched gaine;
      Sighs, nor laments should thus bee spent in vaine:
      True sorrow, never outward wayling beares;

Bee rul'd by mee, keepe all the rest in store,
10   Till noe roome is that may containe one more,
      Then in that sea of teares, drowne haples mee,

And I'le provide such store of sighs as part
      Shalbee enough to breake the strongest hart,
      This dunn, wee shall from torments freed bee.

48.

{P55} How like a fire doth love increase in mee,
      The longer that itt lasts, the stronger still,
      The greater purer, brighter, and doth fill
      Noe eye with wunder more, then hopes still bee

5   Bred in my brest, when fires of love are free
        To use that part to theyr best pleasing will,
        And now impossible itt is to kill
        The heat soe great wher Love his strength doth see.

     Mine eyes can scarce sustaine the flames my hart
10   Doth trust in them my passions to impart,
        And languishingly strive to show my love;

     My breath nott able is to breathe least part
        Of that increasing fuell of my smart;
        Yett love I will till I butt ashes prove.

                    Pamphilia.

12–14. The conclusion resembles that of Sir Robert Sidney in Sonnet 9.12–14:
    I yealde, I love, to yow, then erst, I burn,
    More hott, more pure, like wood oft warme before
    But to yow burnt to dust, kan burn no more.

    14. May N. Paulissen first noted the possibility of a pun on the name "will," but she
was unable to identify the person: "The Love Sonnets of Lady Mary Wroth: A Critical
Introduction" (Ph.D. dissertation, University of Houston, 1976), 48, 152. Many of the
Elizabethan sonneteers, such as Sidney, Drayton, and Shakespeare, used the device of the
embedded name, and in this case the poet may be alluding to her lover, William
Herbert, third Earl of Pembroke. If so, here is one of the very few places in which the
identification of Amphilanthus is made explicit. To conclude the first section of sonnets
(P1–55), Lady Mary Wroth signed the name "Pamphilia" immediately below this
poem.

                    Sonnet.

[P56] Lett griefe as farr bee from your deerest brest
        As I doe wish, or in my hands to ease;
        Then showld itt bannist bee, and sweetest rest
        Bee plac'ed to give content by love to please,

5   Lett those disdaines which on your hart doe seaze
        Doubly returne to bring her soules unrest,
        Since true love will nott, that beelov'd displease
        Or lett least smart to theyr minds bee adrest,

     Butt often times mistakings bee in love,
10   Bee they as farr from faulce accusing right,
        And still truthe governe with a constant might,
        Soe shall you only wished pleasures prove,

     And as for mee, she that showes you least scorne,
     With all despite, and hate bee her hart torne.

Song.

[P57]   O mee the time is come to part,
        And with itt my lyfe-killing smart
        Fond hope leave mee my deer must goe
        To meet more joy, and I more woe;

5   Wher still of mirth injoye thy fill
        One is enough to suffer ill
        My hart soe well to sorrow us'd
        Can better bee by new griefs brusd;

        Thou whom the heav'ns them selves like made
10 Showld never sitt in mourning shade
        Noe I alone must mourne, and end
        Who have a lyfe in grief to spend,

        My swiftest pace to waylings bent
        Shews joy had butt a short time lent
15 To bide in mee wher woes must dwell,
        And charme mee with theyr cruell spell.

        And yett when they theyr wichrafts try
        They only make mee wish to dy
        Butt ere my faith in love they change
20 In horrid darknes will I range.

      17. This song develops the idea of witchcraft found in *AS* Song 5.77–78: "My feete
are turn'd to rootes, my hart becommeth lead, / No witchcraft is so evill, as which man's
mind destroyeth."

Song.

[P58]   Say Venus how long have I lov'd, and serv'd you heere?
        Yett all my passions scorn'd or doubted allthough cleere
        Alas thinke love deserveth love, and you have lov'd
        Looke on my paines, and see if you the like have prov'd:

5   Remember then you ar the Goddess of desire,
        And that your sacred powre hath touch'd, and felt this fire,
        Parswade thes flames in mee to cease, or them redress
        In mee, poore mee who stormes of love have in excess.

        My restles nights may show for mee how much I love
10 My sighs unfain'd can wittnes what my hart doth prove
        My saddest looks doe show the greife my soule indures
        Yett, all thes torments from your hands noe help procures.

        Command that wayward child your sonn to grant your right,
        And that his bowe, and shafts hee yeeld to your fayre sight

15   To you who have the eyes of joye the hart of love,
       And then new hopes may spring that I may pitty move:

       Lett him nott triumph that hee can both hurt, and save,
       And more brag that to you your self a wound hee gave.
       Rule him, or what shall I expect of good to see
20   Since hee that hurt you, hee alas may murder mee.

13–14. According to Ovid's *Metamorphoses*, Cupid's arrows struck Venus and Mars: IV, 171 and following. Sir Philip Sidney refers to the myth in *AS* 17.1–4, as does Greville, *Caelica*, 13.
    20. *AS* 20.2: "See there that boy, that murthring boy I say."

Song.

[P59]   I, that ame of all most crost
       Having, and that had, have lost,
       May with reason thus complaine
       Since love breeds love, and lovs paine;

5   That which I did most desire
       To allay my loving fire
       I may have, yett now must miss
       Since an other ruler is:

       Would that I noe ruler had,
10   Or the service nott soe bad,
       Then might I, with blis injoy
       That which now my hopes destroy;

       And that wished pleasure gott
       Brings with itt the sweetest lott:
15   I, that must nott taste the best
       Fed must sterve, and restles rest.

Song.

[P60]   Love as well can make abiding
       In a faythfull sheapheards brest
       As in Princese whose thoughts sliding
       Like swift rivers never rest.

5   Chang to theyr minds is best feeding
       To a sheapheard all his care
       Who when his love is exceeding
       Thinks his faith his richest fare;

       Beauty butt a slight inviting
10   Can nott stirr his hart to chang;

117

Constancy his chiefe delighting
   Strives to fle from phant'sies strang;
Fairnes to him is noe pleasure
   If in other then his love
15 Nor can esteeme that a tresure
   Which in her smiles doth nott move:

This a sheapheard once confessed
   Who lov'd well butt was nott lov'd
Though with scorne, and griefe opressed
20   Could nott yett to chang bee mov'd
Butt him self hee thus contented
   While in love hee was accurst:
This hard hap hee nott repented
   Since best lovers speed the wurst.

17–24. This lament is similar to Sir Robert Sidney's Pastoral 9. 17–18 in which a shepherd complains of his beloved's falsehood: "Thus whyle, the worlds fayre frame, such chang approves / Shee will as fals as it bee, [and] as fayre." The shepherd in P60 concludes by acceptance of his misery, as does the speaker of Sidney's poem (ll. 47–48): "Now loves his wrongs, sais, under shame and sinn / I had bin lost, if lost I had not bin."

Song.

[P61]   Deerest if I by my deserving
    May maintaine in your thoughts my love,
      Lett mee itt still injoy
        Nor faith destroy
5   Butt, pitty love wher itt doth move,

    Lett noe other new love invite you
    To leave mee who soe long have serv'd,
      Nor lett your powre decline
        Butt purely shine
10   On, mee, who have all truth preserv'd;

    Or had you once found my hart straying
    Then would nott I accuse your chang,
      Butt beeing constant still
        Itt needs must kill
15   One, whose soule knowes nott how to rang;

    Yett may you loves sweet smiles recover
    Since all love is nott yett quite lost
      Butt tempt nott love too long
        Least soe great wrong
20   Make him think hee is too much crost.

Song.

[P62]   Fairest, and still truest eyes
Can you the lights bee, and the spies
      Of my desires?
Can you shine cleere for loves delight,
5   And yett the breeders bee of spite,
      And jealous fires?

Mark what lookes doe you beehold,
Such as by jealousie are told
      They want your love:
10   See how they sparcle in distrust
Which by a heat of thoughts unjust
      In them doe move;

Learne to guide your course by art
Chang your eyes into your hart,
15   And patient bee
Till fruitles jealousie gives leave
By safest absence to receave
      What you would see;

Then lett Love his triumph have,
20   And suspition such a grave
      As nott to move,
While wished freedome brings that bliss
That you injoy what all joy is
      Happy to love.

2nd section (P63–P72)

Sonnet. I.

[P63]   In night yett may wee see some kind of light
    When as the Moone doth please to show her face,
    And in the sunns roome yeelds her light, and grace
    Which otherwise must suffer dullest night,

5   Soe ar my fortunes, bard from true delight
    Colde, and unsertaine, like to this strang place,
    Decreasing, changing in an instant space,
    And even att full of joy turn'd to despite;

Justly on Fortune was beestow'd the wheele
10   Whose favors ficle, and unconstant reele;
    Drunk with delight of chang, and sodaine paine;

Wher pleasure hath noe settled place of stay

Butt turning still for our best hopes decay,
And this (alas) wee lovers often gaine.

1. Following an interlude of songs, this poem begins the second section of sonnets
(P63–72).
    9. See *AS* 66.6: "Fortune wheeles still with me in one sort slow"

2.

[P64] Love like a jugler, comes to play his prise,
     And all minds draw his wonders to admire,
     To see how cuningly hee, wanting eyes,
     Can yett deseave the best sight of desire:

5   The wanton child, how hee can faine his fire
     So pretely, as none sees his disguise!
     How finely doe his tricks, while wee fooles hire
     The badge, and office of his tirannies,

For in the end, such jugling hee doth make
10   As hee our harts, in stead of eyes doth take
     For men can only by theyr slieghts abuse

The sight with nimble, and delightfull skill;
     Butt if hee play, his gaine is our lost will:
     Yett childlike, wee can nott his sports refuse.

5–7. The description of childish games recalls that of *AS* 11.12–14, where Cupid
romps:
    And in her brest bopeepe or couching lyes,
    Playing and shining in each outward part:
    But, foole, seekst not to get into her heart.

3.

[P65] Most blessed Night, the happy time for love,
     The shade for Lovers, and theyr loves delight,
     The Raigne of Love for servants, free from spite,
     The hopefull seasons, for joy's sports to move;

5   Now hast thou made thy glory higher prove
     Then did the God, whose pleasant reede did smite
     All Argus eyes into a deathlike night
     Till they were safe, that non could love reprove,

Now thou hast clos'd those eyes from priing sight
10   That nourish jealousie more than joyes right
     While vaine suspition fosters theyr mistrust,

Making sweet sleepe to master all suspect
    Which els theyr privatt feares would nott neglect
    Butt would imbrace both blinded, and unjust.

6- 8. Ovid records how Mercury, playing the pipe of Syrinx, lulled the thousand-eyed Argus to sleep and destroyed him: *Metamorphoses*, I. 717. Sir Philip Sidney also refers to the myth of jealous Argus, *AS* Song 11. 41−42.

4.

[P66] Cruell suspition, O! bee now att rest,
    Lett dayly torments bring to thee some stay;
    Alas make nott my ill thy ease-full pray,
    Nor give loose raines to rage when love's oprest.

5 I ame by care sufficiently distrest,
    Noe rack can strech my hart more, nor a way
    Can I find out for least content to lay
    One happy foote of joye, one step that's blest;

Butt to my end thou fly'st with greedy eye,
10   Seeking to bring griefe by bace jealousie,
    O in how strang a cage ame I kept in?

Noe little signe of favor can I prove
    Butt must bee way'de, and turnd to wronging love,
    And with each humor must my state begin.

11. *AS* 104.7−8: "this dungeon darke, / Where rigrows exile lockes up all my sense."

5.

[P67] How many nights have I with paine indur'd
    Which as soe many ages I esteem'd
    Since my misfortune? yett noe whitt redeem'd
    Butt rather faster tide, to griefe assur'd?

5 How many howrs have my sad thoughts indur'd
    Of killing paines? yett is itt nott esteem'd
    By cruell love, who might have thes redeem'd,
    And all thes yeers of howres to joy assur'd:

Butt fond child, had hee had a care to save
10   As first to conquer, this my pleasures grave
    Had nott bin now to testify my woe;

I might have binn an Image of delight,
  As now a Tombe for sad misfortunes spite,
  Which Love unkindly for reward doth showe.

6.

[P68] My paine, still smother'd in my grieved brest,
  Seekes for some ease, yett cannott passage finde
  To bee discharg'd of this unwellcome ghest;
  When most I strive, more fast his burdens bind,

5 Like to a ship, on Goodwines cast by wind
  The more she strives, more deepe in sand is prest
  Till she bee lost; so am I, in this kind
  Sunk, and devour'd, and swallow'd by unrest,

Lost, shipwrackt, spoyl'd, debar'd of smallest hope
10 Nothing of pleasure left; save thoughts have scope,
  Which wander may: Goe then, my thoughts, and cry

Hope's perish'd; Love tempest-beaten; Joy lost
  Killing dispaire hath all thes blessings crost
  Yett faith still cries, Love will nott falsefy.

5. The Goodwins, or Goodwin Sands, a treacherous shoal off the coast of Kent: see Edward H. Sugden, *A Topographical Dictionary to the Works of Shakespeare and his Fellow Dramatists* (Manchester: Manchester University Press, 1925), 227. In *The Merchant of Venice* Salerio mentions "the Goodwins . . . a very dangerous flat, and fatal, where the carcasses of many a tall ship lie buried" (III. i. 4–6).
  9. Although the metaphor of the shipwrecked lover goes back to Petrarch (*Rime*, 189), Sir Robert Sidney's sonnets frequently use the same imagery—22 and 23.3–4: "If perisht barck on shore by tempest cast / Which late praide for the land, now on it dyes."

7.

[P69] An end fond jealousie alas I know
  Thy hidenest, and thy most secrett art
  Thou canst noe new invention frame butt part
  I have allreddy seene, and felt with woe,

5 All thy dissemblings which by fained show
  Wunn my beeleefe, while truth did rule my hart
  I, with glad mind imbrace'd, and deemd my smart
  The spring of joy, whose streames with bliss showld flow;

I thought excuses had bin reasons true,
10 And that noe faulcehood could of thee ensue;
  Soe soone beeleefe in honest minds is wrought;

Butt now I find thy flattery, and skill,
    Which idly made mee to observe thy will;
    Thus is my learning by my bondage bought.

8.

[P70] Poore Love in chaines, and fetters like a thiefe
    I mett led forthe, as chast Diana's gaine,
    Vowing the untaught Lad should noe reliefe
    From her receave, who glory'd in fond paine,

5 She call'd him theife; with vowes hee did maintaine
    Hee never stole; butt some sadd slight of griefe
    Had given to those who did his powre disdaine,
    In which reveng, his honor, was the chiefe:

She say'd hee murder'd, and therfor must dy;
10   Hee, that hee caus'd butt love: did harmes deny
    Butt, while she thus discoursing with him stood

The Nimphs unty'd him, and his chaines tooke off
    Thinking him safe; butt hee loose, made a scofe
    Smiling, and scorning them, flew to the wood.

1. The First Idyll of Moschus, translated by Barnabe Barnes, portrays the flight of Cupid: Sir Sidney Lee (ed.), "The First Eidillion of Moschus describing Love," *Elizabethan Sonnets* (2 vols.; 1904; New York: Cooper Square, 1964), I, 268–69. The motif of Cupid as Fugitive became a common one, as Lisle John records in *Elizabethan Sonnet Sequence*, 195: AS 8; Barnes, *Parthenophil and Parthenope*, 75, 93; Greville, *Caelica*, 13, 33, 35. Lady Mary adds the figures of Diana and her nymphs.

9.

[P71] 'Pray doe nott use thes words I must bee gone,
    Alas doe nott foretell mine ills to come,
    Lett nott my care bee to my joyes a tombe,
    Butt rather finde my loss with loss alone;

5 Cause mee nott thus a more distressed one
    Nott feeling blis because of this sad dombe
    Of present cross, for thinking will orecome,
    And loose all pleasure, since griefe breedeth none;

Lett the misfortune come att once to mee,
10   Nor suffer mee with griefe to punnish'd bee,
    Lett mee bee ignorant of mine owne ill:

Then now with the foreknowledg quite to lose
   That which with soe much care, and paines love chose
   For his reward, butt joye now, then mirth kill.

> 3. Sir Robert Sidney uses a similar image in Sonnet 30.8: "I was loves cradle once, now loves grave right."
> 8. loose: obs. form of lose

10.

[P72] Folly would needs make mee a lover bee
   When I did litle thinke of loving thought
   Or ever to bee ty'de; while shee told mee
   That non can live, butt to thes bands are brought;

5 I, ignorant, did grant, and soe was bought,
   And solde againe to lovers slaverie;
   The duty to that vanitie once taught
   Such band is, as wee will nott seeke to free,

Yett when I well did understand his might
10   How hee inflam'de, and forc'd one to affect
   I lov'd, and smarted, counting itt delight
   Soe still to wast, which reason did reject.

When love came blindfold, and did chaleng mee
Indeed I lov'd butt wanton boy nott hee.

> 1. The portrayal of Folly as a woman is traditional: see Erasmus, *Praise of Folly*, trans. Betty Radice (Baltimore: Penguin, 1971), 64–65.
> 9–14. Margaret Witten-Hannah, in "Lady Mary Wroth's *Urania*: The Work and the Tradition" (Ph.D. dissertation, University of Auckland, 1978), 152, argues that the author's revision of the poem was incomplete because the masculine pronouns remain in the sestet, but it is more likely that they refer to the "wanton boy."

Interlude

Song.

[P73] The springing time of my first loving
   Finds yett noe winter of removing
   Nor frosts to make my hopes decrease
   Butt with the sommer still increase.

5 The trees may teach us loves remaining
   Who suffer chang with little paining
   Though winter make theyr leaves decrease
   Yett with the sommer they increase.

As Birds by silence show theyr mourning
10   In colde, yett sing att springs returning
Soe may love nipt awhile decrease
Butt as the sommer soone increase.

Those that doe love butt for a season
Doe faulcefy both love, and reason,
15   For reason wills if love decrease
Itt like the sommer should increase.

Though love some times may bee mistaken
The truth yett ought nott to bee shaken,
Or though the heate awhile decrease
20   Itt with the sommer may increase.

And since the spring time of my loving
Found never winter of removing
Nor frosts to make my hopes decrease
Shall as the sommer still increase.

Song.

[P74]   Love a child is ever criing,
    Please him, and hee straite is flying,
    Give him hee the more is craving
    Never satisfi'd with having;

5   His desires have noe measure,
    Endles folly is his treasure,
    What hee promiseth hee breaketh
    Trust nott one word that hee speaketh;

    Hee vowes nothing butt faulce matter,
10   And to cousen you hee'l flatter,
    Lett him gaine the hand hee'll leave you,
    And still glory to deseave you;

    Hee will triumph in your wayling,
    And yett cause bee of your fayling,
15   Thes his vertus ar, and slighter
    Ar his guiftes, his favors lighter,

    Feathers ar as firme in staying
    Woulves noe fiercer in theyr praying.
    As a child then leave him crying
20   Nor seeke him soe giv'n to flying.

[Song.]

[P75] Beeing past the paines of love
Freedome gladly seekes to move,
Says that loves delights were pritty
Butt to dwell in them 't'were pitty,

5   And yett truly says that love
Must of force in all harts move
Butt though his delights are pritty
To dwell in them were a pitty.

Lett love slightly pas like love
10 Never lett itt too deepe move
For though loves delights are pritty
To dwell in them were great pitty;

Love noe pitty hath of love
Rather griefes then pleasures move,
15 Soe though his delights are pritty
To dwell in them would bee pitty.

Those that like the smart of love
In them lett itt freely move
Els though his delights are pritty
20 Doe nott dwell in them for pitty.

[P76] O pardon, Cupid I confess my fault
Then mercy grant mee in soe just a kind
For treason never lodged in my mind
Against thy might soe much as in a thought,

5   And now my folly I have deerly bought
Nor could my soule least rest or quiett find
Since rashnes did my thoughts to error bind
Which now thy fury, and my harme hath wrought;

I curse that thought, and hand which that first fram'd
10 For which by thee I ame most justly blam'd,
Butt now that hand shall guided bee aright,

And give a crowne unto thy endless prayse
Which shall thy glory, and thy greatnes raise
More then thes poore things could thy honor spite.

1. This formal apology to Cupid announces the sequence of fourteen poems, the *corona*, to follow. Note that the speaker now labels as "folly" her chastisement of Cupid's faults. This reversal recalls the end of Thomas Watson's *The Tears of Fancie*, Sonnet 59, where the narrator concludes by honoring Love as a god.

A Crowne of Sonetts dedicated to Love — 3rd section
(a corona)
[P77–90]

The Crowne, or *corona*, was an Italian poetic form in which the last line of either a sonnet or stanza served as the first line of the next. The number of sonnets (stanzas) could vary, from seven to as many as fourteen: see Louis Martz, *The Poetry of Meditation* (Rev. ed.; New Haven: Yale University Press, 1962), 106. One of the best continental examples is the "Corona di Madriali" by Tasso, which appeared in *Rime per Lucrezia Bendidio*, ed. Bruno Maier, in *Opere*, 175 (5 vols.; Milan: Rizzoli Editore, 1963), I, 335–38. Tasso's *corona*, written probably in 1561–62, consisted of twelve madrigals linked together in praise of the lady, called Laura. The *corona* could be used to condemn as well as praise; Annibale Caro wrote a vituperative *corona* of nine sonnets, in which he attacked one of his enemies: *Opere*, ed. Vittorio Turi (Bari, Italy, 1912), I, 161–65.

Sir Philip Sidney included in the *Old Arcadia* one of the first examples of the *corona* in English, in which he linked ten dizains (Ringler, *OA* 72). Sidney called attention to his use of this intricate poetic form in the *Old Arcadia* by describing it as "that kinde of verse, which is called the Crowne." In the final version of *Delia* (1594), Samuel Daniel linked together five sonnets in his collection: Alexander Grosart (ed.), *The Complete Works in Verse and Prose of Samuel Daniel* (4 vols.; London: privately printed, 1885), 34–38. George Chapman later used the form of the *corona* in his "A Coronet for his Mistress Philosophy," which consisted of ten linked sonnets and was published in 1595 with *Ovid's Banquet of Sense:* Phyllis B. Bartlett (ed.), *Poems* (Oxford: Clarendon, 1941), 83–86. John Donne also employed the form in "La Corona," a collection of seven linked sonnets, written probably in 1607: Helen Gardner (ed.), *The Divine Poems* (Oxford: Clarendon, 1952), 1–5.

Perhaps the most immediate influence was Lady Mary Wroth's father, Sir Robert Sidney, who wrote an incomplete crown of sonnets, including four poems and a quatrain of the fifth: ff. 13ᵛ–15. His *corona* was written in praise of a specific lady, whom he identified in the second sonnet by the first name only: "my first breath I had drawn, upon the day / Sacred to yow, blessed in yowr faire name" (ll. 10–11). Because he was born on November 19 (St. Elizabeth's day), his poem implied that the lady's name was Elizabeth: Kelliher and Duncan-Jones, "A Manuscript of Poems by Robert Sidney," 122. In the manuscript a note of explanation in Sir Robert Sidney's hand states, "The rest of the 13 sonnets doth want" (f. 15). Unlike her father, Lady Mary completed a larger *corona* in honor of a more universalized concept of love.

A crowne of Sonetts
dedicated to Love.

[P77]   In this strang labourinth how shall I turne?
        Wayes are on all sids while the way I miss:
        If to the right hand, ther, in love I burne;
        Lett mee goe forward, therin danger is;

5   If to the left, suspition hinders bliss,
        Lett mee turne back, shame cries I ought returne

Nor fainte though crosses with my fortunes kiss;
Stand still is harder, allthough sure to mourne;

Thus lett mee take the right, or left hand way;
10   Goe forward, or stand still, or back retire;
I must thes doubts indure with out allay
Or help, butt traveile find for my best hire;

Yett that which most my troubled sence doth move
Is to leave all, and take the thread of love.

    1. Petrarch included the image of the labyrinth of love in the *Rime*: "nel laberinto intrai; ne veggio ond'esca" (211, l. 14). Lisle John (*Elizabethan Sonnet Sequence*, 231) has recorded the subsequent use of the image of the labyrinth or maze. The image, which became popular with the English sonneteers, was employed by Thomas Watson in *Hekatompathia*, where he referred specifically to the "doubtful Labyrinth of *Love*" and in a preface to the poem explained the mythological allusion to Ariadne's rescue of Theseus from the Minotaur: "My Love is Past" (95), *Poems*, ed. Edward Arber (London: Constable, 1910), 131.

    7. Nor: The author occasionally used nor, without including other negatives (*OED*, 3b).

    12. traveile: The 1621 text used "travel," probably to insure the regularity of meter.

    14. thread of love: See U35.15−21 for the myth of Ariadne and the thread. Sir Robert Sidney alluded to the same myth in his song Pastoral 9.41−44 (italics added):
So hee whose senses foild, no cure cowld breed
In her faults, safety to his ruins fownd.
Those the good Dolfin were, *the saving threed,*
Which stayde the seas deep jawes, *the maze unwound.*

2.

[P78] Is to leave all, and take the thread of love
Which line straite leads unto the soules content
Wher choyse delights with pleasures wings doe move,
And idle phant'sie never roome had lent,

5 When chaste thoughts guide us then owr minds ar bent
To take that good which ills from us remove,
Light of true love, brings fruite which none repent
Butt constant lovers seeke, and wish to prove;

Love is the shining starr of blessings light;
10   The fervent fire of zeale, the roote of peace,
The lasting lampe fed with the oyle of right;
Image of fayth, and wombe for joyes increase.

Love is true vertu, and his ends delight;
His flames ar joyes, his bands true lovers might.

10–12. The religious imagery resembles that of Sir Robert Sidney in Sonnet 4.5–8, which he designed as the introductory poem of his sequence:

True Vestale like, which with most holy care
Preserve the sacred fyres, relligiously
I doe mantein, and that no end they try
Of my best parts their subject I prepare.

A marginal note in the upper left-hand corner of the manuscript indicates the importance he attached to this poem: "This showld be first" (f. 4ᵛ).

3.

[P79] His flames ar joyes, his bands true lovers might,
   Noe staine is ther butt pure, as purest white,
   Wher noe clowde can apeere to dimm his light,
   Nor spott defile, butt shame will soone requite,

5 Heere are affections, tri'de by loves just might
   As gold by fire, and black deserND by white,
   Error by truthe, and darknes knowne by light,
   Wher faith is vallwed for love to requite,

 Please him, and serve him, glory in his might,
10   And firme hee'll bee, as innosencye white,
   Cleere as th'ayre, warme as sunn beames, as day light,
   Just as truthe, constant as fate, joy'd to requite,

 Then love obay, strive to observe his might,
 And bee in his brave court a glorious light.

1. Sir Philip Sidney's monorhymed sonnet, *OA* 42, used the same ending words: light, might.

6. deserND: "discern'd" in the 1621 text

14. In contrast to the Anacreontic Cupid (the figure of the small, mischievous boy) which had appeared earlier in the sonnet sequence, the speaker now turns to examine an opposed concept of Cupid as a noble monarch. References to the ruler Cupid in his Court of Love reappear throughout the *corona*: P80, P82, P85, P86, P89.

4.

[P80] And bee in his brave court a gloriouse light,
   Shine in the eyes of faith, and constancie,
   Maintaine the fires of love still burning bright
   Nott slightly sparkling butt light flaming bee

5 Never to slack till earth noe stars can see,
   Till Sunn, and Moone doe leave to us dark night,
   And secound Chaose once againe doe free
   Us, and the world from all devisions spite,

Till then, affections which his followers are
10   Governe our harts, and prove his powers gaine
To taste this pleasing sting seek with all care
For hapy smarting is itt with smale paine,

Such as although, itt pierce your tender hart
And burne, yett burning you will love the smart.

    7. secound Chaose: ultimate destruction of the world

5.

[P81] And burne, yett burning you will love the smart,
       When you shall feele the weight of true desire,
       Soe pleasing, as you would nott wish your part
       Of burden showld bee missing from that fire;

5   Butt faithfull and unfained heate aspire
       Which sinne abolisheth, and doth impart
       Saulves to all feare, with vertues which inspire
       Soules with devine love, which showes his chaste art,

And guide hee is to joyings; open eyes
10   Hee hath to hapines, and best can learne
       Us means how to deserve, this hee descries,
       Who blind yett doth our hidenest thoughts deserne.

Thus wee may gaine since living in blest love
Hee may our profitt, and owr Tuter prove.

    9. hee: Cupid
    14. profitt: a pun on profit (gain) and prophet (spelling used in the 1621 text)

6.

[P82] Hee may owr profitt, and our Tuter prove
       In whom alone wee doe this power finde,
       To joine two harts as in one frame to move;
       Two bodies, butt one soule to rule the minde;

5   Eyes which must care to one deere object bind
       Eares to each others speech as if above
       All els they sweet, and learned were; this kind
       Content of lovers wittniseth true love,

Itt doth inrich the witts, and make you see
10   That in your self, which you knew nott before,
       Forcing you to admire such guifts showld bee
       Hid from your knowledg, yett in you the store;

Millions of thes adorne the throne of Love,
How blest bee they then, who his favours prove.

3. To joine two harts as in one: In *Poems Written by the Right Honorable William Earl of Pembroke* (1660), a lyric entitled, "On one heart made of two," is attributed to Pembroke: Gaby E. Onderwyzer (ed.), *Poems Written by the Right Honorable William Earl of Pembroke*, Augustan Reprint Society, no. 79 (Los Angeles: William A. Clark Memorial Library, 1959), 43–44.
4. Two bodies, butt one soule: For a survey of this Renaissance *topos*, see Laurens J. Mills, *One Soul in Bodies Twain* (Bloomington, Ind.: Principia Press, 1937).
14. prove: experience

7.

[P83] How blest bee they then, who his favors prove
    A lyfe wherof the birth is just desire,
    Breeding sweet flame which hearts invite to move
    In thes lov'd eyes which kindle Cupids fire,

5   And nurse his longings with his thoughts intire,
    Fixt on the heat of wishes formd by love,
    Yett wheras fire distroys this doth aspire,
    Increase, and foster all delights above;

    Love will a painter make you, such, as you
10   Shall able bee to drawe your only deere
    More lively, parfett, lasting, and more true
    Then rarest woorkman, and to you more neere,

    Thes be the least, then all must needs confess
    Hee that shunns love doth love him self the less.

8.

[P84] Hee that shunns love doth love him self the less
    And cursed hee whos spiritt nott admires
    The worth of love, wher endles blessednes
    Raines, and commands, maintaind by heavnly fires

5   Made of vertu, join'de by truth, blowne by desires
    Strengthned by worth, renued by carefullnes
    Flaming in never changing thoughts, briers
    Of jelousie shall heere miss wellcomnes;

    Nor coldly pass in the pursuites of love
10   Like one longe frozen in a sea of ise,
    And yett butt chastly lett your passions move
    Noe thought from vertuouse love your minds intise.

Never to other ends your phant'sies place
Butt wher they may returne with honors grace.

9.

[P85] Butt wher they may returne with honors grace
Wher Venus follyes can noe harbour winn
Butt chased ar as worthles of the face
Or stile of love who hath lasiviouse binn.

5 Oure harts ar subject to her sunn; wher sinn
Never did dwell, or rest one minutes space;
What faults hee hath, in her, did still begin,
And from her brest hee suckd his fleeting pace,

If lust bee counted love t'is faulcely nam'd
10 By wikednes a fayrer gloss to sett
Upon that vice, which els makes men asham'd
In the owne frase to warrant butt begett

This childe for love, who ought like monster borne
Bee from the court of Love, and reason torne.

  1–8. The distinction between Venus as the goddess of sensual love and her son as the
god of "*l'amour du coeur*" follows the Court of Love tradition: Neilson, *Origins and Sources of
the Court of Love*, 55. She developed further the contrast in P88 of the *corona*.
  9–11. Shakespeare's Adonis contrasted love and lust in a similar fashion: "Love
surfeits not, Lust like a glutton dies; / Love is all truth, Lust full of forged lies." *Venus
and Adonis*, ll. 803–804.
  5. sunn: "Sonne" in the 1621 text
  12. In the owne: From the fourteenth to the seventeenth centuries, "the own" was
often used in the sense of its own (*OED*).
  12. frase: phrase

10.

[P86] Bee from the court of Love, and reason torne
For Love in reason now doth putt his trust,
Desert, and liking are together borne
Children of love, and reason parents just,

5 Reason adviser is, love ruler must
Bee of the state which crowne hee long hath worne
Yett soe as neither will in least mistrust
The government wher noe feare is of scorne,

Then reverence both theyr mights thus made of one,
10 Butt wantones, and all those errors shun,

Which wrongers bee, impostures, and alone
Maintainers of all follyes ill begunn;

Fruit of a sowre, and unwholsome ground
Unprofitably pleasing, and unsound.

3. Desert: merit
13. sowre: cold and wet, as a result of retaining stagnant moisture

11.

[P87] Unprofitably pleasing, and unsound
When heaven gave liberty to frayle dull earth
To bringe forth plenty that in ills abound
Which ripest yett doe bring a sertaine dearth.

5   A timeles, and unseasonable birth
Planted in ill, in wurse time springing found,
Which hemlock like might feed a sick-witts mirthe
Wher unruld vapors swimm in endles rounde,

Then joy wee nott in what wee ought to shun
10   Wher shady pleasures showe, butt true borne fires
Ar quite quench'd out, or by poore ashes wunn
Awhile to keepe those coole, and wann desires.

O noe lett love his glory have and might
Bee given to him who triumphs in his right.

7. John Gerarde described the properties of hemlock, which is often grown in water:
"It is one of the deadly poisons which killeth by its colde qualities, as Dioscorides
writeth, saying, Hemlocke is a very evill, dangerous, hurrfull, and poisonous herbe,"
The Herball or a Generall Historie of Plantes (London: J. Norton, 1595), STC 11750, 904.
Sir Robert Sidney alludes to hemlock in Song 22.1 – 3:
  But alas why do yow nowrish
  Poisnous weeds of colde despayre
  In Loves garden...

12.

[P88] Bee given to him who triumphs in his right
Nor vading bee, butt like those blossooms fayre
Which fall for good, and lose theyr coulers bright
Yett dy nott, butt with fruite theyr loss repaire

5   Soe may love make you pale with loving care
When sweet injoying shall restore that light
More cleare in beauty then wee can compare
If nott to Venus in her chosen night,

And who soe give them selves in this deere kind
10   Thes hapinesses shall attend them still
To bee suplyd with joys, inrichd in mind
With treasures of content, and pleasures fill,

Thus love to bee devine doth heere apeere
Free from all fogs butt shining faire, and cleere.

13.

[P89] Free from all fogs butt shining faire, and cleere
Wise in all good, and innosent in ill
Wher holly friendship is esteemed deere
With truth in love, and justice in our will,

5   In love thes titles only have theyr fill
Of hapy lyfe maintainer, and the meere
Defence of right, the punnisher of skill,
And fraude; from whence directions doth apeere,

To thee then lord commander of all harts,
10   Ruller of owr affections kinde, and just
Great King of Love, my soule from fained smarts
Or thought of change I offer to your trust

This crowne, my self, and all that I have more
Except my hart which you beestow'd beefore.

14.

[P90] Except my hart which you beestow'd before,
And for a signe of conquest gave away
As worthles to bee kept in your choyse store
Yett one more spotles with you doth nott stay.

5   The tribute which my hart doth truly pay
Is faith untouch'd, pure thoughts discharge the score
Of debts for mee, wher constancy bears sway,
And rules as Lord, unharm'd by envyes sore,

Yett other mischiefs faile nott to attend,
10   As enimies to you, my foes must bee;
Curst jealousie doth all her forces bend
To my undoing; thus my harmes I see.

Soe though in Love I fervently doe burne,
In this strange labourinth how shall I turne?

3. store: treasure

14. The final sonnet in the *corona* shows that despite the speaker's efforts to idealize passion, the base emotion of jealousy continues to exist. The image of entrapment in the labyrinth is hence appropriate to this exploration of the nature of love. In the Newberry MS of the second part of *Urania*, Lady Mary Wroth later repeated phrases from this poem: "I have confidence to love, and yett that is master'd with dispaire, In this strange labourinth, help, and aide poore afflicted mee" (II. ii. f. 61).

Interlude

Song. I.

[P91] Sweet lett mee injoye thy sight
     More cleere, more bright then morning sunn,
  Which in spring time gives delight
     And by which sommers pride is wunn;

5 Present sight doth pleasures move
     Which in sad absence wee must miss,
  Butt when mett againe in love
     Then twise redoubled is our bliss,

  Yett this comfort absence gives,
10   And only faithfull loving tries
  That though parted, loves force lives
     As just in hart as in our eyes,

  Butt such comfort bannish quite
     Farr sweeter is itt still to finde
15 Favour in thy loved sight
     Which present smiles with joyes combind

  Eyes of gladnes, lips of love,
     And harts from passion nott to turne,
  Butt in sweet affections move
20   In flames of faith to live, and burne,

  Deerest then this kindnes give,
     And grant mee lyfe which is your sight
  Wherin I more blessed live
     Then graced with the sunns faire light.

1. This poem resembles Sir Robert Sidney's Song 20. 1–2: "Senses by unjust force banisht / From the objects of yowr pleasure."

2.

[P92] Sweet Silvia in a shadie wood
     With her faire Nimphs layde downe

Sawe nott farr off wher Cupid stood
  The Monarck of loves crowne;

5   All naked playing with his wings
    Within a mirtle tree
Which sight a soddaine laughter brings
    His godhead soe to see;

And fondly they beegan to jest
10   With scofing, and delight,
Nott knowing hee did breed unrest,
    And that his will's his right;

When hee perseaving of theyr scorne
    Grew in such desp'rate rage
15   Who butt for honor first was borne
    Cowld nott his rage aswage;

Till shooting of his murdring dart
    Which nott long lighting was
Knowing the next way to the hart
20   Did through a poore nimph pas;

This shott, the others made to bow
    Beesids all those to blame
Who scorners bee, or nott allow
    Of powrfull Cupids name;

25   Take heede then, nor doe idly smyle
    Nor loves commands despise
For soone will hee your strength beeguile
    Although hee want his eyes.

6. mirtle: traditionally the tree of love; see also P96.12.
7–8. The speaker abruptly switches back to the Anacreontic Cupid, the mischievous boy, after failed efforts to idealize Cupid as a noble ruler in the *corona*.

3.

[P93] Come merry spring delight us
    For winter long did spite us
    In pleasure still persever,
    Thy beauties ending never,
5   Spring, and growe
    Lasting soe
    With joyes increasing ever;

    Lett colde from hence bee banisht
    Till hopes from mee bee vanisht,

10 Butt bless thy dainties growing
   In fullnes freely flowing
     Sweet birds sing
     For the spring
   All mirthe is now beestowing;

15 Philomeale in this arbour
   Makes now her loving harbour
   Yett of her state complaining
   Her notes in mildnes straining
     Which though sweet
20   Yett doe meete
   Her former luckles payning.

15. Ovid recounts the story of Philomela's transformation into a nightingale following the rape by Tereus: *Metamorphoses*, VI, 668. Sir Philip Sidney used the myth in *CS*4, where the speaker also celebrates the coming of spring and gives advice to Philomela to cheer herself.

4.

[P94] Lovers learne to speake butt truthe
    Sweare nott, and your othes forgoe,
   Give your age a constant youth
    Vowe noe more then what you'll doe.

5 Thinke itt sacrilidg to breake
    What you promise shall in love,
   And in teares what you doe speake
    Forgett nott when the ends you prove;

   Doe nott think itt glory is
10   To intisce, and then deseave,
   Your chiefe honors ly in this
    By worth what wunn is, nott to leave;

   'T'is nott for your fame to try
    What wee weake nott oft refuse
15 In owr bownty owr faults ly
    When you to doe a fault will chuse;

   Fy, leave this, a greater gaine
    'T'is to keepe when you have wunn
   Then what purchaced is with paine
20   Soone after in all scorne to shun;

   For if worthles to bee priz'd
    Why att first will you itt move,

And if worthy, why dispis'd
    You can nott sweare, and ly, and love,

25   Love (alas) you can nott like
    'T'is butt, for a fashion mov'd
Non can chuse, and then dislike
    Unles itt bee by faulshood prov'd.

Butt your choice is, and your love
30   How most number to deseave,
As if honors claime did move
    Like Popish lawe, non safe to leave;

Fly this folly, and returne
    Unto truth in love, and try,
35   None butt Martirs hapy burne
    More shamefull ends they have that lye.

32. The hostile reference to "Popish lawe" is to be expected from a member of the staunchly Protestant Sidney family. The author is probably making a general allusion to papal absolutism, but one instance of papal law that had particularly disturbed Englishmen was the bull of February 5, 1570, which pronounced judgment against "Elizabeth, pretended queen of England, and her heretical followers": see A. O. Meyer, *England and the Catholic Church under Elizabeth*, trans. J. R. McKee (1916; New York: Barnes and Noble, 1967), 77–79, and Patrick McGrath, *Papists and Puritans under Elizabeth I* (London: Blandford Press, 1967), 20.

Final section (P95 – 103)

I.

[P95]   My hart is lost, what can I now expect,
    An ev'ning faire; after a drowsie day?
    (Alas) fond phant'sie this is nott the way
    To cure a morning hart, or salve neglect,

5   They who should help, doe mee, and help reject,
    Imbrasing looce desires, and wanton play,
    While wanton bace delights doe beare the swaye,
    And impudencie raignes without respect:

O Cupid! lett thy mother know her shame
10   'T'is time for her to leave this youthfull flame
    Which doth dishoner her, is ages blame,
    And takes away the greatnes of thy name;

Thou God of love, she only Queene of lust,
Yett strives by weakning thee, to bee unjust.

1. After an interlude of four songs, this poem introduces the final section of sonnets (P95–103).
4. morning: "mourning" in the 1621 text

10. Ovid describes Venus' pursuit of Adonis: *Metamorphoses*, X, 524. Lady Mary gives an extended account of the paradoxical relationship in the Newberry manuscript of *Urania*: "Adonis was in a kinde diefied by the Idolatrie of his Goddess Venus, who was his suppliant, hee her God, and she the great Queene of love, yett his vassall" (II. ii. f. 9).

2.

[P96]   Late in the Forest I did Cupid see
      Colde, wett, and crying hee had lost his way,
      And beeing blind was farder like to stray:
      Which sight a kind compassion bred in mee,

5   I kindly tooke, and dride him, while that hee
      Poore child complain'd hee sterved was with stay,
      And pin'de for want of his accustom'd pray,
      For non in that wilde place his hoste would bee,

   I glad was of his finding, thinking sure
10   This service should my freedome still procure,
      And in my armes I tooke him then unharmde,

   Carrying him safe unto a Mirtle bowre
      Butt in the way hee made mee feele his powre,
      Burning my hart who had him kindly warmd.

9–10. The ultimate source of this poem is the *Anacreontea*, 33, with its account of Cupid as a beggar, who seeks food and shelter only to reward his benefactor with darts. As Lisle John (*Elizabethan Sonnet Sequence*, 195) notes, the motif of Cupid as beggar was an extremely common one; AS 65; Barnes, *Parthenophil*, 93; Constable, *Diana*, Dec. II, 6 and 7; Drayton, *Idea*, 33, 48; Greville, *Caelica*, 12.1–4.

3.

[P97]   Juno still jealouse of her husband Jove
      Desended from above, on earth to try
      Whether she ther could find his chosen love
      Which made him from the heavens so often fly;

5   Close by the place, wher I for shade did ly
      She chaseing came; butt when she saw mee move
      Have you nott seene this way sayd shee to hy
      One, in whom vertue never ground did prove,

   Hee, in whom love doth breed to stirr more hate,
10   Courting a wanton Nimph for his delight
      His name is Jupiter, my Lord by fate
      Who, for her leaves mee, heav'n, his throne, and light,

I sawe him nott, sayd I, although heere are
Many in whose harts love hath made like warr.

> 1–4. Ovid recounts Juno's journeys in search of Jupiter: *Metamorphoses*, I, 601ff; II, 466ff; III, 261ff; VI, 332ff; IX, 295ff. See also Greville, *Caelica*, ll. 1–2. Lady Mary described Jupiter's amorous activities in a passage from the Newberry MS of *Urania*: "never did any old man smug up him self soe, nott Jupiter when hee fell to a new love pleased himself better in his joyfull hopes" (II. ii. f. 15ᵛ).

4.

[P98] When I beeheld the Image of my deere
　　　　With greedy lookes mine eyes would that way bend,
　　　　Fear, and desire did inwardly contend;
　　　　Feare to bee mark'd, desire to drawe still neere,

5　　　And in my soule a speritt wowld apeer,
　　　　Which boldnes waranted, and did pretend
　　　　To bee my genius, yett I durst nott lend
　　　　My eyes in trust wher others seemed soe cleere,

　　　　Then did I search from whence this danger 'rose,
10　　　If such unworthynes in mee did rest
　　　　As my sterv'd eyes must nott with sight bee blest;
　　　　When jealousie her poyson did disclose;

　　　　Yett in my hart unseene of jealous eye
　　　　The truer Image shall in triumph lye.

> 7. genius: tutelary spirit; also the arch-priest of the Court of Love; see Neilson, *Origins and Sources of the Court of Love*, 257.
> 14. Sir Philip Sidney refers to the "image" of the beloved: *AS* 32. 13–14: "But from thy heart, while my sire charmeth thee, / Sweet *Stella's* image I do steale to me."

5.

[P99] Like to huge clowds of smoke which well may hide
　　　　The face of fairest day though for awhile,
　　　　Soe wrong may shadow mee, till truth doe smile,
　　　　And justice (sun like) hath those vapors tyde,

5　　　O doting Time, canst thou for shame lett slide
　　　　Soe many minutes while ills doe beguile,
　　　　Thy age, and worth, and faulshoods thus defile
　　　　Thy ancient good, wher now butt crosses 'bide,

　　　　Looke butt once up, and leave thy toyling pace,
10　　　And on my myseries thy dimm eye place,
　　　　Goe nott soe fast, butt give my care some end,

140

Turne nott thy glas (alas) unto my ill
　　Since thou with sand itt canst nott soe farr fill
　　Butt to each one my sorrows will extend.

6.

[P100]　O! that noe day would ever more appeere,
　　　　Butt clowdy night to governe this sad place,
　　　　Nor light from heav'n thes haples rooms to grace
　　　　Since that light's shadow'd which my love holds deere;

　5　Lett thickest mists in envy master heere,
　　　　And sunn-borne day for malice showe noe face,
　　　　Disdaining light wher Cupid, and the race
　　　　Of Lovers are dispisde, and shame shines cleere.

　　　Lett mee bee darke, since bard of my chiefe light;
　10　　And wounding jealousie commands by might;
　　　　Butt stage play like disguised pleasures give;

　　　To mee itt seems as ancient fictions make
　　　　The starrs all fashions, and all shapes partake
　　　　While in my thoughts true forme of love shall live.

7.

[P101]　No time, noe roome, noe thought, or writing can
　　　　Give rest, or quiett to my loving hart,
　　　　Or can my memory or phantsie scan
　　　　The measure of my still renuing smart,

　5　Yett would I nott (deere love) thou shouldst depart
　　　　Butt lett my passions as they first began
　　　　Rule, wounde, and please, itt is thy choysest art
　　　　To give disquiett which seemes ease to man;

　　　When all alone, I thinke upon thy paine
　10　　How thou doest traveile owr best selves to gaine;
　　　　Then howerly thy lessons I doe learne,

　　　Think on thy glory which shall still assend
　　　　Untill the world come to a finall end,
　　　　And then shall wee thy lasting powre deserne.

8.

[P102]　How gloewoorme like the sunn doth now apeere
　　　　Colde beames doe from his gloriouse face desend

141

Which showes his days, and force draw to an end,
Or that to leave taking his time growes neere;

5   This day his face did seeme butt pale though cleere,
The reason is hee to the north must lend
His light, and warmth must to that climate bend
Whose frozen parts cowld nott loves heat hold deere,

Alas if thou (bright sunn) to part from hence
10   Grieve soe, what must I haples? who from thence
Wher thou dost goe my blessing shall attend;

Thou shalt injoye that sight for which I dy,
And in my hart thy fortunes doe envy,
Yett grieve, I'le love thee, for this state may mend.

    1. The picture of the winter sun resembles Donne's description of "A Nocturnall upon S. Lucies Day," 1–9.

9.

[P103]   My muse now hapy, lay thy self to rest,
Sleepe in the quiett of a faithfull love,
Write you noe more, butt lett thes phant'sies move
Some other harts, wake nott to new unrest,

5   Butt if you study, bee those thoughts adrest
To truth, which shall eternall goodnes prove;
Injoying of true joye, the most, and best,
The endles gaine which never will remove;

Leave the discource of Venus, and her sunn
10   To young beeginers, and theyr brains inspire
With storys of great love, and from that fire
Gett heat to write the fortunes they have wunn,

And thus leave off, what's past showes you can love,
Now lett your constancy your honor prove,

Pamphilia.

    9. sunn: "sonne" in the 1621 text
    13–14. See AS 70.13–14: "I give you here my band for truth of this, / Wise silence is best musicke unto blisse." According to the 1621 Urania, Pamphilia embodies the virtue of Constancy in the symbolic episode when she accepts the keys to the Throne of Love, "at which instant Constancy vanished, as metamorphosing her self into her breast" (I. i. 141).

[F1]   Venus unto the Gods a sute did move,
        That since she was of love the godess stil'd
        She only might the pouer have of love,
        And nott as now a partner with her child,

5   The cause to this which stird the Godess milde
        Was that of late her servant faulse did prove
        Hurt as she sayd afresh by Cupid wilde,
        And to a Nimph his passions did remove;

        Or els that they would eyes unto him give
10   That hee might see, how hee his shafts did drive;
        This they deny'd: For if hee blind did ill

        What would hee seeing? Butt thus much they did
        To shoote without her leave they him forbid
        Hee this observ'd, and since obays her will.

      1–4. The struggle between Venus and Cupid for dominance is a frequent theme in
the sequence: see P58 and P95.

Song.

[F2]   The birds doe sing, day doth apeere
        Arise, arise my only deere,
        Greete this faire morne with thy faire eyes
        Wher farr more love, and brightnes lies,

5   All this long night noe sleepe, nor rest
        My love commanded soule possest
        Butt wachfully the time did marck
        To see those starrs rise in the darck,

        Arise then now, and lett those lights
10   Take Pheabus place as theyr due rights
        For when they doe together shine
        The greater light is still held thine,

Then with those eyes inrich thy love
From whose deere beams my joye doth move,
15 Shine with delight on my sad hart,
And grace the prize wun by theyr dart.

Sonett

[F3] Eyes, can you tell mee wher my hart remaines?
Have you nott seene itt in these lovely eyes?
With pride showe you the place itt ther retaines,
And baby-like still passtime as itt lies?

5 Or can you in that blessed brest surprise
The run-away? when itt new triumph gaines
To lodg wher greatest harts for mercy cries?
Have you nott seene itt ther joye att theyr paines?

Iff neither wher? wher lives itt? wher abides
10 This careles sprite who from mee closely slides,
And hartles leavs mee? O, alas I knowe

Itt is petitioning for pitty's place
Wher love hath purest, and still during grace;
Thus while I thought itt sor'de, itt creeps beelowe.

6. run-away: See P30 for a similar treatment of the *topos* of the migration of the heart.
13. during: enduring

Sonett

[F4] Can the lov'd Image of thy deerest face
Soe miroir like present thee to my sight
Yett Cristalls coldenes gaine loves sweetest place,
When warmth with sight hath ever equall might.

5 You say t'is butt the picture of true light
Wherof my hart is made the safest case
Faithfully keeping that rich pourtraits right
From change or thought that relique to displace,

My brest doth nourish itt, and with itt lives
10 As oyle to Lamps theyr lasting beeing gives
Each looke alures a wish of meeting joye;

Iff butt a picture, then restore with ease
The lyfe peece of my soule, and lett itt seaze
This chillnes into heate, and barrs destroy.

Sonett

[F5] Oft did I wounder why the sweets of Love
    Were counted paines, sharp wounds, and cruell smarts
    Till one blow sent from heavnly face prov'd darts
    Enough to make those deem'd-sweets bitter prove,

5 One shaft did force my best strength to remove,
    And armies brought of thoughts, which thought imparts,
    One shaft soe spent may conquer courts of harts,
    One shott butt dubly sent my sprite did move,

    Two sparckling eyes were gainers of my loss
10 While love-begetting lips theyr gaine did cross,
    And chaleng'd hauf of my hart-master'd prise,

    Itt humbly did confess they wan the field,
    Yett equall was theyr force, soe did itt yeeld
    Equally still to serve those lips, and eyes.

9–12. See Sir Robert Sidney's Sonnet 15.9–11:
Yowr face, the feelde where beauties orders shine
What can resist? Yowr eies, loves Canons strong,
The brave directions of yowr lips devine!

Sonett

[F6] Fly traiter joye whose end brings butt dispaire
    Soone high, and prowd, and att the heith downe cast
    Like stately trees, whose leav'y crowns have past
    To brave the clowds, and with theyr state compare,

5 When for theyr heds the grownd theyr pillows are,
    And theyr dispised roots by one poore blast
    Rais'd up in spite, theyr tops by earth imbrast
    Glad of decline, for from thence springeth care,

    Even soe fond joye, thou raisest up our heads,
10 When coms dispaire, and on thy pleasure treads,
    Then languishingly dost thou pine, and cry,

    Haples joye that can nott act joys kind part
    Butt must bee mastered by dispayrs sharp smart,
    Thus faine thou wouldst bee kind, butt must deny.

1–2. See the opening of P33 for a close parallel in phrasing.
2. heith: height

The Countesse of Montgomery's Urania

In both the published first part of the *Urania* (1621) and the unpublished second part (Newberry MS), Lady Mary Wroth created the major characters of her romance as members of an imaginary royal family. The accompanying charts identify those figures who are most frequently designated as the speakers of the verse. The poems are printed in the order in which they appear in the *Urania*. Because the prose context often enhances the meaning of the verse, the notes provide a brief account of the speaker and situation for each poem.

{U1}   Unseene, unknowne, I here alone complaine
        To Rocks, to Hills, to Meadowes, and to Springs,
    Which can no helpe returne to ease my paine,
        But back my sorrowes the sad Eccho brings.
5   Thus still encreasing are my woes to me,
        Doubly resounded by that monefull voice,
    Which seemes to second me in miserie,
        And answere gives like friend of mine owne choice.
    Thus onely she doth my companion prove,
10   The others silently doe offer ease:
    But those that grieve, a grieving note doe love;
        Pleasures to dying eies bring but disease:
    And such am I, who daily ending live,
    Wayling a state which can no comfort give.

> The shepherdess Urania recites this sonnet as she walks among the rocks of "Pantalaria" (Pantelleria), an island in the Mediterranean Sea, where the action of Lady Mary Wroth's romance begins. Urania laments the fact that she is ignorant of her own identity and parentage (I. i. p. 2).
> 9. she: According to Ovid's *Metamorphoses* (III, 356ff), Echo was a mountain nymph who pined away for love of the handsome youth Narcissus, until only her voice remained.

{U2}   Here all alone in silence might I mourne:
        But how can silence be where sorrowes flow?
        Sighs with complaints have poorer paines out-worne;
        But broken hearts can only true griefe show.

MAJOR CHARACTERS IN THE TWO PARTS OF
The Countesse of Montgomery's Urania

NOTE: The Kings of Morea, Naples, and Pamphilia are brothers, and their descendants form the two royal families in Charts A and B. Because the King of Pamphilia has no immediate heirs, he selects his niece Pamphilia as his successor to the throne.

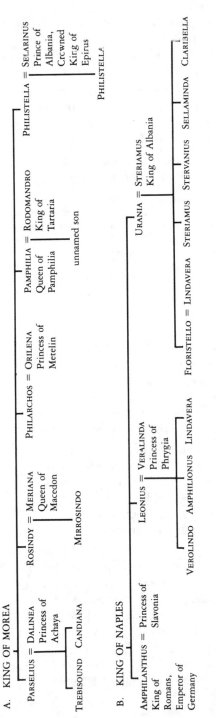
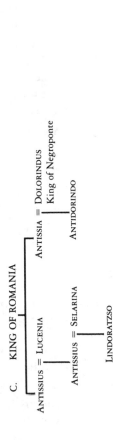

A. KING OF MOREA

PARSELIUS = DALINEA Princess of Achaya

TREBISOUND   CANDIANA

ROSINDY = MERIANA Queen of Macedon

MIRROSINDO

PHILARCHOS = ORILENA Princess of Metelin

PAMPHILIA Queen of Pamphilia = RODOMANDRO King of Tartaria

unnamed son

PHILISTELLA = SELARINUS Prince of Albania, Crowned King of Epirus

PHILISTELLA

B. KING OF NAPLES

AMPHILANTHUS = Princess of Slavonia King of Romans, Emperor of Germany

VEROLINDO   AMPHILIONUS   LINDAVERA

LEONIUS = VERALINDA Princess of Phrygia

FLORISTELLO = LINDAVERA   STERIAMUS

URANIA = STERIAMUS King of Albania

STERIAMUS   STERVANIUS   SELLAMINDA   CLARIBELLA

C. KING OF ROMANIA

ANTISSIUS = LUCENIA

ANTISSIUS = SELARINA

LINDORATZSO

ANTISSIA = DOLORINDUS King of Negroponte

ANTIDORINDO

5 Drops of my dearest bloud shall let Love know
   Such teares for her I shed, yet still do burne,
   As no spring can quench least part of my woe,
   Till this live earth, againe to earth doe turne.

   Hatefull all thought of comfort is to me,
10   Despised day, let me still night possesse;
   Let me all torments feele in their excesse,
   And but this light allow my state to see.

   Which still doth wast, and wasting as this light,
   Are my sad dayes unto eternall night.

When Urania discovers this sonnet in a hidden room within a rock, she wonders about its author: "How well doe these words, this place, and all agree with thy fortune? sure poore soule thou wert heere appointed to spend thy daies, and these roomes ordain'd to keepe thy tortures in" (I. i. p. 3). The poem was written by Perissus, the King of Sicily's unhappy nephew, who is in love with Limena.

13. this light: a candle. Urania's discovery of this sonnet is based on a similar episode in Sir Philip Sidney's *Old Arcadia*, in which Cleophila enters a darkened cave, illuminated by the light of a single candle, and finds a poem on top of a stone table (*OA*, 181).

[U3] Heart drops distilling like a new cut-vine
   Weepe for the paines that doe my soule oppresse,
           Eyes doe no lesse
   For if you weepe not, be not mine,
5   Silly woes that cannot twine
           An equall griefe in such excesse.

   You first in sorrow did begin the act,
   You saw and were the instruments of woe,
           To let me know
10   That parting would procure the fact
   Wherewith young hopes in bud are wrackt,
           Yet deerer eyes the rock must show.

   Which never weepe, but killingly disclose
   Plagues, famine, murder in the fullest store,
15   But threaten more.
   This knowledge cloyes my brest with woes
   T'avoid offence my heart still chose
           Yet faild, and pity doth implore.

Anguished by her feelings of jealousy, Pamphilia fears that Amphilanthus may be in love with another woman, Antissia. Unable to sleep, Pamphilia "took pen and paper, and being excellent in writing, writ thes verses following" (I. i. p. 51).

[U4]   Adieu sweet Sun
        Thy night is neare
        Which must appeare
        Like mine, whose light but new begun
5   Weares as if spun
        By chance not right,
        Led by a light
        False, and pleasing, ever wun.

        Come once in view
10   Sweet heat, and light
        My heavy sp'rit
        Dull'd in thy setting, made anew
        If you renew,
        Daysies doe grow,
15   And spring below
        Blest with thy warm'th, so once I grew.

        Wilt thou returne,
        Deare blesse mine eyes
        Where loves zeale lyes
20   Let thy deere object mildly burne
        Nor flie, but turne
        'Tis season now
        Each happy bow
        Both buds and blooms, why should I mourne?

> Amphilanthus hears Steriamus, Prince of Albania, perform this song, accompanied by the lute. Both are love-lorn over Pamphilia, and their thoughts are exactly matched: "like two Lutes tun'd alike, and placed, the one struck, the other likewise sounds: so did these speeches agree to his incumbred thoughts" (I. i. p. 54).

[U5]   Beare part with me most straight and pleasant Tree,
        And imitate the Torments of my smart
        Which cruell Love doth send into my heart,
        Keepe in thy skin this testament of me:

5   Which Love ingraven hath with miserie,
        Cutting with griefe the unresisting part,
        Which would with pleasure soone have learnd loves art,
        But wounds still curelesse, must my rulers bee.

        Thy sap doth weepingly bewray thy paine,
10   My heart-blood drops with stormes it doth sustaine,
            Love sencelesse, neither good nor mercy knowes

Pitiles I doe wound thee, while that I
Unpitied, and unthought on, wounded crie:
Then out-live me, and testifie my woes.

Pamphilia carves this poem into the bark of an ash tree, "causing that sapp to accompany her teares for love, that for unkindness" (I. i. p. 75).
1–2. See *OA* 47.1–2, in which Pamela inscribes a similar sonnet on a tree: "Do not disdaine, ô streight up raised Pine, / That wounding thee, my thoughtes in thee I grave."

[U6]   My thoughts thou hast supported without rest,
My tyred body here hath laine opprest
With love, and feare: yet be thou ever blest;
Spring, prosper, last; I am alone unblest.

On the roots of the same ash tree as in U5 Pamphilia inscribes these words (I. i. p. 76).
1–4. This verse postscript derives from Sidney's account of how Pamela engraves a couplet (*OA* 48) on the roots of the same tree into which she had previously carved the lines of her sonnet.

[U7]   Drowne me not you cruell teares,
Which in sorrow witnes beares
          Of my wailing,
          And Loves failing.

5   Flouds but cover, and retire
Washing faces of desire
          Whose fresh growing
          Springs by flowing.

Meadowes ever yet did love
10   Pleasant streames which by them move:
          But your falling
          Claimes the calling

Of a torrent curstly fierce
Past wits power to rehearse;
15   Only crying,
          Or my dying
May instead of verse or prose
My disasterous end disclose.

Leandrus, Prince of Achaya, who is in love with Pamphilia, writes these verses concerning his frustrated passions (I. i. pp. 83–84).

[U8]   The Sunne hath no long journey now to goe
        While I a progresse have in my desires,
        Disasters dead-low-water-like do show
        The sand, that overlook'd my hop'd-for hyres.

5   Thus I remaine like one that's laid in Briers,
        Where turning brings new paine and certaine woe,
        Like one, once burn'd bids me avoid the fires,
        But love (true fire) will not let me be slow.

    Obedience, feare, and love doe all conspire
10   A worth-lesse conquest gain'd to ruine me,
        Who did but feele the height of blest desire
        When danger, doubt, and losse, I straight did see.
    Restlesse I live, consulting what to doe,
    And more I study, more I still undoe.

> Antissia, believing that Amphilanthus has rejected her, composes a sonnet: "shee was invited, either by her owne passion, or the imitation of that excellent Lady [Pamphilia], to put some of her thoughts in some kind of measure, so as shee perplexed with love, jealousie, and losse as shee beleev'd, made this Sonnet, looking upon the Sunne, which was then of a good height" (I. i. p. 94).

[U9]   Sweete solitarines, joy to those hearts
        That feele the pleasure of Loves sporting darts,
        Grudge me not, though a vassall to his might,
        And a poore subject to curst changings spite,
5   To rest in you, or rather restlesse move
        In your contents to sorrow for my love.
        A Love, which living, lives as dead to me,
        As holy reliques which in boxes be,
        Plac'd in a chest, that overthrowes my joy,
10   Shut up in change, which more then plagues destroy.
        These, O you solitarinesse, may both endure,
        And be a Chirurgion to find me a cure:
        For this curst corsive eating my best rest
        Memorie, sad memorie in you once blest,
15   But now most miserable with the weight
        Of that, which onely shewes Loves strange deceit;
        You are that cruell wound that inly weares
        My soule, my body wasting into teares.
        You keepe mine eies unclos'd, my heart untide,
20   From letting thought of my best dayes to slide.
        Froward Remembrance, what delight have you,

Over my miseries to take a view?
Why doe you tell me in this same-like place
Of Earths best blessing I have seene the face?
25 But maskd from me, I onely see the shade
Of that, which once my brightest Sun-shine made.
You tell me, that I then was blest in Love,
When equall passions did together move.
O why is this alone to bring distresse
30 Without a salve, but torments in excesse?
A cruell Steward you are to inrole
My once-good dayes, of purpose to controle
With eyes of sorrow; yet leave me undone
By too much confidence my thrid so sponne:
35 In conscience move not such a spleene of scorne,
Under whose swellings my despaires are borne.
Are you offended (choicest Memorie),
That of your perfect gift I did glorie?
If I did so offend, yet pardon me.
40 Since 'twas to set forth your true exelencie.
Sufficiently I thus doe punish'd stand,
While all that curst is, you bring to my hand.
Or, is it that I no way worthy was
In so rich treasure my few dayes to passe?
45 Alas, if so and such a treasure given
Must I for this to Hell-like paine bee driven?
Fully torment me now, and what is best
Together take, and mem'ry with the rest,
Leave not that to me, since but for my ill,
50 Which punish may, and millions of hearts kill.
Then may I lonely sit downe with my losse
Without vexation, for my losses crosse:
Forgetting pleasures late embrac'd with Love,
Linck'd to a faith, the world could never move;
55 Chain'd with affection, I hop'd could not change,
Not thinking Earth could yeeld a place to range:
But staying, cruelly you set my blisse
With deepest mourning in my sight, for misse
And thus must I imagine my curse more,
60 When you I lov'd add to my mischiefs store:
If not, then Memory continue still,
And vex me with your perfectest knowne skill,
While you deare solitarinesse accept
Me to your charge, whose many passions kept

65 In your sweet dwellings have this profit gaind,
   That in more delicacie none was paind:
Your rarenesse now receive my rarer woe
   With change, and Love appoints my soule to know.

As he wandered by himself, thinking of his thwarted love, Dolorindus, Prince of Negroponte, wrote these verses. His journey led him to "a Mount cast up by nature, and more delicate then Art could have fram'd it, though the cunningest had undertaken it" (I. i. p. 109). A seventeenth-century manuscript copy (not holograph) of an earlier version of this poem is in the British Library: Addit.MS 23229, ff. 91–92. The manuscript poem is entitled "Penshurst Mount," the name given to a piece of high ground on the Sidney estate, which Ben Jonson referred to in his poem "To Penshurst": "Thou hast thy walks for health as well as sport: / Thy Mount, to which the dryads do resort" (ll. 9–10).

   1. The first line echoes *OA* 34.1: "O sweet woods the delight of solitarines!"

[U10] Deare Love, alas, how have I wronged thee,
     That ceaselesly thou still dost follow me?
My heart of Diamond cleare, and hard I find,
     May yet be pierc'd with one of the same kind,
5 Which hath in it ingraven a love more pure,
     Then spotlesse white, and deepe still to endure,
Wrought in with teares of never resting paine,
     Carv'd with the sharpest point of curs'd disdaine.
Raine oft doth wash away a slender marke,
10   Teares make mine firmer, and as one small sparke
In straw may make a fire: so sparkes of love
     Kindles incessantly in me to move;
While cruelst you, due onely pleasure take,
     To make me faster ty'd to scornes sharpe stake;
15 Tis harder, and more strength must used be
     To shake a tree, then boughes we bending see:
So to move me it was alone your power
     None else could ere have found a yeelding hower.
Curs'd be subjection, yet blest in this sort,
20   That 'gainst all but one choice, my heart a fort
Hath ever lasted: though beseig'd, not mov'd,
     But by their misse my strength the stronger prov'd
Resisting with that constant might, that win
     They scarce could parly, much lesse foes get in.
25 Yet worse then foes your slightings prove to be,
     When careles you no pitie take on me.
Make good my dreames, wherein you kind appeare,
     Be to mine eyes, as to my soule, most deare.

From your accustomed strangenesse, at last turne;
30   An ancient house once fir'd, will quickly burne,
And wast unhelp'd, my long love claimes a time
   To have aid granted to this height I clime.
A Diamond pure, and hard, an unshak't tree
   A burning house find helpe, and prize in mee.

Early in the morning Pamphilia walks by herself in the forest, while "her passionate breast scarce allowing her any respite from her passions, brought these Verses to her mind, wherein shee then imprinted them" (I. i. p. 121).

[U11]   Stay mine eyes, these floods of teares
    Seeme but follies weakely growing,
  Babes at nurse such wayling beares,
    Frowardnesse such drops bestowing:
5   But *Niobe* must shew my fate,
  She wept and griev'd her selfe a state.

My sorrowes like her Babes appeare
    Daily added by increasing;
She lost them, I loose my Deare,
10   Not one spar'd from woes ne're ceasing:
She made a rock, heaven drops downe teares,
Which pitie shewes, and on her weares.

Before parting from her friend Pamphilia, Antissia sings this song "or rather part of one." The narrator comments at its conclusion that "assuredly more there was of this Song, or else she had with her unframed and unfashioned thoughts, as unfashionably framd these lines" (I. i. p. 122). Lady Mary Wroth probably created this brief poem with its central image of Niobe's tears, from the original version of U9, "Penshurst Mount," in which six lines were omitted after l. 60 of the final version (see the lines quoted in the textual note to U9). The author thus calls attention to her own process of revising the poetry for inclusion in the *Urania*.

Dialogue
Sheapherd, and Sheapherdess

[U12]   She: Deare how doe thy wining eyes
        My sences wholy ty?
    Sh 2: Sence of sight wherin most lies
        Chang, and variety,
5   She: Chang in mee?
    Sh 2: Choyse in thee some new delights to try;
    She: When I chang, or chuse butt thee
        Then changed bee mine eyes;

Sh 2: When you absent see nott mee
10   Will you nott breake thes tyes?
She: How can I
          Ever fly wher such parfection lies?
Sh 2: I must yett more try thy love
          How if that I should chang?
15 She: In thy hart can never move
          A thought soe ill, soe strang.
Sh 2: Say I dy?
She: Never I could from thy love estrang:
Sh 2: Dead what can'st thou love in mee
20   When hope, with lyfe is fled?
She: Vertue, beauty, fayth in thee
          Which live will, though thou dead:
Sh 2: Beauty dies
She: Nott wher lies a minde soe richly sped;
25 Sh 2: Thou dost speake soe faire, soe kind
          I can nott chuse butt trust:
She: None unto soe chaste a minde
          Should ever bee unjust
Sh 2: Then thus rest
30   True possest of love without mistrust.

    The climax of Book One of the first part of the *Urania* is the arrival of Pamphilia and
Amphilanthus at the Throne of Love, located on the island of Cyprus, which is known as
the birthplace of Venus and Adonis (Ovid, *Metamorphoses*, x). Young lovers who are
trapped within the three towers may be released from enchantment only after "the
valiantest Knight, with the loyallest Lady come together, and open that gate, when all
these Charmes shal have conclusion" (I. i. p. 40). To celebrate the liberation from
enchantment, the King of Cyprus has his shepherds and shepherdesses present songs,
which imitate the eclogues following the individual books of Sir Philip Sidney's *Old
Arcadia*. This dialogue between "a neate, and fine shepheard, and a dainty loving Lasse"
(I. i. p. 143) is also similar to Sir Robert Sidney's Pastoral 2, in which the nymph tests the
authenticity of her shepherd's love.

Song

[U13] Love what art thou? A vaine thought
          In our minds by phant'sie wrought,
          Idle smiles did thee beegett
          While fond wishes made the nett
5   Which soe many fooles have caught;

          Love what art thou? light, and faire,
          Fresh as morning cleer as th'Aire,

       Butt too soone thy evening chang
       Makes thy worth with coldenes rang
10   Still thy joy is mixt with care:

Love what art thou? A sweet flowre
       Once full blowne, dead in an howre,
       Dust in winde as stayd remaines
       As thy pleasure, or our gaines
15   If thy humor chang, to lowre.

Love what art thou? childish, vaine,
       Firme as bubbles made by raine:
       Wantones thy greatest pride,
       Thes foule faults thy vertues hide
20   Butt babes can noe staydnes gaine.

Love what art thou? causeles curst
       Yett alas thes nott the wurst
       Much more of thee may bee say'd
       Butt thy law I once obay'd
25   Therfor say noe more att first.

Among the eclogues that conclude Book One of the *Urania*, the following song is performed by a shepherdess, "being as it seemd falne out with Love, or having some great quarell to him" (I. i. p. 143).

Song

[U14] Who can blame mee if I love?
        Since love beefore the world did move:

        When I lov'd nott, I dispaird;
        Scarce for hansomnes I car'd,
5   Since, soe much I ame refin'd
        As new fram'd of state, and mind;
        Who can blame mee?

        Some, in truth of love beeguil'de
        Have him blinde, and childish stil'de,
10   Butt lett non in thes persist
        Since soe judging, judgment mist;
        Who can blame mee?

        Love in Chaose did appeere,
        When nothing was, yett hee seem'd cleere,
15   Nor when light could bee descride
        To his crowne a light was ty'de;

Who can blame mee?

Love is truth, and doth delight
Wher as honor shines most bright,
20   Reasons self doth love aprove
Which makes us, our selves to love;
Who can blame mee?

Could I my past time beeginn
I would nott committ such sinn
25   To live an howre, and nott to love
Since love makes us parfaite prove;
Who can blame mee?

    Because Amphilanthus disagreed with the mocking treatment of love found in the previous song, a Cypriot shepherd sings these verses for his satisfaction; other members of the group sing "the burden" (refrain) of the song: "Who can blame mee if I love? / Since love beefore the world did move" (I. i. pp. 144–45).

[U15]   Pray thee *Diana* tell mee, is it ill,
    As some doe say, thou think'st it is, to love?
  Me thinks thou pleased art with what I prove,
    Since joyfull light thy dwelling still doth fill.

5   Thou seemst not angry, but with cheerefull smiles
    Beholdst my Passions; chaste indeed thy face
  Doth seeme, and so doth shine, with glorious grace;
    For other loves, the trust of Love beguiles.

  Be bright then still, most chast and cleerest Queene,
10   Shine on my torments with a pittying eye:
  Thy coldnesse can but my despaires discry,
    And my Faith by thy clearenesse better seeme.

  Let those have heat, that dally in the Sunne,
    I scarse have knowne a warmer state then shade;
15   Yet hottest beames of zeale have purely made
    My selfe an offring burnt, as I was wonne.

  Once sacrific'd, but ashes can remaine,
    Which in an Ivory box of truth inclose
  The Innocency whence my ruines flowes,
20   Accept them as thine, 'tis a chast Loves gaine.

    Steriamus reflects on his mistress' rejection, as he looks at the Moon, "who seem'd chastly to behold her selfe in the smooth face of the Sea, which yet sometimes left her plainnes, rising, as catching at her face; or, as with love to embrace it, or rather keepe her in her dwellings" (I. ii. p. 152).

[U16] Teares some times flow from mirth, as well as sorrow,
Pardon me then, if I againe doe borrow
Of thy moist rine some smiling drops, approoving
Joy for true joy, which now proceeds from loving.

> Pamphilia returns to the ash tree, where her sad sonnet was carved (U5), and engraves four additional lines, vowing eternal love for Amphilanthus: "Yet 'tis all one, deere love, maintaine thy force well in my heart, and rule as still thou hast: more worthy, more deserving of all love, there breaths not then the Lord of my true love. Joy then *Pamphilia*, if but in thy choice, and though henceforth thy love but slighted be, joy that at this time he esteemeth me" (I. ii. p. 161).

[U17] How doe I find my soules extreamest anguish
With restles care my harts eternall languish?
Torments in lyfe increasing still with anguish,
Unquiet sleepes which breed my sences languish.

5 Hope yett appeares which somwhat helpes my anguish
And lends a sparcke of lyfe to salve this languish
Breath to desire, and ease to forgon anguish,
Baulmes butt nott cures to bitter tasting languish.

Yett strait I feele hope proves butt greater anguish
10 Faulse in ittself to mee brings cruell languish.
Could I nott hope, I suffer might my anguish
At least with lesser torture smart and languish.

For rebell hope I see thy smiles are anguish,
Both Prince, and subject, of e'relasting languish.

> Philarchos, youngest son of the King of Morea, sings this song, but it is overheard by Nereana, who is lost in the woods (I. ii. pp. 166–67). Suffering from a thwarted love for Steriamus, she wanders alone in circles, as a reflection of her distressed mental condition: "a thousand thoughts at this time possessing her, and yet all those as on a wheele turnd, came to the same place of her desperate estate." She begins to recover when the last line of Philarchos' poem reminds her of her own royal blood.
>
> 1–2. This sonnet, like P79, is monorhymed. The use of only one pair of rhymed words is a device found in Sir Philip Sidney's *OA* 39 and *AS* 89.
>
> 14. Lady Mary Wroth heavily revised this poem for inclusion in the *Urania* by changing its verb tense from past to present and by altering the imagery of the last line to refer to the speaker's rank.

Song

[U18] Gon is my joy while heere I mourne
In paines of absence, and of care,
The heav'ns for my sad griefs doe turne
Theyr face to stormes, and show dispayre;

5   The days ar dark, the nights oprest,
      With cloud'ly weeping for my paine,
    Which in theyr acting seeme destrest
      Sighing like griefe for absent gaine.

The Sunn gives place, and hids his face
10   That day can now bee hardly knowne,
    Nor will the starrs in night yeeld grace
      To sunn-robd heav'n by woe orethrowne;

Our light is fire in fearfull flames,
    The aire tempestious blasts of winde
15 For warmth wee have forgott those names
    Such blasts, and stormes are us assinde:

And still you blessed heav'ns remaine
    Distemperd while this cursed powre
Of absence rules, which brings my paine,
20   Lett your care bee more still to lowre.

Butt when my sunn doth back returne
    Call yours againe to lend his light
That they in flames of joye may burne
    Both equall shining in our sight.

Pamphilia recalls this song as she walks alone in the garden: "for so stilly did she moove, as if the motion had not been in her, but that the earth did goe her course, and stirre, or as trees grow without sence of increase. But while this quiet outwardly appear'd, her inward thoughts more busie were, and wrought, while this Song came into her mind" (I. ii. p. 177).
    12. robd: robbed

[U19]   When I with trembling aske if you love still,
      My soule afflicted lest I give offence,
    Though sensibly discerning my worst ill;
      Yet rather then offend, with griefe dispence.

5   Faintly you say you must; poore recompence
      When gratefull love is fore, I see the hill
    Which marres my prospect love, and Oh from thence
      I tast, and take of losse the poison'd pill.

While one coale lives, the rest dead all about
10   That still is fire: so your love now burnd out
    Tells what you were, though to deceiving led.

The Sunne in Summer, and in Winter shewes
    Like bright, but not like hot, faire false made blowes
    You shine on me, but your loves heate is dead.

In an attempt to win back her beloved, the shepherdess Allarina composes these verses "knowing that they might speake in kind for me, and yet my selfe not beg againe" (I. ii. p. 186).

12—14. Sir Robert Sidney uses similar imagery in Sonnet 21.12—14:
Or if on mee, from my fayre heaven are seen,
Some scattred beames: know sutch heate gives theyr light
As frosty mornings Sun: as Moonshyne night.

[U20]   You powers divine of love-commanding eyes,
        Within whose lids are kept the fires of love;
    Close not your selves to ruine me, who lies
        In bands of death, while you in darkenesse move.

5   One looke doth give a sparck to kindle flames
        To burne my heart, a martyr to your might,
    Receiving one kind smile I find new frames
        For love, to build me wholly to your light.

My soule doth fixe all thoughts upon your will,
10   Gazing unto amazement, greedy how
To see those blessed lights of loves-heaven, bow
        Themselves on wretched me, who else they kill.

You then that rule loves God, in mercy flourish:
        Gods must not murder, but their creatures nourish.

The shepherd Alanius, in love with Liana, performs a lyric for Pamphilia, who commends it as "a proper song, and well composd" (I. ii. p. 212).

[U21]   You pure and holy fire
        Which kindly now will not aspire
        To hot performance of your Nature, turne
        Crosse to your selfe and never burne
5   These Reliques of a blessed hand,
        Joynd with mutuall holy band
        Of love and deare desire.

Blame me not dearest lines,
        That with loves flames your blacknesse twines,
10   My heart more mourning doth for you expresse,
        But griefe for sorrow is no lesse.
        Deepest groanes can cover, not change woe,
        Hearts the tombe, keepes in the showe,
        Which worth from ill refines.

15   Alas yet as you burne,
        My pitie smarts, and groanes to turne

Your paines away, and yet you must consume
Content in me, must beare no plume,
Dust-like Dispaire may with me live,
20   Yet shall your memory out-drive
These paines wherein I mourne.

You reliques of pure love
To sacred keepe with me remoove,
Purg'd by this fire from harme, and jealous feare,
25   To live with me both chast and cleare:
The true preserveresse of pure truths,
Who to your grave gives a youth
In faith to live and moove.

Famous bodys still in flames,
30   Did anciently preserve their names,
Unto this funerall nobly you are come,
Honour giving you this tombe.
Teares and my love performe your rights,
To which constancie beares lights
35   To burne, and keepe from blame.

Melasinda, Queen of Hungary, composed this poem after she burned a letter from her suitor Ollorandus, King of Bohemia, and put the ashes in her cabinet. The poem witnesses "the sorrow for the burning, and the vowes she made to them burned" (I. ii. p. 227).
    1–2. See Sir Robert Sidney's Song 4.1–3:
My sowle in purest fyre
Doth not aspyre
To rewarde of my paine

[U22]   Love peruse me, seeke, and finde
How each corner of my minde
       Is a twine
       Woven to shine.
5   Not a Webb ill made, foule fram'd,
Bastard not by Father nam'd,
       Such in me
       Cannot bee.
Deare behold me, you shall see
10   Faith the Hive, and love the Bee,
       Which doe bring.
       Gaine and sting.
Pray desect me, sinewes, vaines,
Hold, and loves life in those gaines;

15   Lying bare
     To despaire,
  When you thus anotamise
  All my body, my heart prise;
     Being true
20   Just to you.
  Close the Truncke, embalme the Chest,
  Where your power still shall rest,
     Joy entombe,
    Loves just doome.

A young maid, overcome by love, sings this lyric as she fishes by a stream; she is overheard by Amphilanthus and Ollorandus, who observe her: "shee held her angle as neglectively, as love the ill causer of her paine held her, when the poore little fish did plaie with the baite, or offer to swallow it, too big for them, yet made the corke stirre: so (would she say) doth Love with me, play with me, shew me pleasures, but lets me enjoy nothing but the touch of them" (I. ii. p. 241).

  10. See P37.10–14 for a similar image.

[U23] From victory in love I now am come
    Like a commander kild at the last blow:
    Instead of Lawrell, to obtaine a tombe
    With triumph that a steely faith I show.
5   Here must my grave be, which I thus will frame
    Made of my stony heart to other name,
    Then what I honor, scorne brings me my tombe,
    Disdaine the Priest to bury me, I come.

  Cloath'd in the reliques of a spotlesse love,
10   Embrace me you that let true lovers in;
    Pure fires of truth doe light me when I moove,
    Which lamp-like last, as if they did begin.
    On you the sacred tombe of love, I lay
    My life, neglect sends to the hellish way,
15   As offering of the chastest soule that knew
    Love, and his blessing, till a change both slew.

  Here doe I sacrifise worlds time of truth,
    Which onely death can let me part with all,
    Though in my dying, have perpetuall youth
20   Buried alone in you, whereby I fall.
    Open the graves where lovers Saints have laine,
    See if they will not fill themselves with paine
    Of my affliction, or strive for my place,
    Who with a constant honour gaine this grace.

25   Burne not my body yet, unlesse an Urne
        Be fram'd of equall vertue with my love
        To hold the ashes, which though pale, will burne
        In true loves embers, where he still will move;
        And by no meanes, let my dust fall to earth,
30   Lest men doe envy this my second birth,
        Or learne by it to find a better state
        Then I could doe for love immaculate.

        Thus here, O here's my resting place ordain'd,
        Fate made it ere I was; I not complaine,
35   Since had I kept, I had but blisse obtain'd,
        And such for loyalty I sure shall gaine.
        Fame beares the torches for my last farewell
        To life, but not to love, for there I dwell,
        But to that place, neglect appoints for tombe
40   Of all my hopes; thus Death I come, I come.

Emilena, Princess of Styria (a province of Austria), who has been betrayed by a man whom she takes to be Amphilanthus, composes a song that is performed by one of her maids. The princess is described as "perfect in all noble qualities, as subject to love, and so to bee for too much faith deceived" (I. ii. p. 249).

[U24]   I, who doe feele the highest part of griefe
        Shall I bee left without reliefe:
        I, who for you doe cruell torments beare
        Will you alas leave mee in feare;
5   Know comfort never could more wellcom bee
        Then in this needfull time to mee,
        One drop of comfort will bee higher priz'd
        Then seas of joyes, if once dispisd;
        Turne nott the tortures which for you I try
10   Upon my hart to make mee dy;
        Have I offended? t'was att your desire
        When by your vowes, you felt lov's fire;
        What I did erre in, was to please your will,
        Can you gett, and the ofspring kill?
15   The greatest fault which I committed have
        Is, you did ask, I freely gave,
        Kindly relent, lett causeless curstnes fly
        Give butt one sigh, I blest shall dy:
        Butt O you can nott, I have much displeasd,
20   Striving to gaine, I losse have seaz'd;
        My state I see, and you your ends have gain'd

I'me lost, since you have mee obtain'd,
And since I can nott please your first desire
I'le blow, and nourish scorners fire,
25 As Salimanders in the fire doe live
Soe shall those flames my being give,
And though against your will, I live, and move
Forsaken creatures live and love;
Doe you proceed; and you may well confess
30 You wrong'd my care, when I care less.

Antissia begins to realize that Amphilanthus loves Pamphilia rather than her, and she composes these verses in that mood: "far-well delights, the truest flatterers, and thou dispaire infold me, I am thine" (I. ii. p. 271). The poem shows considerable revision, probably to adapt it to the highly emotional character of Antissia: "she was a meere *Chaos*, where unfram'd, and unorder'd troubles had tumbled themselves together without light of Judgement" (I. i. p. 95).
25. Salimanders: According to Pliny, the salamander lives in the fire (*Natural History*, X, 86). Examples include Lodge's *Phillis*, "Now am I a salamander by his [Love's] power, / Living in flames" (Sonnet 38.12–13) and *Henry IV, Part I* (III. iii. 47). See critical introduction, p. 51.

[U25] Blame me not dearest, though grieved for your sake,
Love mild to you, on me triumphing sits,
Sifting the choysest ashes of my wits,
Burnt like a Phoenix, change but such could shake.

5 And a new heat, given by your eyes did make
Embers dead cold, call Spirits from the pits
Of darke despaire, to favour new felt fits,
And as from death to this new choice to wake.

Love thus crownes you with power, scorne not the flames,
10 Though not the first, yet which as purely rise
As the best light, which sets unto our eyes,
And then againe ascends free from all blames.

Purenesse is not alone in one fix'd place,
Who dies to live, finds change a happy grace.

Although disappointed in their first loves, both Steriamus and Urania recover to find happiness with each other, as the seer Lady Mellissea had predicted: "from death in shew [they] rose unto a new love" (I. ii. p. 276). Steriamus composes a "booke of Verses" for Urania, in which one sonnet specifically commends "a second love" (I. ii. p. 276).

[U26] Love among the clouds did hover
Seeking where to spie a lover:
In the Court he none could find,

Townes too meane were in that kind,
5   At last as he was ripe to crying,
In Forrest woods he found one lying

Under-neath a tree fast sleeping,
Spirit of Love her body keeping,
Where the soule of *Cupid* lay
10   Though he higher then did stay,
When he himselfe in her discrying,
He hasted more then with his flying.

And his tender hand soft laying
On her breast his fires were playing,
15   Wak'd her with his baby game,
She who knew love was no shame
With his new sport; smild as delighted,
And homeward went by *Cupid* lighted.

See the shady Woods bestowing
20   That, which none can aske as owing
But in Courts where plenties flow,
Love doth seldome pay, but owe,
Then still give me this Country pleasure,
Where sweet love chastly keepes his treasure.

A country swain (actually "third sonne to an Earle") sings this song to a forest nymph "with as much amorosnesse as his young yeares could entertaine, or love be pleased to inrich him withall" (I. iii. p. 294).

[U27]   Infernall Spirits listen to my moanes,
From Cavy depths, give hearing to my groanes,
Great *Pluto*, let thy sad abiding move
With Hellish fires, to flame for fires of love;
5   Let *Charon* passe my woes unto thine eares:
His boate if empty they shall load it well,
With tortures great, as are the paines of Hell,
And waightier then the Earth this body beares.

Take downe my spirit, cloyd with griefe and paine,
10   Conjure the darkest Pits, to let me gaine
Some corner for a rest; if not, let mee
O *Pluto* wander, and complaine to thee:
No corsive can make wounds have torture more,
Nor this disfavor vex a forelorne soule;
15   (If all thy furys were put in a role)
Then Love gives me; ah bitter eating sore.

Call thy great Counsell, and afflicted Sp'rits,
   Examine well their woes, with all their nights,
   And you shall find none there that are not mine,
20 Nay, my least, with their greatest joyntly twine.
   Let saddest Echo from her hollow Cave,
   Answere the horrid plaints my sorrow gives,
   Which in like mournefull, and vast caverne lives;
   Then judge the murdering passions which I have.

25 My Judge is deafe, then, O thy justice prove,
   Mend thou the fault of proud forgetfull love,
   Release me from thy Court, and send me out
   Unto thy Brother *Jove*, whose love and doubt
   Hath oft transform'd him from his heavenly kind:
30 So now from thee transforme my killing care
   To blessing, and from Hell into the Ayre,
   Darke griefe should not a loving fancy bind.

The daughter of Plamergus, who laments the death of her lover Polydorus, begins "to turne, and twine her sorrowes: but now she had spun them into Rime, like the Swan in a most weeping Verse" (I. iii. p. 303). She reads her poem aloud from within a tomb of red marble, where she dies of grief.
   5. *Charon*: son of Erebos, an aged and dirty ferryman who conveyed in his boat the shades of the dead across the rivers of the lower world.

[U28] The joy you say the Heavens in motion trie
   Is not for change, but for their constancy.
   Should they stand still, their change you then might move,
   And serve your turne in praise of fickle love.
5 That pleasure is not but diversified,
   Plainely makes proofe your youth, not judgement tried.
   The Sunnes renewing course, yet is not new,
   Since tis but one set course he doth pursue,
   And though it faigned be, that he hath chang'd,
10 'Twas when he from his royall seate hath raing'd:
   His glorious splendor, free from such a staine,
   Was forc'd to take new shapes, his end to gaine.
   And thus indeed the Sunne may give you leave,
   To take his worst part, your best to deceive.
15 And whereof he himselfe hath been ashamd,
   Your greatnesse praiseth, fitter to be blamd,
   Nothing in greatnes loves a strange delight,
   Should we be governd then by appetite?
   A hungry humour, surfetting on ill,

20   Which Glutton-like with cramming will not fill.
     No Serpent can bring forth so foule a birth,
        As change in love, the hatefullst thing on earth.
     Yet you doe venture this vice to commend,
        As if of it, you Patron were, or Friend.
25   Foster it still, and you shall true man be
        Who first for change, lost his felicitie.
     Rivers (tis true) are clearest when they run,
        But not because they have new places won;
     For if the ground be muddy where they fall,
30   The clearenesse with their change, doth change with all,
     Lakes may be sweet, if so their bottoms be;
        From rootes, not from the leaves our fruit we see.
     But love too rich a prize is for your share,
        Some little idle liking he can spare
35   Your wit to play withall; but true love must
        Have truer hearts to lodge in, and more just,
     While this may be allow'd you for loves might,
        As for dayes glory framed was the night.
     That you can outward fairenesse so affect,
40   Shewes that the worthier part you still neglect.
     Or else your many changings best appeares;
        For beauty changeth faster then the yeares:
     And that you can love greatnesse, makes it knowne,
        The want of height in goodnesse of your owne.
45   Twas not a happinesse in ancient time
        To hold plurality to be no crime,
     But a meere ignorance, which they did mend,
        When the true light did glorious lusture lend.
     And much I wonder you will highly rate
50   The brutish love of Nature, from which state
     Reason doth guide us, and doth difference make
        From sensuall will, true reasons lawes to take.
     Wer't not for Reason, we but brutish were,
        Nor from the beasts did we at all differ;
55   Yet these you praise, the true stile opinion,
        By which truths government is shroudly gon.
     Honor by you esteemd a title, true,
        A title cannot claimd by change as due.
     It is too high for such low worth to reach,
60   Heaven gifts bestow'th as to belong to each.
     And this true love must in revenge bestow
        On you, his sacred power, with paine to know:

THE POEMS OF LADY MARY WROTH

A love to give you fickle, loose, and vaine,
   Yet you with ceaselesse griefe, seeke to obtaine
65 Her fleeting favours, while you wayling prove,
   Meerely for punishment a steddy love:
Let her be faire, but false, great, disdainefull,
   Chast, but to you, to all others, gainefull,
Then shall your liberty and choice be tide
70   To paine, repentance, and (the worst sinne) pride.
But if this cannot teach you how to love,
   Change still, till you can better counsell prove:
Yet be assur'd, while these conceits you have,
   Love will not owne one shot (you say) he gave.
75 His are all true, all worthy, yours unjust,
   Then (changing you) what can you from him trust.
Repentance true felt, oft the Gods doth win,
   Then in your Waine of love, leave this foule sin:
So shall you purchase favour, bannish shame,
80   And with some care obtaine a lovers name.

The wife of Polydorus writes these lines in answer to the amorous longings of
Nicholarus, who attempted to usurp the throne of Albania. He had composed verses
praising variety in love, but she answers with a defense of constancy (I. iii. pp. 318–19).
   1–12. Spenser's "Cantos of Mutability" raise a similar issue, whether the motion of
the planets is proof of the dominance of change or constancy (VII. vii. 51–58).

[U29] As these drops fall: so Hope drops now on me
   Sparingly, coole, yet much more then of late,
   As with Dispaire I changed had a state
   Yet not posses'd, governe but modestly.

5 Deerest, let these dropps heavenly showers prove
   And but the Sea fit to receive thy streames,
   In multitudes compare but with Sun beames,
   And make sweete mixture, twixt them, and thy love.

The Seas rich plenty joynd to our delights,
10   The Sunn's kind warmth, unto thy pleasing smiles
   When wisest hearts thy love-make-eyes beguiles,
   And vassell brings to them the greatest Sprites.

Raine on me rather then be drye; I gaine
   Nothing so much as by such harmeles teares,
15   Which take away the paines of loving feares,
   And finely winns an everlasting raigne.

But if like heate drops you do wast away
　　Glad, as disburden'd of a hot desire;
　　Let me be rather lost, perish in fire,
20　　Then by those hopefull signes brought to decay.

Sweete be a lover puer, and permanent,
　　Cast off gay cloathes of change, and such false slights:
　　Love is not love, but where truth hath her rights,
　　Else like boughs from the perfect body rent.

Bellamira, prompted by renewed hope in her love for the King of Dalmatia, wrote verses as she sat in an orchard while the rain drops began to fall. Amphilanthus commended her art and remarked that "pittie it is, that you should hide, or darken so rare a gift" (I. iii. p. 337). For the autobiographical similarities between the character Bellamira and Lady Mary Wroth, see the introduction, p. 29.

[U30]　You, who ending never saw
　　　　Of pleasures best delighting,
　　　You that cannot wish a thaw.
　　　　Who feeles no frost of spighting,
5　　　Keeping Cupids hand in awe,
　　　　That sees but by your lighting.
　　　Bee not still too cruell bent
　　　　Against a soule distressed,
　　　Whose heart love long since hath rent,
10　　　　And pittilesse oppressed:
　　　But let malice now be spent,
　　　　And former ills redressed.
　　　Grieve I doe for what is past,
　　　　Let favour then be granted,
15　　　Theeves by judgement to dye cast,
　　　　Have not of mercy wanted;
　　　But alone at feasts I fast,
　　　　As Chiefe of pleasure scanted:
　　　You accuse me that I stole
20　　　　From you your hearts directing,
　　　All your thoughts at my controule,
　　　　Yet passions still rejecting;
　　　But you place me in the roule
　　　　Of left loves new electing.
25　　　Though I kinder was to it,
　　　　My heart in place bestowing,
　　　To make roome for yours more fit,
　　　　As just exchange truth flowing,

Till you fondly gain'd the bit,
30   And flying, left love owing.
Which debt resting still unpaid,
    Let this at last be gained,
When your new loves have you staid,
    With welcome choyce obtained:
35   Let change on your brest be laid,
    While I live still unstained.

> In searching for his wife Urania, Steriamus mistakes her for another woman, Lady Pastora, who is dressed as a shepherdess and who sings a lyric as she combs her hair: "Love said shee, hath tyranniz'd over me, as well as plaid with you" (I. iii. p. 356).
> 1. Kelliher and Duncan-Jones ("A Manuscript of Poems by Robert Sidney," 114) call attention to the similarities between this poem and Sir Robert Sidney's Song 20.

[U31]   Cruell Remembrance alas now be still,
    Put me not on the Racke to torture me:
I doe confesse my greatest misery
    Lives in your plenty, my last harme your skill.

5   Poyson, and Venome onely once doe kill,
    While you perpetually new mischiefes see,
To vexe my soule with endlesse memory,
    Leaving no thought that may increase my ill.

Els have you neede to tell me I was blest,
10   Rich in the treasure of content, and love,
When I like him, or her had sweetest rest
    But passd like daies, you stay and vexings prove.

Chang'd from all favours you add unto despaire
Who under these waights grone, most wretched are.

> After she suspects that Amphilanthus has abandoned her, this time for a woman named Musalina, Pamphilia exclaims: "'Cruell remembrance will you also add to my misery: flye me, or if you stay, serve then to vexe me while I accuse onely you;' then shee cast some verses Sonnet-waies in her thoughts, which were these" (I. iii. p. 390).

Sonett

[U32]   Unquiet griefe search farder, in my hart
    If place bee found which thou hast nott possest
    Or soe much space can build hopes smalest nest:
    Take itt t'is thine, mine is the lodg of smart,

5   Despaire, dispaire hath us'd the skilfulst art
    To ruin hope, and murder easfull rest,

O mee, dispaire my vine of hope hath prest,
Ravisht the grapes the leaves left for my part:

Yett ruler griefe, not thou dispaire deny,
10   This last request proclaimes t'was nott suspect
Grafted this bud of sorrow in my brest:

Butt knowledge dayly doth my loss descry
Colde love's now match'd with care; chang with respect
When true flames liv'd thes faulse fires were supprest.

When Meriana, Queen of Macedon, requests to hear some of Pamphilia's poetry, the author is reluctant to share her verses, "so sad they are, as only fit me to heare, and keepe." She finally agrees to read her work, but she defends her choice of genre: "I seldome make any but Sonnets, and they are not so sweet in rehearsing as others that come more roundly off" (I. iii. p. 392).

[U33]   Losse my molester at last patient be,
    And satisfied with thy curst selfe, or move
    Thy mournefull force thus oft on perjurd love,
    To wast a life which lives by mischeifes fee.

5   Who will behould true misery, view me,
    And find what wit hath fain'd, I fully prove;
    A heaven-like blessing chang'd throwne from above,
    Into Dispaire, whose worst ill I doe see.

Had I not happy beene, I had not knowne
10   So great a losse, a King depos'd, feeles most
    The torment of a Throne-like-want, when lost,
    And up must looke to what late was his owne.

Lucifer downe cast, his losse doth grieve,
    My Paradice of joy gone, doe I live?

Pamphilia reads this sonnet as she sits by a stream waiting for the nymph Silviana, who had vowed to dedicate her life to Diana. After reading the last line of the poem, Pamphilia answers her own question: "Yes I doe live, cry'd she, but to what end? only to mourne, lament, and moane a state all pitty wants" (I. iii. p. 409).
    14. Paradice of joy: See *AS* 68.13: "O thinke I then, what paradise of joy."

[U34]   O! that I might but now as senceles bee
    Of my felt paines, as is that pleasant tree
    Of the sweet musique thou deere bird dost make,
    Who I immagin doth my woes partake,
5   Yett contrary wee doe owr passions move
    Since in sweet notes thou doest thy sorrowes prove.

I, butt in sighs and teares can show I grieve
And those best spent, if worth doe them beeleeve;
Yett thy sweet pleasure makes mee ever finde
10   That hapines to mee, as love is blinde,
And these thy wrongs in sweetnes to attire
Throwse downe my hopes, to make my woes aspire,
Beesids of mee th'advantage thou hast gott
Thy griefe thou utterest, mine I utter nott,
15   Yett thus att last wee may agree in one
I mourne for what still is, thou what is gone.

    As the ladies gather in a grove, the Queen of Naples writes these impromptu verses
when she hears "a Nightingale most sweetly singing, upon which she grounded her
subject" (I. iii. p. 416).

[U35]   Deare, though unconstant, these I send to you
As witnesses, that still my Love is true.
Receive these Lines as Images of Death,
That beare the Infants of my latest breath,
5   And to my tryumph, though I dye in woe,
With welcome glory, since you will it so,
Especially, my ending is the lesse,
When I Examples see of my distresse.
As *Dido*, one whose misery was had
10   By Love, for which shee in Deathes robes was clad;
Yet lost shee lesse then I, for I possest
And love enjoy'd, she lik'd, what was profest
Most cruell, and the death-lik'st kind of ill,
To lose the blessing of contentments will.
15   Faire *Ariadne* never tooke more care,
Then I did how you might in safety fare,
Her thrid my life was to draw you from harme,
My study wholly how I might all charme
That dangerous were, while pleasures you optain'd,
20   And I the hazard with the labour gain'd:
Yet shee this his life sav'd, he her honor lost,
That false Prince *Theseus* flying, left her crost
With his abandoning her truth, and love
Leaving her desolate, alone to prove
25   His Love, or ended, or but given for neede,
Caus'd her with misery to gaine that meed.
I *Ariadne* am alike oppress'd,
Alike deserving, and alike distress'd:

172

Ungratefull *Demophon*, to *Phillis* faire
30 A Thracian Lady, caus'd by like dispaire,
Or greater farr, for after fervent love,
In which bless'd time he freely still did prove:
What is desir'd, or lov'd, he left this Queene
And bliss, for a lesse Kingdome which had beene
35 Before his fathers, and by reason right,
For *Theseus* was his Sire that King of spight.
Thus did he both inherit state, and ill,
While *Phillis* selfe, her lovely selfe did kill,
Making a Tree her Throne, a Cord the end
40 Of her affections, which his shame did send.
I strangled am, with your unkindnes choak'd
While cruelty is with occasions cloak'd.
Medea Witch, with her enchanting skill
Did purchase what was craved by her will,
45 Yet was by *Jason* left at last, which showes
Love only free from all bewitching blowes.
But his owne witchcraft, which is worst of ills,
Never absenting till all joy it spills.
Charms it may be, with-held you now from me,
50 Breake through them, leave that Circes so oft free,
The Syrens songe, *Calypsoes* sweete delights
And looke on faith, which light is of true lights.
Turne backe the eyes of your chang'd heart, and see
How much you sought, how fondly once sought me,
55 What travell did you take to win my love?
How did you sue that I as kind would prove?
This is forgot as yesterdayes lik'd sport,
Love winning lasting long, once won proves short.
I like *Penelope* have all this time
60 Of your absenting, let no thought to clime
In me of change, though courted, and pursu'd
By love, perswasions, and even fashons rude
Almost to force extending, yet still she
Continued constant, and as I am free.
65 Ten yeares a cause was for *Ulisses* stay
While *Troy* beseiged was, but then away
Was homeward bent by all, save him who stayd,
And ten yeares more on forraine beautyes pray'd.
Against his will, he oft his will enjoyed.
70 And with variety at last was cloy'd.
Chainge wearyed him, when weary he return'd,

And from his wandring then to staydnes turn'd.
Come you now backe, I thus invite you home,
And love you, as if you did never roame:
75   I have forgot it as if never done,
And doe but thinke me a new to be wone.
I shall appeare, it may be, as I did,
And all passd falts shall in my breast be hid,
Try me againe, and you shall truely find,
80   Where fairenesse wanteth, clearenes of a minde;
Fairer, and richer then the masse of all
Their persons, which from me have made you fall,
If joyn'd together, and from thence to frame
A minde of beauteous faith, fit for the name
85   Of worthy Constancy inrich'd with truth,
Which gave me to you, and so held my youth
In young desires, still growing to your love,
Nourish them now, and let me your love prove.
Leave the new powerfull charms of strangers tongus,
90   Which alwayes truth with their faire falshood wrongs.
Come backe to me, who never knew the plot
To crosse your minde, or to thy will an nott:
Come, I say, come againe, and with *Ulisses*
Enjoy the blessings of your best blisses;
95   Happy the comfort of a chaste loves bed,
Blessed the pillow that upholds the head
Of loyall loving, shame's the others due,
Leave those for me who cannot be but true.
Come, and give life, or in your stay send death
100   To her that lives in you, else drawes no breath.

> After her lover betrayed her, Dorolina composed this long poem on "the subject of
> many unhappy Women, but bringing them all to my sadd estate" (I. iii. p. 418).
> Although she cautions that "the Verses are long and teadious," her audience insists on
> hearing her account of famous women deceived by men.
> 29. All of the women appear in Ovid's *Heroides*; one of the lesser known figures,
> Phyllis, the daughter of the Thracian King Sithon, fell in love with Demophon. Before
> the nuptials were celebrated, he went to Attica to settle his affairs at home, but he
> delayed returning longer than she expected. When Phyllis committed suicide, she was
> metamorphosed into a tree (*Heroides*, II).

[U36]   Why doe you so much wish for raine, when I,
Whose eyes still showring are, stand you so nigh?
Thinke you that my poore eyes now cannot lend

You store enough? alas, but rightly bend
5 Your looks on me, and you shall see a store
Able to moisten Earth, and ten earths more:
Sighs to make Heaven as soft as tender wooll,
And griefe sufficient to make up the full
Of all despaires, then wish not, since in me
10 Contained are teares, griefe, and misery.

> When she arrives at her home in Romania, Musalina finds the country suffering from
> a great drought, with everyone wishing for rain. She writes this poem to describe her
> sorrow on parting from Amphilanthus; although Musalina was not originally a writer,
> "she was grown likewise a Poet as being a necessary thing, and as unseparable from a
> witty lover as love from youth" (I. iii. p. 422).

Lindamira's Complaint
[U37–43]

The account of Lindamira's life exactly parallels that of Lady Mary Wroth in such
details as family background, education, marriage, and participation in court activi-
ties. The prose narrative introduces a series of seven poems, which describe the inner
turmoil resulting from a lover's betrayal. By including a fictionalized self-portrait, the
author follows one of the oldest traditions of pastoral, arising from Virgil's appearance
under the assumed name of Tityrus in the *Eclogues*. Other examples include Sannazaro
as Sincero in his *Arcadia* and Spenser as Colin Clout in the *Shepheardes Calender*. Lady
Mary Wroth's most likely model was Sir Philip Sidney's autobiographical character,
Philisides, who tells his life story, followed by love poems to "Mira" (*OA*, 334–44).

I.

[U37] Deare eyes farewell, my Sunne once, now my end,
        While your kinde willing grace I felt, all joy
        In soule I knew withdrawne, you now destroy
        The house that being gave to loves best friend.

5 You now alas to other objects bend
        That warmth of blisse which best delights enjoy,
        Striving to win an oft won idle toy,
        By falshood nurs'd, such creatures seldome mend.

Try your new loves, affect the choyce of store,
10   And be assur'd they likewise will choose more,
        Which I yet grieve; for though the losse I beare

I would have none with you to challenge right;
        But beare you must for making choyce so light:
        Yet still your beames Ile love, shine you elsewhere.

2.

[U38] O deadly rancour to a constant heart,
      Frownes, and neglect, my only favours be:
      Sometimes a cold respect is granted me;
      But hot flames to those eyes joy in my smart.

5   Once yet for Justice sake weigh my hard part,
      In gratefulnesse I should kinde usage see;
      For being tied alone to you, els free,
      Till by your wrongs now joynd with heart-broke smart.

    A glorious triumph you no doubt shall have,
10   To crowne your victory on murders grave,
      While falshood beares the armes my life hath won.

    I onely twise seaven yeares love shall gaine
      Change, worse then absence, or death's cruelst paine:
      The last yet got, you have your labour done.

      12. twise seaven yeares: According to the *Urania*, the queen banished Lindamira
after fourteen years of service (I. iii. p. 425).

3.

[U39] A surgeon I would aske, but 'tis too late,
      To stay the bleeding wound of my hurt heart:
      The roote is toucht, and the last drops depart
      As weeping for succeeding others fate.

5   Alas that my kild heart should waile my state,
      Or leisure have to thinke on ought but smart,
      Nor doth it, but with pitie beare a part,
      With her embrac'd yours like a loving mate.

    But now unmarried by a new disdaine
10   Cold death must take the body from her love
      And thou poore heart must end for my unworth.

    Conscience is lost, and outward fairenes gaines
      The place where worth did, or else seemd to move,
      Thus world like change new triall still brings forth.

4.

[U40] O Memorie, could I but loose thee now,
      At least learne to forget as I did move
      My best, and onely thoughts to waite on love,
      And be as Registers of my made vow.

5 Could I but let my mind to reason bow,
  Or see plaine wrongs, neglects, and slightings prove
  In that deare Sphear, which as the Heavens above
  I prizd, and homage to it did allow.

 Canst thou not turne as well a Traitor too
10 Since Heaven-like powers teach thee what to doo?
  Canst not thou quite forget thy pleasures past;

 Those blessed houres, the onely time of blisse,
  When we feard nothing but we time might misse
  Long enough to enjoy what's now off cast.

5.

[U41] Leave me vaine Hope, too long thou hast possest
  My mind, made subject to thy flattring skill,
  While Aprill mornings did my pleasures fill,
  But cloudy dayes soone changd me from that rest;

5 And weeping afternoones to me adrest,
  My utter ruine framd by Fortunes will,
  When knowledge said Hope did but breed, and kill,
  Producing only shadowes at the best.

 Yet Hope tis true, thy faults did faire appeare
10 And therefore loth to thinke thou counseldst me
  Or wilfully thy errors would not see
  But catch at Sunne moates which I held most deare

 Till now alas with true felt losse I know,
  Thy selfe a Bubble each faire face can blow.

   12. Sunne moates: particles of dust seen floating in sunbeams; recalls the reverse
situation in Matthew 7.3

6.

[U42] Though you forsake me, yet alas permit
  I may have sorrow, for my poysn'd crosse;
  Thinke not, though dead, to joy I cannot hit
  Upon a torture, for my soule-pierc'd losse.

5 Or if by chance I smile, I hopes ingrosse,
  Nor for I die not, I doe bliss admit,
  Most griefe will oft give leave for show to toss
  Upon the waves, where Shipwrack'd comfort split.

177

Thinke then your will, and left, leave me yet more:
10   Vexe not my loathed life, to ruine bent;
Be satisfied with glut of your bad change:

Lay me unthought on, in the love-kill'd store,
My griefe's my owne, or since for you 'tis sent,
Let me have that part from you while you range.

7·

[U43]   Some doe, perhaps, both wrong my love, and care,
Taxing me with mistrust, and Jelousie,
From both which sinnes in love like freedome, free
I live, these slanders but new raised are.

5   What though from griefe, my soule I doe not spare,
When I perceive neglect's slight face on me?
While unto some the loving smiles I see,
I am not Jealous, they so well doe fare.

But doubt my selfe lest I lesse worthy am,
10   Or that it was but flashes, no true flame,
Dazl'd my eyes, and so my humour fed.

If this be jealousie, then doe I yeeld,
And doe confesse I thus goe arm'd to field,
For by such Jealousie my love is led.

[U44]   From a long way, and Pilgrimage for Love,
I am return'd weary'd with Travels paine,
Not finding ease, or those vexations moove;
First, to my soule they are, where to remaine
5   They vow to setle; then alas, can I
Thinke of a rest, but travell till I die.

Dressed as a pilgrim who has traveled to Jerusalem in repentance for her sins, Pelarina sings this song, while Perselina, the King of Macedon's daughter, overhears it (I. iv. p. 449).
    1. Sir Robert Sidney's longest poem, Song 6, presents a dialogue between a pilgrim who has returned from the East and a woman who questions him concerning the fate of her beloved. In Lady Mary Wroth's poem, a woman conducts her own "Pilgrimage for Love."

[U45]   Did I boast of liberty?
'Twas an insolency vaine:

I doe onely looke on thee,
    And I captive am againe.

Despite the cruel treatment she has received, Pelarina is still committed to her love; she admits, "I could but like a poore miserable Poet confesse my selfe in Rime" (I. iv. p. 453).

[U46]   Love farewell I now discover
        Thee a Tyrant o're a lover,
    All thy promis'd sweets prove crosses,
    Thy rewards are only losses.

5   A pritty thing I did deeme thee,
        Innocent, and mild esteeme thee,
    But I find thee as curst matter
    As a swelling high wrought water.

    Cupids name a pleasant folly
10   Hath beguiled hearts most holly,
    Even to sacrifize in homage,
    Life and soule unto their domage.

    Mine an offering once I profferd,
        Happily refusd when offerd,
15   Ile keepe now but to revile thee,
    From the craft which did beguile me.

Pamphilia and Amphilanthus, now rejoined, overhear the queen's shepherd Sidurno playing upon a rebeck and singing this song (I. iv. pp. 482–83).

[U47]   Faithfull lovers keepe from hence
        None but false ones here can enter:
    This conclusion hath from whence
    Falsehood flowes, and such may venter.

The climactic enchantment of part one of the *Urania* is the Hell of Deceit, which Pamphilia discovers when she arrives at a mysterious configuration of rocks, known as the Crown of Stones. Within the largest stone, she sees "a place like a Hell of flames, and fire, and as if many walking and throwing pieces of men and women up and downe the flames: partly burnt, and they still stirring the fire, and more brought in, and the longer she looked, the more she discernd, yet all as in the hell of deceit" (I. iv. p. 494). When she witnesses the torture of Amphilanthus, with his breast cut open to reveal her name written on his heart, Pamphilia attempts to rescue him, but she is driven back by the flames. After failing to save the prince, Pamphilia sadly reads this inscription on the rock, which serves as a warning to prevent her entry. The entire episode bears a strong similarity to Spenser's account in the *Faerie Queene* of Scudamour's attempt to rescue Amoret from torture at the hands of Busyrane, who appears to extract her heart (III. xii. 21).

[U48]   *Egypts* Pyramids inclose their Kings,
        But this farr braver, nobler things;
    Vertue, Beauty, Love, Faith, all heere lye
        Kept in *Myras* Tombe, shut from eye:
5   The *Phoenix* dyes to raise another faire,
        Borne of her ashes, to be heire;
    So this sweete Place may claime that right in woe,
        Since heere she lyes, Heaven willing so.

> While traveling to the city of Myra in Lycia, the Duke of Bavaria observes an unusual pyramid decorated "with rare Trophies belonging to Love, which shewed that it was dedicated to that God, but one thing seemed strangest to him, which was a Garland hanging on the one side of it, of flowers dead, and withered, some fallen off, others decayed, following them that were gone before, and under it these lines graven in a peece of Brasse" (I. iv. p. 498). The pyramid memorializes the devotion of the lady Myra, who chose to die rather than forsake her love for Alarinus. A song attributed to William Herbert, third Earl of Pembroke, develops a similar theme:
>
> Death's living tomb thus will I be,
> And living dye continually.
> To Birds and Worms I'le it expose,
> That on my body when I dye
> They may engrave this Elegie:
> No solemn burial will I crave,
> My Cell shall be my Tomb and Grave;
> And ere I breath my last thereon,
> I'le write this sad Inscription;
> *Here lies inclosed in this Tomb,*
> *He that indur'd Loves Martyrdom.*
>   Onderwyzer (ed.), *Poems,* 103

[U49]   If a cleere fountaine still keeping a sad course,
        Weepe out her sorrowes in drops, which like teares fall;
        Marvell not if I lament my misfortune,
                    Brought to the same call.

5   Who thought such faire eyes could shine, and dissemble?
        Who thought such sweete breath could poyson loves shame?
        Who thought those chast eares could so be defiled?
                    Hers be the sole blame.

    While love deserv'd love, of mine still she fail'd not,
10   Foole I to love still where mine was neglected,
        Yet faith, and honor, both of me claim'd it,
                    Although rejected.

    Oft have I heard her vow, never sweete quiet
        Could once possesse her while that I was else where,
15   But words were breath then, and as breath they wasted
                    Into a lost Ayre.

So soone is love lost, not in heart imprinted,
  Silly I, knew not the false power of changing,
  Love I expected, yet (ah) was deceived,
20   More her fond ranging.

Infant Love tyed me not to mistrust change,
  Vowes kept me fearelesse, yet all those were broken:
  Love, faith, and friendship by her are dissolved,
                 Suffer'd unspoken.

The Duke of Brunswick sings these verses to his lady "in manner or imitation of Saphiks" (I. iv. p. 511). The sapphic is a form of quantitative verse, with the following pattern of scansion:

– ˘ – – – ˘ ˘ – ˘ – –
– ˘ – – – ˘ ˘ – ˘ – –
– ˘ – – – ˘ ˘ – ˘ – –
           – ˘ ˘ – –

Sir Philip Sidney experimented with sapphics in three poems: *OA* 12 and 59, *CS* 5. Mary, Countess of Pembroke, used sapphics in Psalm 125; see Gary F. Waller, *Mary Sidney, Countess of Pembroke: A Critical Study of Her Writings and Literary Milieu* (Salzburg: Institut für Anglistik und Amerikanistik, 1979), 126.

[U50]   That which to some their wishes ends present,
         Is counted day, which former crosses mend,
         Yet night-like day my blessings do prevent,
         And brings that losse, whereto my mischeifs tend.

5   By dayes approach, alasse, that light doth end,
         Which is the only light of my content,
         And more I see, day strive her light to lend
         The darker am I, by sad parting rent.

     Like one long kept in prison, brought to light;
10   But for his end, condemned nere to bee
         Freed from his Dungeon, till that wretched hee,
         Conclude his living with his latest sight.

So now with griefe, doth day appeare to mee,
And Oh! too early since we parting see.

Although the Duke of Brunswick presents this sonnet as a gift to his lady, it was actually written by his friend, the Duke of Wertenberg; the narrator comments somewhat cynically: "great pitty it was not his owne worke, but as it was, it was liker a Lovers present, counterfeite as his vowes, and protestations, yet true beguilers of welbeleeving women, who were happier to be Hereticks, then such beleevers" (I. iv. p. 514).

9–12. Sir Robert Sidney includes a very similar image in Sonnet 23.9–10: "For as the condemnd man from dungeon ledd / Whoe with first light hee sees, ends his last breath."

[U51]

Wo. Fond aged man, why doe you on me gaze,
     Knowing my answer? resolution take;
     Follow not fondly in an unusd Maze
     As if impossibilities to shake.
5   For know I hate you still, and your poore love
        Can mee as soone as Rocks to pitie move.

Man. Alas my dearest soule, too long I knew
     I lov'd in vaine, your scorne I felt likewise,
     Your hate I saw; yet must I still pursue
10   Your fairest sight, though you doe me despise;
        For love is blind, and though I aged be,
        I can nor part from it, nor it from me.

Wo. What blame dost thou deserve, if thou wilt still
     Follow my hate, who will not breath to change,
15   And strive to gaine as if from scorne, or ill
     Loving disdaine as Juels rich, and strang:
        Or canst thou vainely hope thy wailing cries
        Can move a pitty? no let this suffice.

Man. Pitie, alas I nere could looke to see
20   So much good hap; yet Deere be not too cruell,
     Though you thus young hate aged love in me,
     My love hath youth, or you shall see loves fuell
        Deserving your reward, then not denie,
        Let me now see those eyes kind, or I die.

25 Wo. These eyes of mine thou never shalt behold,
     If clouds of true disdaine may dim desire,
     They shall as blacke be as thy faults are bold,
     Demanding what's unfit; a poore old fire
        Wasted like Triumphs, sparcles onely live,
30   And troubled rise from embers which outlive.

Man. I doe confesse a boldnesse tis in me
     Ought to resist, if your sweet selfe command;
     Yet blind me needs you must, for if I see,
     Mine eyes must rest on you, and gazing stand:
35   Heaven not forbids the bacest worme her way,
        Hide that deare beauty, I must needs decay.

Wo. My beauty I will hide, mine eyes put out,
     Rather then be perplexed with thy sight,
     A mischiefe certaine worse is, then a doubt,
40   Such is thy sight, thy absence my delight;

Yet mine the ill, since now with thee I stay.
Tyred with all misfortune cannot stray.

Man. Thy beautie hide? O no, still cruell live
To me most haplesse; dim not that bright light
45 Which to this Earth all lights and beauties give.
Let me not cause for ever darkest night,
No, no, blessed be those eyes and fairest face,
Lights of my soule, and guides to all true grace.

My sweet commanderesse shall I yet obay
50 And leave you here alas unguarded? shall
I not then for sorrow ever stray
From quiet peace, or hope, and with curst thrall
Sit downe and end? yet if you say I must
Here will I bide in banishment accurst:
55 While you passe on be cruell, happy still
That none else triumph may upon mine ill.

The Dukes of Brunswick and Wertenberg overhear a dialogue sung by an old man and a young damsel. Although the lady admits that her suitor may have some positive qualities, she rejects his love: "hee hath carried himselfe honestlie, but foolishly loveth mee, who cannot requite him" (I. iv. p. 517).
1–2. See Sir Robert Sidney's Pastoral 8. 1–2, a dialogue between a shepherd and a nymph, who refuses him: "Shepheard why doest thow so looke still on mee, / From whence doe these new humors grow in thee?"

1.

[U52] A sheapherd who noe care did take
Of aught butt of his flock
Whose thoughts noe pride cowld higher make
Then to maintaine his stock,
5 Whose sheepe his love was, and his care,
Theyr good his best delight,
The lambs his joye, theyr sport his fare,
His pleasure was theyr sight,

2.

Till love, an envier of mans blis
10 Did turne this merry lyfe
To teares, to wishes which ne're miss
Incombrances with strife,
For wheras hee was best content
With looking on his sheepe:
15 His time in woes must now bee spent,
And broken is his sleepe;

3.

Thus first his woefull chang began
    A lambe hee chanc'd to miss
Which to find out about hee ran
20   Yett finds nott wher itt is,
Butt as hee past O! fate unkind
    His ill lead him that way
Wheras a willow tree behind
    A faire young mayden lay;

4.

25 Her bed was on the humble ground
    Her hed upon her hand
While sighs did show her hart was bound
    In lov's untying band,
Clear tears her cleerest eyes lett fall
30   Upon her love borne face
Which heavnly drops did sorrow call
    Prowd wittnes of disgrace;

5.

The sheapherd stayd, and fed his eyes
    Nor furder might hee pas
35 But ther his freedome to sight ties
    His bondage his joye was.
His lambe hee deems nott haulf soe faire
    Though itt were very white,
And liberty hee thinks a care
40   Nor breathes butt by her sight,

6.

His former lyfe is alterd quite,
    His sheep feed in her eyes,
Her face his field is of delight,
    And flocks hee doth dispise,
45 The rule of them hee leaves to none
    His scrip hee threw away,
And many hee forsakes for one,
    One hee must now obay:

7.

Unhapy man whose loosing found
50   What better had bin lost

Whose gaine doth spring from such a grownd
    Wherby hee must bee crost,
The worldly care hee now neglects
    For Cupids service ties
55 Care only to his fond respects
    Wher wavelike treasure lies,

8.

As this lost man still gazing stood
    Amased att such a sight
Immagining noe heavnly food
60   To feed on butt her sight
Wishing butt her beams to behold
    Yett grievd hee for her griefe
When mournfully hee did unfolde
    Her woes without reliefe.

9.

65 His new sun rose, and rising sayd
    Farwell faire willow tree
The roote of my estate decayd
    The fruit for haples mee,
What though thy branch a signe be made
70   Of labor lost in love?
Thy beauty doth noe sooner vade
    Then those best fortunes prove;

10.

My songs shall end with willow still,
    Thy branches I will weare:
75 Thou wilt accompany my ill,
    And with mee sorrow beare,
True freind sayd she, then sigh'd, and turn'd,
    Leaving that restles place,
And sheapheard who in passions burn'd
80   Lamenting his sad case;

11.

This mayd now gon, alone he left,
    Still on her foot steps gaz'd,
And hartles growne by love bereft
    Of mirth, in spiritt raysed,
85 To satisfy his restles thought

Hee after her will hy,
His ruin to bee sooner brought,
And sooner harme to try,

12.

Then thus his latest leave hee tooke,
90   My sheepe sayd hee farwell,
Lett som new sheapherd to you looke
    Whose care may mine excell,
I leave you to your freedome now
    Loves lawes soe fast mee bind
95 As noe time I can you allow;
    Or goe poore flock, and find

13.

The mayd whom I soe deerly love;
    Say itt was her deere sight
Which from your keepe doth me remove,
100   And kills my first delight,
Goe you my dog who carefull were
    To guard my sheepe from harme,
Looke to them still noe care forbear
    Though love my sences charme;

14.

105 Butt you my pipe that musique gave,
    And pleasd my silent rest
Of you I company will crave
    Our states now suteth best,
For if that faire noe pitty give
110   My dying breath shall cry
Through thee the paines wherin I live
    Wherby I breathe to dy;

15.

Madly hee ran from ease to paine
    Nott sick yett far from well,
115 Hart rob'd by two faire eyes, his gaine
    Must prove his worldly hell,
After his hart hee fast doth hy,
    His hart to her did fly,
And for a byding place did cry,
120   Within her brest to ly;

16.

She that refus'd: when hee her spide
    Her whom hee held most deere
Ly weeping by a rivers side
    Beholding papers neere.
125 Her ruling eyes must yett bee dimd
    While pearlike tears she shed
Like shadowes on a picture limd,
    Att last thes words she read.

17.

When I unconstant am to thee
130   Or faulse doe ever prove,
Lett hapines bee banisht mee
    Nor have least taste of love;
Butt this alas too soone cride she
    Is (Ô) by thee forgott
135 My hopes, and joys now murderd bee,
    And faulshood is my lott;

18.

Too late I find what t'is to trust
    To words, or othes, or tears,
Since they that use them prove unjust,
140   And couler butt owr fears.
Poore fooles ordain'd to bee deceav'd;
    And trust to bee betraide,
Scornd when owr harts ar us bereav'd
    Sought to, awhile delay'd;

19.

145 Yett though that thou soe faulse hast bin
    I still will faithfull bee
And though thou think'st to leave, noe sin
    I'le make my loyalty
To shine soe cleere as thy foule fault
150   To all men shalbee knowne,
Thy chang to thy changd hart bee brought,
    My faith abroad bee blowne.

20.

This having sayd againe she rose
    The papers putting by,

155 And once againe a new way chose
    Striving from griefe to fly;
Butt as she going was along
    That pleasant runing streame
She saw the sallow trees amonge
160   The sheapherd Aradeame.

21.

For soe this woefull lad was call'de,
    But when she him beheld,
What wichcraft hath thee now inthralld,
    And brought thee to this field?
165 What can the cause or reason bee
    That thou art hether come
Wher all must taste of misery,
    And mirth with griefe intombe?

22.

Iff mirthe must heere intombed bee
170   Faire sheapherdes sayd hee
This place the fittest is for mee
    If you use crueltie,
For know I hether com to see
    Your self, wherin now lies
175 My lyfe, whose absence martir'd mee
    Whose sight my powre tyes.

23.

Give mee butt leave to live with you,
    Itt is the lyfe I crave:
To you I bound am to bee true,
180   My lyfe to you I gave,
When first I did behold you ly
    In shade of willow tree
That time, my soule did to you ty,
    Those eyes did murther mee.

24.

185 Is this the reason? ah cride she
    The more I waile your cace
Who thus partaker needs little bee
    In griefe, and in disgrace,
I pitty you, butt can nott ayde

190 You, nor redress your ill
    Since joy, and paine together payd
     Scarce satisfies the will;

25.

    Iff I doe ty you I release
     The bond wherin you are,
195 Your freedome shall nott finde decrease
     Nor you accuse my care,
    The paine I have is all my owne
     Non can of itt beare part,
    Sorrow my strength hath overthrowne:
200   Disdaine hath kil'd my hart;

26.

    And sheapherd if that you doe love
     This counsell take of mee
    This humour fond, in time remove
     Which can butt torture thee,
205 Take itt from her who too too well
     Can wittnes itt is soe,
    Whose hope seem'd heav'n, yett prov'd a hell,
     And comfort chang'd to woe.

27.

    For I was lov'd, or soe I thought
210   And for itt lov'd againe,
    But soone those thoughts my ruin brought,
     And nourisht all my paine,
    They gave the milk that fed beliefe
     Till wean'd they proved dry,
215 Theyr latter nourishment was griefe
     Soe famish'd I must dy;

28.

    Then see your chance; I can nott chang
     Nor my affection turne
    Disdaine, which others move to rang
220   Makes mee more constant burne;
    My sighs I'me sure can nott you please,
     My griefe noe musique prove,
    My flowing teares your passions ease,
     Nor woes delight your love,

29.

225 Iff my sight have your freedome wunn
      Receave itt back againe
Soe much my self I find undun
      By guifts which prove noe gaine
As I lament with them that love
230   Soe true in love I ame,
And liberty wish all to prove
      Whose harts waste in this flame,

30.

Yett give mee leave (sigh'd hee with tears)
      To live butt wher you are,
235 My woes shall waite upon your fears,
      My sighs attend your care,
I'le weepe whenever you shall waile,
      If you sigh I will cry
When you complaine, I'le never faile
240   To waile my misery.

31.

I will you guard, and safely keepe
      From danger, and from feare,
Still will I wach when you doe sleep,
      And for both sorrows beare,
245 Make mee nott free I bondage crave
      Nor seek els butt to serve,
This freedom will procure my grave,
      Thes bonds my lyfe preserve.

32.

For lyfe, and joye, and ease, and all
250   Alas lies in your hands
Then doe nott cause my only fall,
      I tyde ame in such bands.
Part hence I can nott, nor love leave,
      Butt heer must ever byde
255 Then pitty lett my paine receave,
      Doe nott from mercy slide;

33.

Iff that sayd she you constant are
      Unto your coming ill

I'le leave this place yett lett all care
260   Accompany mee still;
And sheapherd live, and hapy bee,
    Lett judgment rule your will,
Seeke one whose hart from love is free,
    And who your joye may fill;

34.

265 For I lov's bondslave ame, and tyde
    In fetters of disdaine:
My hopes ar frozen, my spring dri'de,
    My sommer drownd with paine;
I lov'd, and wurse, I sayd I lov'd,
270   Free truth my ruin brought
And soe your speech the like hath mov'd,
    And loss for gaining bought,

35.

With that away she hasted fast,
    Left him his cares to hold
275 Who now to sorrow makes all hast,
    Woes drive his hopes to fold,
Now hee can see, and weeping say
    His fortune blind hee finds
A hart to harbour his decay,
280   A state which mischief binds.

36.

This now hee feels, and woefully
    His birth, and lyfe hee blames,
Yett passion rules when reasons ly
    In dark, or quenched flames;
285 That place hee first beheld her in
    His biding hee doth make:
The tree his liberty did win
    Hee calls his martir stake;

37.

And pleasingly doth take his fall,
290   His griefe accounts delight,
Freedome, and joye his bitter thrall,
    His food her absent sight,
In contraries his pleasures bee

While mourning gives him ease,
295   His tomb shall bee that haples tree
     Wher sorrow did him seaze.

38.

And thus did live, though dayly dide
   The sheapherd Aradeame
Whose ceasles tears which never drid
300   Were turn'd into a streame
Him self the hed, his eyes the spring
   Which fed that river cleere,
And to true harts this good doth bring
   When they aproach itt neere;

39.

305 And drinke of itt to banish quite
   All ficle thoughts of chang
Butt still in one choyce to delight,
   And never think to rang;
Of this sweet water I did drink
310   Which did such faith infuse
As since to change I can nott think
   Love will death sooner chuse.

The Duke of Wertenberg recites this long narrative poem, composed by his lady Lycencia, who used the form of the pastoral to conceal her identity and "to cover her owne ill fortune the better" (I. iv. p. 520).
   300. The transformation of Aradeame's tears into a stream recalls the tale of Alpheus and Arethusa in Ovid's *Metamorphoses* (v). Lady Mary Wroth also alluded to the tale in the *Urania*: "turne this sweet water into a spring of love, that as it hath beene ever called by that blessed name of *Arethusa*" (I. i. p. 168).

[U53]   Rise, rise from sluggishnes, fly fast my Deere,
     The early Larke prevents the rising lights:
     The Sunne is risen, and shines in the rights
     Of his bright glory, till your eyes appeare.

5   Arise, and make your two Sunnes so cleare show,
     As he for shame his beames call backe againe,
     And drowne them in the Sea for sorrowes paine,
     That you, Commandresse of the light may know,

   The dutie Sunne, and all must yeeld to you
10   Where richnesse of desert doth lie imbracd,

Night by your brightnes wholly now defac'd,
And Day alone left to you as lights due.

Yet be as waighty still in love to me,
   Presse me with love, rather then lightly flie
15   My passions like to women, made to tie
   Of purpose to unloose, and oft be free.

Thus may your lightnesse shewing ruine me,
   I cannot live if your affections dye,
   Or leave off living in my constancy
20   Be light and heavy too, so wee agree.

The Talkative Knight, a Florentine, composes these verses "in commendation of his Mistresses eyes, and blaming her being sleepy in the morning, when shee should have beene up to entertaine him" (I. iv. p. 538). The narrator emphasizes the Florentine's erratic, impulsive speech, as he "talk'd on, and regarded, or not, said Verses, spake Prose, and Rime againe, no more heeding answers."

I

[U54]   Have I lost my liberty,
   And my selfe, and all, for thee
       O Love?
   Yet wilt thou no favour give
5   In my losse thy blame will live;
       Alas remove.

2

Pitie claimes a just reward,
But proud thoughts are thy best guard
       Once smile:
10   Glory tis to save a life
When deceivers are in strife
       Which to beguile.

3

Your gaine hath my paine begot,
But neglect doth prove my lot,
15   O turne,
Say it was some other harme,
And not your still sought for Charme
       Did make me burne.

4

Thus may you all blame recall,
20   Saving me from ruins thrall
        Then love
Pitie me, Ile no more say
You to cruelty did sway,
        But loyall prove.

5

25   Else be sure your tricks Ile blaze,
And your triumph Castle raze
        Take heed,
Conquerours cannot remaine
Longer then mens hearts they gaine,
30   Worse will you speed.

6

You a King set up by Love,
Traytors soone may you remove
        From hy,
Take this counsell serve loves will
35   And seeke not a heart to kill,
        Least both doe cry.

    Leurenius, Prince of Venice, sings this lyric to the shepherdess Celina. Once having
mocked Cupid, she is chastised for her rash behavior: "insolent thou wert to love;
scornfully, peevishly reviling him, and now but deservedly thou art pained, and he justly
revenged" (I. iv. pp. 544–45).

[U55]   Love growne proud with victory,
        Seekes by sleights to conquer me,
        Painted showes he thinks can bind
        His commands in womens mind.
5   Love but glories in fond loving,
I most joy in not removing.

Love a word, a looke, a smile,
        In these shapes can some beguile,
        But he some new way must move
10   To make me a vassell prove.
Love but &

Love must all his shadowes leave
        Or himselfe he will deceive,
        Who loves not the perfect skie,

15 More then clouds that wanton flie.
Love but &

Love, yet thus thou maist me win,
   If thy staidnesse would begin
   Then like friends w' would kindly meete
20   When thou proov'st as true as sweete
Love then glory in thy loving
   And Ile joy in my removing.

Lemnia, a shepherdess, sings this song, which is overheard by Celina and another fellow sufferer. She sings "merrily and carelesly," unconcerned if Cupid or human witnesses listen (I. iv. p. 549); although scorning passion, she soon experiences Cupid's revenge by falling in love with the Prince of Venice. The central theme is similar to that of Lady Mary Wroth's play, *Love's Victorie*.

1. Compare the opening line to the play's title and Cupid's boast to Venus: "then take noe care loves victory shall shine / when as your honor shall bee raisd by mine: (f. 5).

[U56] This no wonder's of much waight,
'Tis the hell of deepe deceit.

Amphilanthus undergoes an enchantment at the Hell of Deceit parallel to the one experienced earlier by Pamphilia (see U47). Although he attempts to rescue Pamphilia from torture, he is thrown out of the cave in a trance and awakens to find "these words onely written in the place of the entrance" (I. iv. p. 554).

The Secound Part of
the Countesse of Montgomery's Urania

[N1] Why doe you thus torment my poorest hart?
Why doe you cleerest eyes obscure all day,
From mee loves poorest vassall? Can my smart
Ad triumph to your Crowne? Make noe delay
5 Butt quickly O conclude, and doe nott stay,
Rebellions must bee crusht by present art
Yett I a subject ame without dismaye,
For loyalty I justly claime great part,
Butt if thos cruell eyes will nott impart
10 A favourable sensure, Oh poore claye
How can an new mould bee to ease my smart?
Noe an new death must all thes ills repay,
Then wellcom death since by thos eyes I dy,
Love looke, are any cleerer in your skye?

> A young prince of Corinth, who has fallen in love with an extremely vain and peevish woman, sings these verses "to an od kinde of musick, his voice suteable to his ditty" (II. i. f. 8ᵛ). The Princess of Elis requires him to forswear the society of all other women for seven years, and he is now ending the period of his isolation.

[N2] See pp. 217–18.

[N3] Most deere, more hapy soverainsing harts,
      Free from flattering;
Murdering peeces prove your sweet eye darts
      Joys from desire scattering,

5 Why alas were you framd if alone to kill?
      You knowe murdering
A crime by all condemn'd, is this your skill,
      Nor caus'd nor furdering?

Yett you alas may certainly controle
10   Thos humours flowing,
Butt if itt bee you love to fleet, and role
      Poor slaves for honors showing,

Certainly you will end att last as wee,
And pitty wanting cry alas wo's mee.

A shepherdess named Fancy, who favors change and variety in lovers, sings this song, which the narrator describes as "truly nott contemptable" (II. i. f. 13). Fancy is already beginning to feel the onset of old age and to regret the rejection of her first beloved.

[N4]   Honor now injoye the day
        Love is falen into desmay,
        Nay is conquer'd, yeeld all right
        To the power of his might
  5   Honor, honor, now is all:
        Captive Cupid sees his fall;

        Never lett a slight love come,
        In honors sight for a doombe
        Or thinke light affections thrall
 10   Dare apeere, noe now 't'is gall;
        Honor Monarck is of Love,
        Under him affections move,

        This is Honors purest throne,
        Heere hee brightly shines alone,
 15   Poore love like meane sphears appeere,
        In him's onely brightnes cleere,
        Had I knowne him thus beefore,
        Myne armes, I had layd att his dore,

        Now I yeeld them to his worthe
 20   This doth knowledg true bring forthe
        Arrowes, bowe, darts, and wings
        Which death brought to mortallings:
        All I offer up to you
        Deere Honor, as the Monarck true.

Rodomandro, the King of Tartaria, presents a masque, in which Cupid is interrupted by Honor, who chastises him and disarms him of his powers. The defeated Cupid must beg pity from the ladies with this song, "confessing thy self noe thing, thy kingdome les, thy power vanitie [and] thy self aire" (II. i. f. 15).

[N5]   This is Honor's holly day
        Now sheapheard swaines, neatheards play
            Cupid wills itt soe:
        Kings, and princes come alonge
  5   You shall safely pass from wronge
            Desire was your foe,

2

Fond·desire is now layd waste
Truth of love in his stead plaste
 Honor guides you now,
10   'T'is true Cupid was desire,
Fondly using wanton fire
 Therfor thus doth bowe,

3

Love's nott Love, that vainely flings
Like a harmfull waspe that stings
15 Therin I did miss
Desire should nott bee stil'd love
Butt with honors wings to move
 Bright love tells us this,

4

Honor like the brightest morne
20 Shines while clowded love is worne
 And consum'd to dust,
Like faire flowrs long beeing pulld
Dy, and wither if nott culld
 Slightest like the wurst,
25 Butt lett harts, and voices singe
Honor's Cupids just borne kinge.

 After Cupid agrees to become "a servant to honor, and a page to truth," the performers sing this last song of Rodomandro's masque, which celebrates the triumph of Honor over Cupid (II. i. f. 15).

[N6]   Come lusty gamesters of the sea
 Billowes, waves, and winds,
Like to most lovers make your plea
 Say love all combinds;
5 Lett nott Dian rule your sprites,
Her pale face shuns all delights,

Venus was borne, of the sea foame
 Queene of love is she
Like her sweet pleasant phantisies roame,
10 This Varietie;
Juno yett a firme wife is,
Soe may I bee in my blis,

Pallas is yett a fierce, sterne lass,
    Wisdome doth profess,
15 Ceares a hous-wife I soone pass,
    Lovers I express;
Venus, my deere sea borne Queene,
Gives mee pleasures still unseene,

And you faire starry sky, beeholde
20   Venus mee commaunds,
That by noe meanes love should grow colde
    Butt blowe the fire brands;
Soll's best heat must fill our vaines,
Thes are true loves highest straines.

Caught in the grips of a poetical fury, the insane woman Antissia constantly creates songs and poems. Her husband Dolorindus attempts to take her to the island of St. Maura, to cure her of her madness. Antissia's lyric is described as a "tedious ditty," only pleasing to her husband (II. i. f. 15 ᵛ).
    1. gamesters: players, especially those attracted to amorous sports

[N7] This night the Moone eclipsed was
    Alas,
Butt quickly she did brightlier shine
    Devine,
5 Prognosticating by sweet raine
That all things showld bee cleere againe,

Sweet raine foretells us good to growe,
    And flowe,
Coole drops sweet moisture, flowers bring
10   To spring,
Which fruict brings forthe, and soe shall wee
Live hopefully all good to see,

Butt in this time the sun is loste
    And crost,
15 Thought in Antipides nott quite beereft
    Nor left,
Butt in just course shall come againe,
And with pure light both shine, and raigne.

The mad woman Antissia sings these verses in greeting to the seer, Lady Mellissea, but her performance is marred by her own strange gestures, as she moves "up and downe like an new broke colte, in a haulter" (II. ii. f. 16).

[N8]   Stay holy fires
        Of my desires
        Flame nott soe fast;
        My loves butt young
5   From bud new sprunge
        Scarce knowes loves taste,

        Flames showld nott rise
        Till sacrifies
        Were reddy made;
10   A love scarce greene
        Was never seene
        In withring shade,

        Stray till 't'is blowne
        If then orethrowne
15   With curst denyes;
        Poore hart swell'out
        Send flames about
        With murdering eyes,

        Summon all men
20   To Court agen
        Wher loves inthround,
        If they persist
        And smiles resist,
        While chast love is scornd,

25   Then spoile their harts
        With fierce lovs darts,
        And with that store
        Of harts which shakes
        Make martir stakes
30   Still framing more,

        Then with thos eyes
        Wher all truth lies
        A blaze of fire frame,
        As Heccatombbe
35   For victors doombe
        To true loves name,

        Soe holy fires
        Of my desirs
        May rise, and flame
40   Pheanix for truth

Consum'de in youth
Burnt to loves fame.

A beautiful young princess of fourteen, who is the King of Tartaria's sister, sings these
lines as she sits in the garden outside a giant's castle. Licandro, son of the Duke of Athens,
instantly falls in love with the woman and finds himself in a worse predicament than
when he was imprisoned by the giant (II. i. f. 24ᵛ).
 37–40. See Sir Robert Sidney's Song 4.52–54.
 And in yow and my fyres
 With pure desyres
 Phenixlike joye and burne.

[N9] Were ever eyes of such devinitie
 Devine? Noe they are of the Gods
  And soe have ods,
 Of the Gods? Noe, more of Eternitie;
5 They are blew, sure they are then heavens sky
  Firmly
 Kings they rule and commaund,
 Motives of government doe ly
  To their imply
10   Readely
 And soe att mercy stand,

2

 Bee they nott two suns, most shiningly
 Beaming? Noe they are meators rare
  Without compare,
15 Meators noe? Thunderbolts killingly
 Were they of Gods, they would deale beningly
  Gently
 Two sunns were never seene
 Att once, devinitie
20 Doth that deny
   Really
 Butt lightnings oft have binn,

3

 Lightnings O noe, they are induring,
 And bright, are they nott Cupids eyes
25 Falen from the skies
 While hee is doubly blinded in aluring?
 Shall I yett name them must, O then say

201

You may
They are of Gods, of eyes,
30 Of the heavens, of ayre most bright,
    Of purest light,
       Fierce sight,
Yett sweetest under skies.

To express his new love, Licandro composes this lyric. The narrator calls attention to the "strange measure" of the verse with its combination of short and long lines (II. i. f. 26).
9. imply: employ
13. meators: The term meteor was loosely applied to any celestial phenomenon (*OED*).
16. beningly: benignly

{N10} Fierce love, alas yett lett mee rest,
       Beeholde my boyling brest:
       Lett mee butt slumber, if nott sleepe
          Continually to weepe
5   Is too great a smart
                 To a hart
       Transform'd like Niobé to watry powers
                 Telling howers
       In drops of my misfortunes arte;

                           2

10   Cruell, alas, why doe thos eyes
       Rule of the heavenly skies
       Joye in my ruin? My poore streames
          Flumes can nott coole your beames
             For loves sacred fire
15   Must aspire
       Transcendant to the highest powers
                 Telling howers
       In flames of my consuming fire,

                           3

       The Firmament may mee imbrace
20   Ther wanderers may finde place
       Transform'd by love into a space
          Borowing of lovers trace
             Wher continuall faire
                Will tell ayre

25   Wee destined by force, earth, water, ayre, fire
            Bred in ire
  May yett to evenings faire aspire,

4

  Butt dull earth I see you contend
  Nott willing I assend,
30   Give mee then fruicts of plenty heere
     True increase of beauties cheere,
       Why doe you create
       Such a bate
  To singe all harts, by such a fire
35   And intire
  Consuming us to our last fate?

The women accompanying the Queen of Argos sing these lines, and they are overheard by Lusandrino, son of the King of Corinth's brother, and Nummurando, son of the Duke of Corona, as they sit beside a brook. The narrator indicates, "the song was this, butt sung in many severall parts" (II. i. f. 27).

[N11]   Beehold this sacred fire
  In waters curstest ire
     Remaines in mee
  Desdaining change to see
5   As hee makes waters touch
  His prowd inclosing my desire
  And in his bosome keeps my fire
  While I lament too much,

2

  This lampe inflamed with love
10   Consumes nott yett doth move
     And spends the oyle
  Soe doe I waste in toile
  To clime to honors high
  Which with water, and the time
15   Doth the flame make higher clime
  And soe I may rise nigh;

3

  Butt while I heere admire
  Water, and flames conspire
     Nott yeeld to mee

20   Yett cunningly agree
     Noe ease unto my burning smart
     Butt extinguish fyry rays
     The aulter for my loving bays
     To act his lastest part;

4

25   Time butt an attome is
     Limited by powers blis
        Of heavenly might
     Made by eternall right
     For heaven erelasting beeing
30   Makes eternitie the name,
     And mee the attome of my flame,
     Consumed, and burnt by seeing.

Lindavera, disguised as a young shepherdess, sings these verses "with as sweet a voice as any earthly creature could have" and is overheard by the three young princes—Floristello, Prince of Albania; Verolindo, Prince of Phrygia; and Antidorindo, Prince of Negroponte, all of whom have been shipwrecked on the island (II. i. f. 36ᵛ).

[N12]   Love lett mee live, ore lett mee dye,
     Use mee nott wurse then poorest fly
     Who finds some comfort, while alone
        I live, and waste in moane;

5   I have noe shrouding place from woe,
     The billowes beare my overthrowe,
     And sands they cover in disgrace
        Of my loves truest face.

     Wretch sayth the sea heer stay, and drowne:
10   Can you nott feare her curstest frowne?
     Alas she chides us that you stay,
        After her just denay,

     She is the Goddesse sole of Love;
     How dare you mortall thus to move?
15   Bow hart, and soule to her least frowne
        And sensur'd thus ly downe.

The sage Lady Mellissea appears in a fiery chariot with a message especially for Queen Pamphilia. The seer presents to the court party a masque, including this song, which is sung by a swain to his beloved sea nymph (II. i. f. 41).

[N13]   Love butt a phantesie light, and vaine
        Fluttering butt in poorest biaine,
        Birds in chimnies make a thunder
        Putting silly soules in wounder
5   Soe doth this love, this all commaunder
        To a weake poore understander;

2

        Slight him, and hee'le your servant bee,
        Adore him, you his slave must bee,
        Scorne him, O how hee will pray you,
10 Please him, and hee'lle sure beetray you,
        Lett nott his faulshood bee esteemed
        Least your self bee disesteemed.

3

        Crush nott your witts to place him high,
        A thought thing, never seene by eye,
15 Implore nott heaven, nor deities
        They know too well his forgeries
        Nor saints by imprications move
        'T'is butt the Idolatry of love.

An old shepherd, who is scornful of love, sings these verses as part of his instruction to a young, enamored sailor. The old man and the young lovers join together in singing the last two lines "in a conting maner" (II. i. f. 41ᵛ), *i.e.* a whining or sing-song fashion. Pamphilia comments on the song that "if every one showld soe soone mend, loves Monarchy would have a quick end," but Lady Mellissea points out that Pamphilia's love is far greater, befitting a royal heart.

7–11. See Sir Philip Sidney's eclogue between old Geron and the young shepherd Philisides: *OA* 9.44–48.

[N14]   Was I to blame to trust
        Thy love like teares when t'is most just
        To judg of others by our owne? While mine
        From heads of love and faith did flow
5   Yett fruictles ran, could I suspect that thine
        When in my hart each teare did write a line
        Showld have noe spring butt outward showe?

2

        My love O never went
        In maske, which made mee confident

10 That thine had binn love too, and noe disguise,
    Nott love put on, butt taken in,
    Nor like a scarfe to bee putt off which lies,
    Att choise to weare ore leave, butt when thine eyes
    Did weepe thy hart had bled within,

                        3

15 Butt as the guilfull raine
    The sky that weeps itt doth nott paine
    Butt weares the place wherein the drops doe fall
    Soe when thy clowdy lids impart
    Thos showers of subtill teares; which seeme to call
20 Compassion when you doe nott grieve att all,
    You weepe them, butt they frett my hart,

                        4

    Deere eyes I wrong'd nott you
    To thinke you were as faire, soe true;
    Why wowld you then yourselves in griefe attire
25 With pitty to inlarge my smart
    When beauty had enough inflam'd desire
    And when you were even cumber'd with my fire?
    Why would you blowe the coales with art?

                        5

    For was less fault to leave
30 Then having left mee to deceave
    For well you might have my unworthe refused,
    Nor cowld I have of wronge complaind
    Butt since your scorne, you with deceipt confusd
    My undesert you have with teares excus'd
35 And with the guilt your self have stained.

    Urania finds Amphilanthus, distraught and wandering, suffering from the guilt of
    having lost again his beloved Pamphilia (II. i. f.50ᵛ).

[N15] Lying upon the beach,
            Beelow mee on the sands,
       I saw within small reach
            A lady ly in bands,
5   With armes across, and hands
            Infolded in thos twines,

Wherby a true love climes
And for loves triumph stands,

2

Alas, cride she, can love
10   Beequeath mee noe small space
Wher I may live, and love
    Butt run in ruins race?
Nor yett to gaine deaths trace,
You locks of his owne haire,
15   Wittnes I still you beare
    In my harts deerest place,

3

Butt O faulse is his hart,
    Yett faithfull is his haire,
Dead is his love, a pretty art
20   If wee thes two compare.
Haire once cutt off hath share
With death, loves lyfe beeing fled,
To shaddow haire is fled,
Soe are my joys to care.

4

25   Unconstant man, yett deere
    Beehold thy haire outlive
Thy faith, thy worthe, and cleere
    As thine eyes, which did drive
Wrack to my hart, take back
30   Thes reliques, lay the rack
On shriveld harts, and cry
Haire outlives Constancy.

Because Amphilanthus still grieves over his betrayal of Pamphilia, a disguised shepherd sings this song to encourage him as he prepares to return to his true love: "the sheapheard presenting the sad knight with his scrip from about his neck, more pretious then can bee vallued beecause fild with hope" (II. i. f. 53ᵛ).

    1. Lady Mary Wroth's verse may ultimately derive from the first song in Book I of Montemayor's *Diana,* in which the lover laments over a lock of hair. Sir Philip Sidney translated the first song in *CS* 28, and his brother also completed one stanza of the same song:
        Translated owt of Spanish
    Shee whome I loved, and love shall still
    Sitting on this then blessed sand
    Wrate with to mee heaven opning hand

207

First will I dy ere chang I will.
Oh unjust force of love unjust
That thus a mans beleef showld rest
On words conceaved in womans brest
And vowes inroled in the dust. (f.37)

Lady Mary reverses the situation by portraying a woman who suffers betrayal and has only a lock of hair to remind her of the past.

[N16]   Come deere, lett's waulke into this spring
Wher wee may heere the sweet birds sing
And lett us leave this darcksum place
Wher Cupid never yett had grace,
5   For loves bright light
Must us delight
And Cupids fire
Must still respire,
And brightest showe in darckest night.

2

10   'T'is nott the shades can harbour love;
Hee lives in highest spheares above,
And from his beames gives worlds ther light,
Hee raigning Crownd with sweets delight,
In darknes spite
15   Hee rules in light,
For Cupids fire
Must still respire
And brightest show in dullest night,

3

Love doth nott dwell in colde fainte shade,
20   Nor lurcks wher warme love growes to vade,
Hee's perfect heat, and strives to move
Wher equall flames with him showes love.
In Coldes despite
Hee rules in might
25   For Cupids fire
Must still aspire
And pow'rfulst show in darckest night.

Steriamus composes this song as he thinks of his wife Urania: "the verces were thes which hee as curiously sange to his lute when hee was left to his owne repose, speaking as if she had bin with him" (II. i. f. 55ᵛ).

[N17]   Most hapy memory bee ever blest
        Which thus brings into my most weary minde
        Joys past though others would them tortures finde,
        Butt I delighted was in them, though rest

5   I never felt, soe was my soule distrest,
        Yett lov'd the fetters did mee slavelike binde,
        O love, what is thy force? Some say thou'rt blind,
        Noe thou canst see best, and can give ease best,

        Then grant my memery may with mee live,
10   And darken nott my first, and deerest choise,
        From which though swervd, I in itt still rejoyse,
        Nor lett the fates from mee those phantsies drive,

        For though a secound love doth mee infolde,
        Non must the former from my soule unfolde.

On seeing the Morean lady's castle, Steriamus falls into a reverie because the estate so resembles the one in which he experienced his first passionate love—for Pamphilia. Fortunately, the sage Mellissea "had a carefull hand over him," so that Steriamus falls "onely into a prety little frency for the time of olde love, and memory which caused him to measure his thoughts a little into verce" (II. i. f. 56ᵛ).

[N18]   Returne my thoughts, why fly you soe?
        Sorrows may my good outgoe,
      Phantsie's butt phantasticks skill
        The soule alone hath onely will,

5   Heathen people had their Gods
        Whom they implor'd to have the odds
      Of mortalls all, butt 't'would nott bee
        For Love was high'st inthron'd to see,

      Soe love of all things hath most sight,
10   And noe thing more then love is light,
      Then Cupid take thy honor right:
        Thou'rt neither God, nor Earthly sprite.

This poem is recited by a beautiful young lady, the Duke of Sabbro's daughter, who once scorned Cupid: "for I contested against his Godhead, I revilde his powers, I scornd in language his all-conquering bowe, his death shooting Arrowes leaded with Gold" (II. ii. f. 59). Andromarcko, a natural son of Polarchos, King of Cyprus, received a copy of these verses and fell in love with the lady's portrait. He presents his own revised version of N18, which Amphilanthus praises as "a very neate peece of poetrye" (II. ii. f. 62).

[H1]   You pleasant floury meade
     Which I did once well love
     Your pathes no more I'le tread
     Your pleasures noe more prove
5   Your beauty more admire
     Your coulers more adore
     Nor gras with daintiest store
     Of sweets to breed desire;

Walks once soe sought for now
10   I shunn you for the darcke,
     Birds to whose song did bow
     My eares your notes nere mark;
     Brooke which soe pleasing was
     Upon whose banks I lay,
15   And on my pipe did play
     Now, unreguarded pass;

Meadowes, pathes, grass, flouers
     Walkes, birds, brooke, truly finde
     All prove butt as vaine shouers
20   Wish'd wellcome els unkind:
     You once I loved best
     Butt love makes mee you leave
     By love I love deseave
     Joy's lost for lives unrest.

    The Huntington manuscript of *Love's Victorie* begins abruptly with this song, per-
formed by the shepherd Philisses, who laments his fruitless love for Musella (f. 1).

[H2]   Joyfull pleasant spring
     Which comforts to us bring
      Flourish in your pride:
     Never lett decay
5   Your delights alay
      Since joye is to you ti'de,

Lett noe frost nor wind
Your dainty coulers blind
　　Butt rather cherish
10　Your most pleasing sight
Lett never winter bite
　　Nor season perish.

When Lissius enters singing these verses, his friend Philisses mistakenly assumes that his happiness results from winning the affections of Musella (f. 1).

[H3]　O my eyes how do you lead
My poore hart thus forth to rang
From the wounted course to strang
Unknowne ways, and pathes to tread?

5　Lett itt home returne againe
Free untouch'd of gadding thought
And your forces back bee brought
To the ridding of my paine.

Butt mine eyes if you deny
10　This smale favor to my hart,
And will force my thoughts to fly
Know yett you governe butt your part.

While the characters gather to exchange the secrets of their hearts, Climena sings of love, but she does not disclose the name of her favorite (f. 3ʳ). Later she aggressively pursues the shepherd Lissius, who criticizes her behavior: "a woman woo, / the most unfittest, shamfullst thing to doo" (f. 14).

[H4]　　When I doe see
　　Thee, whitest thee
Yea whiter then lambs wull,
　　How doe I joy
5　　That thee injoy
I shall with my hart full.

　　Thy eyes do play
　　Like goats with hay
And skip lik kids flying
10　　From the sly fox
　　Soe eye lids box
Shutts up thy sights priing.

　　Thy cheecks as red
　　As okar spred

15 On a fatted sheeps back,
    Thy paps are found
    As aples round,
Noe prayses shall lack.

One of Musella's admirers is the shepherd Rustick, who is a country bumpkin, obsessed with the care of his sheep. Like the characters of low comedy in Sidney's *Old Arcadia*, such as Dametas, Mopsa, and Miso, Rustick adds comic relief to the more refined courtship of the other lovers in the play. His song of praise for Musella's beauty is humorously filled with barnyard diction (f. 4).

    14. okar: ochre, an earthy red or yellow pigment

[H5] By a pleasant rivers side
Hart, and hopes on pleasures tide
Might I see with in a bower
Proudly drest with every floure
5 Which the spring can to us lend
Venus, and her loving freind.

I upon her beauty gas'de,
They mee seeing were amas'de,
Till att last up stept a child
10 In his face, nott actions mild;
Fly away saide hee for sight
Shall both breed, and kill delight.

Come away, and follow me;
I will lett thee beautys see.
15 I obay'd him, then hee staid
Hard besid a heav'nly maide
When hee threw a flaming dart,
And unkindly strooke my hart.

As part of a singing contest, the shepherd Lacon contributes this song (ff. 4–4ᵛ). In keeping with the etymology of his name, Lacon has a very small speaking part in the play.
    17–18. For a previous account of Cupid's treachery, see P96.

[H6] Love, and Reason once att warr
Jove came downe to end the jarr;
Cupid said love must have place
Reason that itt was his grace.

5 Jove then brought itt to this end:
Reason should on love attend
Love takes reason for his guid
Reason can nott from love slide.

This agreed, they pleasd did part
10 Reason ruling Cupids dart
Soe as sure love can nott miss
Since that reason ruler is.

When Philisses chooses a fortune from Arcas' book, the forlorn lover is advised that joy will follow suffering. Philisses then sings this song concerning the war between reason and love (f. 8ᵛ). A similar debate is found in the Second Eclogues of Sidney's *Old Arcadia*, where there is a "skirmish betwixt Reason and Passyon" (*OA* 27). See also P86.

[H7] Cupid blessed bee thy might,
Lett thy triumph see noe night,
Bee thou justly god of love
Who thus can thy glory move,
5 Harts obay to Cupids sway,
Prinses non of you say nay;
Eyes, lett him direct your way
For without him you may stray;
Hee your secrett thoughts can spy
10 Beeing hid els from each eye;
Lett your songs bee still of love,
Write noe satirs which may prove
Least offensive to his name;
If you doe you will butt frame
15 Words against your selves, and lines
Wher his good, and your ill shines,
Like him who doth sett a snare
For a poore betrayed hare
And that thing hee best doth love
20 Lucklesly the snare doth prove;
Love the king is of the mind,
Please him, and hee will be kind;
Cross him you see what doth com,
Harmes which make your pleasures tomb;
25 Then take heed, and make your blis
In his favour, and soe miss
Noe content, nor joy nor pease
Butt in hapines increase.
Love command your harts and eyes
30 And injoy what pleasure tries;
Cupid govern, and his care
Guard your harts from all dispaire.

Venus in *Love's Victorie* is a proud, domineering woman, who spurs Cupid into exercising his powers over the lovers; she specifically requests that "I would have all to wayle, and all to weepe" (f. 4ᵛ). At the end of Act Two she expresses satisfaction with Cupid's show of force in these lines (f. 10).

[H8]   *Silvesta:*

Silent woods with desarts shade
     Giving peace
Wher all pleasures first ar made
     To increase,
5 Give your favor to my mone
Now my loving time is gone.

Chastity my pleasure is
     Folly fled
From hence now I seeke my blis
10   Cross love dead,
In your shadows I repose
You then love I now have chose.

     Musella:

Choise ill made were better left,
     Beeing cross
15 Of such choise to bee bereft
     Were no loss,
Chastity you thus commend
Doth proceed butt from loves end.

And if love the fountane was
20   Of your fire
Love must chastitie surpas
     In desire,
Love lost bred your chastest thought
Chastity by love is wrought.

When Philisses rejects her love, the shepherdess Silvesta vows to dedicate her service to Diana and to abjure the sight of all men. She defends her choice of chastity in a poetic debate with Musella, who argues that love is a superior power (f. 11).

[H9] Love thy powerfull hand withdraw,
All doe yeeld unto thy law;
Rebells now thy subjects bee,
Bound they are who late were free,
5 Most confess thy power, and might,
All harts yeeld unto thy right;

Thoughts directed ar by thee,
Souls doe strive thy joys to see;
Pitty then, and mercy give
10   Unto them wher you doe live;
They your images doe prove,
In them may you see great love;
They your mirours, you theyr eye
By which they true love doe spy.
15   Cease awhile theyr cruell smarts
And beehold theyr yeelding harts;
Greater glory 'tis to save
When that you a conquest have
Then with tiranny to press
20   Which still make the honor les;
Gods doe prinses hands direct,
Then to thes have some respect.

At the conclusion of Act Four, Venus advises Cupid that it is now time for him to show compassion to the long-suffering lovers. The word "musique" appears at the heading of the song and probably signifies that Venus' lines are to follow (f. 20ᵛ).

POEM POSSIBLY BY WILLIAM HERBERT,
EARL OF PEMBROKE

This poem appears in four additional manuscripts at the British Library, three of which ascribe it to William Herbert, Earl of Pembroke (see introduction, p. 44). In Harley MS 6917, ff. 33ᵛ–34 (designated W), the poem is entitled "A Sonnet" and signed "pembrooke." According to the catalogue of the Harley collection, this seventeenth-century manuscript was originally part of Lord Somer's library. It has previously been dated in the early 1630s: Herbert Berry, "Three New Poems by Davenant," *Philological Quarterly*, XXXI, 70–74. The poem also appears in British Library Addit. 25303, f. 130ᵛ (X), where it is headed "E: P:" and in Addit. 21433, ff. 119ᵛ–120ᵛ (Y), also headed "E: P:". It appears anonymously in Addit. 10309, ff. 125–125ᵛ (Z). The poem is not included in the selection of William Herbert's verse, which was edited by John Donne the younger: *Poems, Written by the Right Honorable William Earl of Pembroke* (London, 1660).

[N2]   Had I loved butt att that rate
       Which hath binn ordain'd by fate
           To all your kinde;
       I had full requited binn
5   Nor your slighting mee had seene,
           Nor once repinde
           Neglect to find,

       For I ame soe wholy thinc
       As in least sort to bee mine
10   My hart denies;
       I doe think noe thought butt thee,
       Nor desire more light to see
           Then what doth rise
           From thy faire eyes,

15   Deer I blame nott thy neglect
       In excess of my respect
           The fault doth rest;
       Thou dost pretty love impart,
       As can lodge in woemans hart
20   Non showld bee prest
           Beeyound ther best,

       Butt when I did give thee more,

217

Then againe thou cowldst restore,
    And woeman bee;
25 I made thee against thy will
To remaine ungratefull still
    By binding thee
    Soe much to mee.

According to the narrator, Amphilanthus composed this song originally as a show of love to Antissia, but meant it for a "higher beauty," Pamphilia. For the entertainment of friends, it is performed by Pamphilia, who "by the eare would singe the skillfullest songs the rarest man of skill could singe, and such she called to accompany her, and allthough she were the best, yett did her naturall perfections surpass ther artificiall, as showed how truly Nature excelleth arte" (II. i. f. 10).

SYMBOLS IN THE TEXTUAL NOTES

]	A reading to the left of the bracket is that of the present text
om.	Material omitted by one of the witnesses
ed.	An editorial emendation
∧	A caret indicates the absence of punctuation.
~	A wavy dash replaces a word where punctuation only has been altered.
[cat]	Roman print within square brackets indicates words or letters supplied by the editor.
[*cat*]	Italic print within square brackets indicates words or letters deleted, erased, or written over in the manuscript.
⟨cat⟩	Angle brackets enclose words written as additions or as replacements for deletions in the manuscript.
[⟨*cat*⟩]	Words added in the manuscript and then deleted are in italic print enclosed in angle brackets and square brackets.

PAMPHILIA TO AMPHILANTHUS

Copy-text: The Folger manuscript of *Pamphilia to Amphilanthus* (with the exception of sonnet P4, which does not appear in F).

P1	2	senceses] F; senses 1621
	4	swiftnes] F; switnesse 1621
	10	brest,] 1621; ~∧F
	11	winn;] 1621; ~∧F
	14	I have] 1621; have I F
P2	2	soules] 1621; eyes F
	3	sought for] 1621; Cupids F
	4	Loves] 1621; his F
	9	Two] 1621; Too F
	10	birthe;] ~ reversed semicolon in F; ~, 1621
	12	even] 1621; yett F
P3	3	hart;] ~ reversed semicolon in F; ~, 1621
	5	moving see] 1621; move to bee F
	11	cry;] ~ reversed semicolon in F; ~. 1621
	14	doe lye] 1621; rely F
P4		This poem appears only in the 1621 text.
	12	Snow] *ed.*; Sow 1621
P5	2	a painefull torment] 1621; ever, torments F
	6	too] *ed.*; to F; two 1621
	7	still] 1621; *om.* F mischiefe] 1621; mischiefes F
	9	wunn] F; none 1621
	10	spring;] 1621; ~∧F
	11	doe] 1621; doth F prove:] 1621; ~∧F
	13	unkind;] *ed.*; ~∧F; ~, 1621
P6	8	torturs] F; torture 1621
	10	such thy will] 1621; you soe willd F paine] 1621; paines F
	11	my] F; may 1621

	12	hart-held] 1621; hart-kild F
P7	5	mine] 1621; my F
	8	wee] 1621; I F
	12	treasure.] 1621; ~∧F
	44	tombe:] 1621; ~∧F
P8	3	off] 1621; of F
	6	thy] 1621; your F to] 1621; doe F
	7	thy foe] 1621; your foe F thy claime] 1621; your claime F
	8	thy] 1621; your F
	9	thou would'st] 1621; you would F thee] 1621; you F
	10	thy will made mee] 1621; you, made mee first F
	11	thy] 1621; your F
	12	refuse.] 1621; ~∧F
P9	4	Increase the] 1621; increaseth F
	6	thought:] 1621; ~∧F
	8	ar wrought] 1621; [*as wrought*] ⟨ar brought⟩ F
	12	sight.] 1621; ~∧F
	13	may;] *ed.*; ~∧F; ~, 1621
P10	3	content?] 1621; ~; F
	4	bliss?] 1621; ~; F
	9	beereav'd] F; bereav'd me 1621 harmes] 1621; [*and*] harmes F
P11	6	is] F; his 1621
	13	saith] 1621; says F
P12	11	to] F; so 1621
	14	too] 1621; to F
P13	8	spite.] 1621; ~∧F
P14	3	I say] 1621; and say F
P15	11	the] 1621; that F

P16 2 joy's] F; joyes 1621
5 leave] F; leane 1621
7 Love] 1621; Cupid F
all] 1621; om. F
8 wishings] 1621; Venus F
P18 4 spite.] 1621; ~∧F
10 Doth flow, when] 1621; itt is
while F
11 left free] 1621; then left F
P19 12 care] 1621; cares F
13 with] 1621; ⟨with⟩ F
P20 12 those] 1621; thes F
P21 4 joye] 1621; [joye] ⟨hope⟩ F
19 phant'sie] 1621; phant'sies F
20 haples] 1621; hopeles F
22 mee] 1621; my F
P22 Wroth wrote "For absence"
opposite this poem
in the Kohler copy of
the 1621 Urania.
8 prest.] 1621; ~∧F
P23 4 in] 1621; by F
10 had] 1621; have F
P24 1 last I] 1621; I last F
2 thine] 1621; thy F
8 minute] F; mnute 1621
12 wrought.] 1621; ~∧F
14 thy] 1621; [my] ⟨thy⟩ F
doth] 1621; [doe] ⟨doth⟩ F
P25 4 favors] 1621; favor F
9 receavd's] F; receiv'd 1621
13 of] 1621; doe F
P26 4 doe] 1621; [did] ⟨doe⟩ F
prise.] 1621; ~∧F
12 choose as] 1621; is theyr F
grace.] 1621; ~∧F
14 sweet] 1621; deere F
P28 2 too] 1621; to F
7 needs] 1621; now F
P29 8 before.] 1621; ~∧F
9 thes] 1621; those F
P30 4 blest] F; best 1621
P31 1 tedious] 1621; treacherous F
7 from hands free] 1621; late
from thee F
13 abide;] 1621; ~∧F
14 gaine your liberty] 1621; I will
sett thee free F
P32 3 mine] 1621; my F
5 thou canst] 1621; you can F
P33 2 Too] 1621; to F

3 must] 1621; unjust F
6 mine] 1621; my F
have] 1621; take F
7 I can too late] too late I can F
8 When] 1621; now F
11 soone] 1621; O! F
14 disdaine] 1621; disdaineth F
rests] F; reasts 1621
poorer] 1621; poore F
P34 11 releeve;] 1621; ~∧F
13 My trusty freinds, my faith
untouch'd esteeme] 1621;
and you my, trusty freinds,
my faith esteeme F
14 I could] 1621; I [well] could F
P35 10 minutes] 1621; minute F
12 favors] 1621; favor F
21 thee:] 1621; ~∧F
P36 9 Reward] 1621; Venus F
10 joy:] 1621; ~∧F
12 depend.] 1621; ~∧F
P37 9 love;] ed.; ~∧F; ~, 1621
13 sweet] 1621; sought F
P38 1 poore Love hast thou] 1621;
hast thou poore Love F
2 end?] 1621; ~∧F
9 oft] 1621; thus F
12 compare.] 1621; ~∧F
P39 8 for] 1621; with F
13 mine] 1621; my F
P40 8 theyr greater] 1621; the
greater F
10 a show] 1621; the mask F
11 spent;] 1621; ~∧F
12 kills] F; kill's 1621
blood.] 1621; ~∧F
P41 2 for] author's cor, F; forth 1621
3 Drops] Wroth hand corrected
the initial letter to
lowercase, probably to
indicate the enjambment of
the previous line.
12 see.] 1621; ~∧F
14 of] 1621; they F
P42 Lines 2, 3, 5, and 6 of each stanza
are indented in the 1621 text.
38 Use your most] 1621; then use
your F
P43 There are three quatrains and a coup-
let in the 1621 text.
5 beest] 1621; bee F

11 of] 1621; in F
13 move,] 1621; ~‿F
P44 9 hart;] *ed.*; ~‿F; ~, 1621
P45 5 those] 1621; thes F
P46 4 are farr off] 1621; farr are of F
     5 they] 1621; thes F
        such] 1621; rhem F
    14 kinde] 1621; true F
        blessings] 1621; blessing F
P47 3 though] 1621; if F
     8 grace] 1621; force F
    12 th'eith] F; th'earth 1621
        bliss.] 1621; ~‿F
    13 gives] F; give 1621
P48 4 unrest.] 1621; ~‿F
     7 hartles trunk of harts depart]
        1621; [*body lives deprivd of
        hart*] ⟨hartles trunk of harts
        depart⟩ F
    11 show'd;] 1621; ~‿F
    12 this] 1621; the F
P49 5 yett] 1621; ⟨yett⟩ F
     8 cursed] 1621; wreched F
    22 prove] F; proone 1621
    23 dying] 1621; living F
P50 8 For your cleer lights, to mach
        his beames above.] 1621;
        [*how to bee match'd on earth
        wher you doe move*] ⟨thatt your
        cleer light showld mach his
        beames above⟩ F
    12 of] 1621; in F
    13 showld] 1621; ⟨showld⟩ F
    14 such] 1621; this F
P51 1 sweetest] 1621; swiftest F
     2 waters] F; water 1621
     5 you doe] 1621; doe yow F
     6 t'orerunn] 1621; t'overrunn F
     8 your swiftest course] 1621;
        butt your course to F
    12 That] 1621; which F
        quite.] 1621; ~‿F
P52 2 multituds] F; multitude 1621
    13 might,] 1621; ~‿F
P53 10 flame] F; paine 1621
P54 5 too] 1621; to F
P55 5 when] 1621; wher F
     7 impossible] F; unpossible 1621
    10 passions] 1621; longings F
    12 to breathe] F; to breath 1621
P56 Lines 2 and 4 of the first three stanzas

are indented in the 1621 text.
P57 Lines 2 and 4 of each stanza are
     indented in the 1621 text.
     8 griefs] 1621; griefe F
    13 waylings] 1621; wayling F
    14 a] 1621; some F
P58 There are three stanzas of six lines
     each (with lines 2, 4, and 6 indented)
     and a final couplet in the 1621 text.
     Wroth hand corrected the arrangement of
     the stanzas in the Kohler copy of the
     1621 *Urania*.
     1 heere?] 1621; ~‿F
    12 procures.] 1621; ~‿F
    16 move:] 1621; ~‿F
    18 to you your] *author's cor*, F;
        to your 1621
        gave.] 1621; ~‿F
P59 13 wished] *author's cor*, F;
        wicked 1621
    14 lott:] 1621; ~‿F
P60 There are six quatrains (with lines 2
     and 4 indented) in the 1621 text.
     4 rest.] 1621; ~‿F
    10 chang;] 1621; ~‿F
    12 fle] 1621; fly F
        strang;] *ed.*; ~‿F; ~, 1621
    21 hee thus] 1621; thus hee F
    22 accurst:] 1621; ~‿F
P61 Lines 3 and 4 are indented in each
     stanza of the 1621 text; in the first
     two stanzas line 2 is also indented
     6 new] 1621; ⟨new⟩ F
    18 too] 1621; to F
P62 Lines 3 and 6 are indented a mini-
     mum of 14 spaces in the 1621 text.
    16 gives] F; give 1621
    23 all] 1621; ⟨all⟩ F
P64 8 badge] 1621; [*image*]
        ⟨maske⟩ F
        office] 1621; service F
     9 hee doth] 1621; doth hee F
P65 3 Love for] 1621; Venus' F
     4 seasons] 1621; season F
     8 non could love] 1621; love
        could non F
     9 Now] 1621; Butt F
    10 than] 1621; then F
P66 1 rest,] 1621; ~‿F
     2 stay;] *ed.*; ~‿F; ~, 1621
     4 oprest.] 1621; ~‿F

5 distrest,] 1621; ~∧F

P68 6 strives] F; strive 1621
10 thoughts] 1621; thought's F
13 blessings] 1621; blessing F

P70 6 sadd slight] 1621; slight touch F
12 off] 1621; of F
The catchword at the bottom of P70 in the Folger manuscript is "O Lett," but the following poem is P20, "Which should I better like of, day, or night." None of Lady Mary Wroth's surviving poems begins with "O Lett."

P71 2 mine] 1621; my F
6 because] 1621; for feare F
10 griefe] 1621; paine F
11 bee] 1621; ⟨bee⟩ F
ill:] 1621; ~∧F

P72 1 Folly] 1621; Cupid F
3 while shee] 1621; till hee F
4 thes] 1621; his F
7 that vanitie] 1621; the god of love F
10 forc'd one to] 1621; [tyran-nously] ⟨forc'd one to⟩ F

P73 Lines 2 and 4 are indented in each stanze of the 1621 text.
1 springing] author's cor, F; spring 1621
3 frosts] 1621; frost F
23 frosts] 1621; frost F

P74 Only line 12 is indented in the 1621 text.
17 Feathers] F; Fathers 1621
18 praying.] 1621; ~∧F

P75 3 pritty] [pretty] ⟨pritty⟩ F
8 in] F; on 1621
10 too] 1621; to F
16 pitty.] 1621; ~∧F

P76 6 or] F; of 1621

P77 2 on] 1621; ⟨on⟩ F
7 with] F; which 1621
12 traveile] F; travell 1621

P78 2 line] 1621; [path] ⟨line⟩ F
3 with] 1621; [on] ⟨with⟩ F
11 The] 1621; [the] ⟨that⟩ F
12 increase.] 1621; ~∧F
13 delight;] ed.; ~∧F; ~, 1621

P79 5 are] 1621; ⟨are⟩ F
tri'de] 1621; tri'de [are] F
6 desernd] F; discern'd 1621

11 sunn] F; Sun's 1621

P81 7 feare] 1621; feares F
12 thoughts] 1621; thought F
deserne.] 1621; ~∧F
13 wee may] 1621; may wee F
14 profitt] F; Prophet 1621

P82 1 profitt] F; Prophet 1621
3 two] 1621; tow F
4 Two] 1621; tow F
5 which must] 1621; with much F
9 make] 1621; makes F
13 Love,] 1621; ~∧F
14 bee] F; are 1621

P83 3 flame] 1621: flames F
4 thes] 1621; those F
kindle] 1621; kindles F
7 wheras] 1621; as wher F
aspire] 1621; respire F
12 woorkman] 1621; woorkmen F
13 all must needs] 1621; needs must all F

P84 12 intise.] 1621; ~∧F

P85 4 binn.] 1621; ~∧F
5 subject] 1621; subjects F
sunn] F; Sonne 1621
6 or] 1621; nor F
space;] 1621; ~∧F

P86 9 of] 1621; butt F

P87 4 dearth.] 1621; ~∧F
12 desires.] 1621; ~∧F

P88 2 vading] F; fading 1621
8 night,] ed.; night ∧ F; might. 1621
12 content] 1621; contents F

P89 8 directions] 1621; directnes F

P90 4 stay.] 1621; ~∧F
6 Is faith untouch'd] 1621; faith untouch'd is F
12 see.] 1621; ~∧F

P91 There are three stanzas of eight lines each, with lines 2, 4, 6, and 8 indented, in the 1621 text.
10 only] 1621; butt F

P92 There are three stanzas of eight lines each (with lines 2, 4, 6, and 8 indented) and a final quatrain (with lines 2 and 4 indented) in the 1621 text.
3 off] 1621; of F
9 And] F; An 1621
12 right] 1621; light F

P93		Lines 5 and 6 of each stanza are indented 12 spaces in the 1621 text.		5	slide] F; slid 1621
				7	thus] 1621; ⟨thus⟩ F
P94	4	doe.] 1621; ~∧F		9	butt once] 1621; once butt F
	/	doe] 1621; may F		10	my] 1621; ⟨my⟩ F
	10	deseave,] 1621; ~∧F			eye] 1621; eyes F
	13	fame] 1621; fames F			place,] 1621; ~∧F
	28	faulshood] F; fashood 1621		13	canst] 1621; can F
		prov'd.] 1621; ~∧F		14	will] 1621; [doe] ⟨will⟩ F
	30	number] 1621; number's F	P101	1	or] 1621; nor F
	35	Martirs] F; Martir's 1621		3	Or] 1621; nor F
P95	4	morning] F; mourning 1621		6	my] 1621; thy F
		hart] 1621; hurt F		11	Then] 1621; [when] ⟨then⟩ F
		salve] 1621; soule F			I doe] 1621; doe I F
	7	wanton] 1621; Venus F	P102	5	This] F; The 1621
	9	thy] F; they 1621			cleere,] 1621; ~∧F
P96	12	safe] 1621; om. F		11	attend;] 1621; ~∧F
P97	4	heavens] 1621; heaven F	P103	1	rest,] 1621; ~∧F
	13	him nott] 1621; nott him F		9	sunn] F; sonne 1621
P98	3	contend;] 1621; ~∧F		13	off] 1621; of F
	11	nott] 1621; ⟨nott⟩ F		14	prove, [with the name written beneath] Pamphilia.] F; prove. 1621
P99	3	wrong] 1621; wrongs F			
	4	tyde] 1621; tride F			

Poems from the Folger Manuscript of *PAMPHILIA TO AMPHILANTHUS*

F1	10	drive;] ~ reversed semicolon in F	F3	2	eyes?] *ed.*; ~∧F
			F4	4	might.] *ed.*; ~∧F
F2	4	lies,] *ed.*; ~∧F	F5	7	harts,] *ed.*; ~∧F
	14	move,] *ed.*; ~∧F		9	Two] *ed.*; Tow F

Poems from the Text of *THE COUNTESSE OF MONTGOMERY'S URANIA*

Copy-text: 1621 (with the exception of nine poems that appear in F: U12, 13, 14, 17, 18, 24, 32, 34, and 52).

U2	3	Sighs] *ed.*; Sigh's 1621			boxes] 1621; richest boxes PM
U4	24	blooms] *ed.*; bloom's 1621			
U9		A seventeenth-century copy (not holograph) of the poem, entitled "Penshurst Mount," is in the British Library: Addit. MS 23229, ff. 91– 92. The following substantive variants appear in this copy (PM):		11	These] 1621; Thys PM
				14	you] 1621; itt PM
				17	that] 1621; which PM
				19	mine] 1621; my PM
				21	what] 1621; with PM
	2	Loves sporting] 1621; brave Cupids PM		23	same-like] 1621; very PM
				24	blessing] 1621; blessings PM
	7	which] 1621; though PM		27	then was blest in] 1621; first did here knowe PM
	8	holy reliques] 1621; Jewells PM		28	When equall] 1621; And mayden PM

did together] 1621; in thys
roome did PM

30   torments] 1621; tortures PM
32   once-good dayes] 1621; once
      blest time PM
34   so] 1621; thus PM
36   swellings] 1621; swelling PM
39   yet] 1621; now PM
42   While] 1621; When PM
      that] 1621; which PM
44   treasure] 1621; honor PM
      few] 1621; past PM
46   paine] 1621; gaine PM
47   and] 1621; in PM
48   and mem'ry] 1621; remem-
      brance PM
49   since but] 1621; if not PM
      my] 1621; more PM
54   to] 1621; with PM
55   with] 1621; in PM
      could] 1621; shold PM
56   could yeeld] 1621; had
      left PM
59   thus must] 1621; so shall PM
60   Six lines added in PM follow-
      ing 1.60:
            Then may I live in Niobes
               sad state,
            Who weeping long indur'd
               her Losses fate,
            Till to a Roche transformed
               from her Tears
            She lives to feele more drops
               which on her weares
            Heaven weepes on her then
               thys example take
            And soe I'le ty myselfe at
               Patience stake,
62   vex] 1621; torture PM
      perfectest knowne] 1621;
      best prized PM
68   With] 1621; which PM

U10   11   fire] ed.; fier 1621
       18   hower.] ed.; ~∧ 1621
U11   2   Seeme] ed.; Seemes 1621
U12   Copy-text: F
       6   delights] 1621; delight F
       9   When] 1621; If F
       12   Ever] 1621; from thence F
       18   could] 1621; would F
       19   can'st] 1621; could'st F
       20   is] 1621; were F

21   Vertue, beauty] 1621; Beauty,
      worth, and F
U13   Copy-text: F
       4   the] 1621; that F
       9   worth] 1621; warmth F
       17   raine:] 1621; ~∧F
       18   pride,] 1621; ~∧F
U14   Copy-text: F
Line 2 and the refrain of the first
stanza are indented in the 1621 text,
and in the rest of the poem all lines
are indented except the first line of
each stanza.
       1   love?] 1621; ~∧F
       6   fram'd] 1621; form'd F
       7   Who can blame mee?] 1621;
            Who can— F (refrain fol-
            lows each stanza)
       14   yett hee] 1621; hee F
       25   an howre] 1621; howre F
U17   Copy-text: F
Lines 2, 4, 6, 8, 10, and 14 are
indented in the 1621 text.
       1   doe] 1621; did F
            soules] 1621; paines F
       2   harts] 1621; soules F
            languish?] 1621; ~∧F
       3   still with] 1621; greatest F
            anguish,] 1621; ~∧F
       4   sleepes] 1621; sleep F
            breed] 1621; made F
            languish.] 1621; ~∧F
       5   Hope yett appeares] 1621;
            Till hope apeer'd F
            helpes] 1621; help'd F
       6   lends a sparcke of] 1621;
            gave new F
            to salve this languish,]
            1621; which ending was
            with languish∧ F
       7   ease] 1621; help F
            anguish,] 1621; ~∧F
       8   butt nott cures] 1621;
            to cares F
            to bitter tasting languish.]
            1621; wounds, and cures to
            bitter languish F
       9   Yett strait I feele] 1621; Butt
            O! I now doe find F
            butt greater] 1621; my F
       10   languish.] 1621; ~∧F
       11   Could I nott hope] 1621; had

I nere hop'd F
suffer might] 1621; might
have borne F

12   torture] 1621; torment F
smart and languish.] 1621;
felt my languish F

13   For] 1621; Now F

14   Both Prince, and subject]
1621; Father, and chil-
dren F
of e'relasting] 1621; butt of
endles F

U18   Copy-text: F

1   mourne] 1621; burne F

3   griefs] 1621; grief F

6   cloud'ly] 1621; cloudlike F

12   robd] 1621; lost F

15   those names] F; the name
1621

16   blasts] 1621; colde F

19   brings] 1621; breeds F
paine,] 1621; ~∧F

22   lend] 1621; give F

24   equall shining] 1621; shining
equall F

U19   14   your] ed.; you 1621
U21   29   bodys] ed.; body's 1621
U22   13   vaines,] ed.; ~∧ 1621
U24   Copy-text: F

3   doe cruell torments] 1621; my
torments patient F

4   Will you alas] 1621; now
doe nott F
in] 1621; in my F

5   Know] 1621; O F

7   comfort] 1621; pitty F

8   joyes] 1621; joye F

12   vowes] 1621; words F

13   What] 1621; Iff F
erre in] 1621; ill, itt F

15   greatest] 1621; om. F
committed] 1621; in
this committed F

16   Is] 1621; was F

17   Kindly relent] 1621; show
yett som pitty, then F
causeless curstnes fly] 1621;
torments hy F

19   much] 1621; you F

20   Striving to gaine, I losse have]
1621; and change, from
mee your hart hath F

Four lines added following line
20 in F:
Now lett noe fauning hope
of fained skill
Seeke any joye, butt joyes to
kill;
Lett all conspire to breed
my wrack, and end,
Yett nott enough my days to
spend;

23   And since] 1621; Yett
though F

24   I'le blow, and nourish] 1621; I
yett may joye in F

26   those] 1621; love F
being] 1621; living F

27   will, I live] 1621; minde I
bee F

28   live and] 1621; feede on F

29   and you may well] 1621; you
one day may F

30   when] author's cor, F;
while 1621

U27   2   groanes,] ed.; ~∧1621

9   paine,] ed.; ~∧1621

U28   1   you] ed.; yon 1621

U30   18   Chiefe] author's cor;
Thiefe 1621

U32   Copy-text: F
Lines 2, 4, 6, 8, 10, and 12 are
indented in the 1621 text.

3   nest:] ~∧F; rest: 1621

4   't is thine, mine is] 1621; from
mee, I ame F

7   prest,] 1621; ~∧F

9   deny,] 1621; ~∧F

10   request ∧ proclaimes] 1621;
request, proclaime F

11   brest:] 1621; ~∧F

13   match'd] 1621; maskd F

U33   5   view] ed.; veiw 1621

U34   Copy-text: F

6   prove.]ed.; ~, F; ~, 1621

7   sighs and teares] 1621; teares,
and sighs F

8   those best spent, if worth doe]
1621; best spent too, soe
some will F

9   Yett thy sweet] 1621; butt
yett (allas) thy F
pleasure] F; pleasures 1621
ever] 1621; om. F

	11	these] 1621; thus F
	12	to make my] 1621; while last- ing F
	16	mourne] F; moure 1621
		still] 1621; now F
U35	24	Leaving] *ed.*; Leaning 1621
U37	3	destroy₍] *ed.*; ~. 1621
	11	beare₍] *ed.*; ~. 1621
U42	9	more:] *ed.*; ~₍ 1621
U43	1	perhaps] *ed.*; perhapts 1621
	14	led.] *ed.*; ~: 1621
U48	1	Pyramids] *ed.*; Pyramid's 1621
U49	9	still] *ed.*; ctill 1621
U51	2	take;] *ed.*; ~₍ 1621
	20	too] *ed.*; to 1621
	55	be] *author's cor*; as 1621
U52	Copy-text: F	
	5	care,] 1621; ~₍F
	11	teares] 1621; cares F
	14	sheepe:] 1621; ~₍F
	28	untying] 1621; fast tying F
	34	nor] *author's cor*, F; no 1621
	36	was.] 1621; ~, F
	40	by] 1621; in F
	41	quite,] 1621; ~₍F
	42	eyes,] 1621; ~₍F
	47	one,] 1621; ~₍F
	53	care] 1621; cares F
	58	a] 1621; *om.* F
		sight] 1621; light F
	61	butt her] 1621; her bright F
	63	hee] 1621; she F
	64	reliefe.] 1621; ~₍F
	67	roote] 1621; triumph F
		estate] 1621; state F
	70	love?] 1621; ~₍F
	72	prove] 1621; move F
	73	still,] 1621; ~₍F
	74	weare:] 1621; ~₍F
	77	turn'd,] 1621; ~₍F
	79	passions] 1621; passion F
	81	This] 1621; The F
		now] 1621; thus F
	82	foot steps] 1621; steps he F
	85	restles] 1621; toyling F
	87	sooner] 1621; surer F
		brought] 1621; bought F
	89	tooke,] 1621; ~₍F
	97	love;] *ed.*; ~₍F; ~, 1621
	102	sheepe] 1621; flock F
	112	breathe] F; breath 1621

	114	yett] 1621; butt F
		well,] 1621; ~₍F
	115	two] 1621; tow F
	116	worldly] 1621; earthly F
	123	rivers] 1621; river F
	124	neere.] 1621; ~₍F
	125	must yett] 1621; yett must F
	128	read.] 1621; ~₍F
	130	prove,] 1621; ~₍F
	133	alas too soone] 1621; too soone alas
	140	fears.] 1621; ~₍F
	145	hast] 1621; have F
	147	leave] 1621; chang F
	150	knowne,] 1621; ~₍F
	151	brought,] 1621; ~₍F
	164	field?] 1621; ~, F
	168	intombe?] 1621; ~; F
	174	Your] 1621; thy F
	175	martir'd] 1621; martirs F
	177	you,] 1621; ~₍F
	178	crave:] 1621; ~₍F
	179	true,] 1621; ~₍F
	180	lyfe] 1621; self F
	184	murther] 1621; conquer F
	185	reason?] *ed.*; ~; F: ~₍1621
	186	your] 1621; thy F
	189	you] 1621; thee F
	190	You] 1621; thee F
		your] 1621; thy F
	194	bond] 1621; band F
		are,] 1621; ~₍F
	197	my] 1621; mine F
	198	can of itt] 1621; of itt can F
		part,] 1621; ~₍F
	201	you doe] 1621; thou dost F
	204	thee] 1621; bee F
	208	woe.] 1621; ~₍F
	210	againe,] 1621; ~₍F
	219	move] F; moves 1621
	221	please,] 1621; ~₍F
	222	prove,] 1621; ~₍F
	223	ease,] 1621; ~₍F
	227	my self I find] 1621; I find my self F
	234	are,] 1621; ~₍F
	235	fears,] 1621; ~₍F
	237	whenever you shall] 1621; when you shall ever F
		waile,] 1621; ~₍F
	240	waile] 1621; plaine F

228

248 bonds] 1621; bands F
  preserve.] 1621; ∼∧F
252 bands.] 1621; ∼∧F
253 leave,] 1621; ∼∧F
255 receave,] 1621; ∼∧F
261 bee,] 1621; ∼∧F
262 your] 1621; thy F
264 your] 1621; thy F
266 disdaine:] 1621; ∼∧F
267 dri'de,] 1621; ∼∧F
268 sommer] 1621; autume F
269 lov'd,] 1621; ∼∧F
271 speech] 1621; state F
273 fast,] 1621; ∼∧F
275 makes] F; make 1621
280 binds.] 1621; ∼∧F
283 passion] F; passions 1621
286 make:] 1621; ∼∧F
291 his] *author's cor*, F;
  this 1621

295 shall] 1621; must F
296 sorrow] 1621; sorrows F
298 Aradeame] *author's cor*, F;
  Arideame 1621
299 ceasles] *author's cor*, F;
  causlesse 1621
301 spring] 1621; springs F
303 And to true harts this
  good doth bring] *author's
  cor*; Which to . . . bring
  1621; That unto lovers
  this good brings F
306 thoughts] 1621; thought F

U55 9 prove] *author's cor*; move F,
  1621
  10 move] *author's cor*; prove F,
  1621

Poems from the Newberry Manuscript, THE SECOUND PART OF THE COUNTESSE OF MONTGOMERY'S URANIA

Copy-text: N

N1 3 vassall?] *ed.*; ∼, N
  4 Crowne?] *ed.*; ∼, N
  14 skye?] *ed.*; ∼; N
N3 1 harts,] *ed.*; ∼∧N
  2 flattering;] *ed.*; ∼∧N
  5 framd] *ed.*; fram N
  kill?] *ed.*; ∼∧N
  8 furdering?] *ed.*; ∼, N
  10 flowing,] *ed.*; ∼∧N
  12 showing,] *ed.*; ∼∧N
N4 1 Honor now injoye the day]
  [*Beehold the lovs great God of
  love*] N
  4 power] [*honor*] N
  5 all:] *ed.*; ∼∧N
  6 sees] *ed.*; see's N
  10 gall;] *ed.*; ∼∧N
  22 mortallings:] *ed.*; ∼∧N
N5 3 soe:] *ed.*; ∼∧N
  6 Desire] [*folly*] N
  11 Fondly using wanton] [*and*]
  fondly using [*butt*] wan-
  ton N
  18 this,] *ed.*; ∼∧N

  24 wurst,] *ed.*; ∼∧N
  26 just borne] [*lawfull*] N
N6 2 Billowes,] *ed.*; ∼∧N
  3 most] ⟨most⟩ N
  4 combinds;] *ed.*; ∼∧N
  5 sprites,] *ed.*; ∼∧N
  11 is,] *ed.*; ∼∧N
  16 express;] *ed.*; ∼∧N
  17 Queene,] *ed.*; ∼∧N
  18 unseene,] *ed.*; ∼∧N
  22 brands;] *ed.*; ∼∧N
N7 10 spring,] *ed.*; ∼∧N
  11 brings] *ed.*; bring's N
  12 see,] *ed.*; ∼∧N
  14 crost,] *ed.*; ∼∧N
N8 3 fast;] *ed.*; ∼∧N
  9 made;] *ed.*; ∼∧N
  15 denyes;] *ed.*; ∼∧N
  24 scornd,] *ed.*; ∼∧N
  30 more,] *ed.*; ∼∧N
  33 frame,] *ed.*; ∼∧N
  36 name,] *ed.*; ∼∧N
N9 12 two] *ed.*; tow N
  13 Beaming?] *ed.*; ∼, N

	18	Two] *ed.*; tow N
N10	12	ruin?] *ed.*; ~, N
	18	fire,] *ed.*; ~_∧N
	25	earth, water, ayre, fire] [*water, fire, ayre, earth*] N
	34	To singe all harts, by such a fire] [*To make all harts obay a sainte*] N
	36	fate?] *ed.*; ~; N
N11	11	And] [*Yett*] N
	20	Yett] [*Butt*] N
N12	8	face.] *ed.*; ~_∧N
	9	drowne:] *ed.*; ~_∧N
	13	Love;] *ed.*; ~, N
	14	move?] *ed.*; ~, N
N13	7	bee,] *ed.*, ~_∧N
	10	you,] *ed.*; ~_∧N
	12	disesteemed.] *ed.*; ~_∧N
	13	high,] *ed.*; ~_∧N
	15	deities] *ed.*; dieties N
	16	too] *ed.*; to N
N14	3	owne?] *ed.*; ~, N
	4	and faith did flow] [*butt fruictles flow*] N
	5	Yett fruictles ran] [*cowld I suspect that thine*] N

	7	showe?] *ed.*; ~, N
	10	too] *ed.*; to N
	12	off] *ed.*; of N
	23	true;] *ed.*; ~_∧N
	27	fire?] *ed.*; ~_∧N
	28	art?] *ed.*; ~_∧N
N15	9	love_∧] *ed.*; ~? N
	21	off] *ed.*; of N
	24	care.] *ed.*; ~_∧N
N16	4	grace,] *ed.*; ~_∧N
	9	night.] *ed.*; ~_∧N
	10	love;] *ed.*; ~_∧N
	20	warme] [*true*] N
N18	1	soe?] *ed.*; ~_∧N
	11	right:] *ed.*; ~_∧N

N18 is recopied in the Newberry Manuscript, with the following changes:

	2	Sorrows] sorrow may] will
	4	alone] above powrs onely] the
	8	was] from inthron'd to] heigth did
	10	And noe thing more then love] nott Venus darling that

Songs from the Huntington Manuscript of LOVE'S VICTORIE

Copy-text: H

H1	5	more admire] more [*more*] admire H
	8	desire] [*delight*] H
H3	4	tread?] *ed.*; ~_∧H
	8	paine.] *ed.*; ~_∧H
H4	3	wull,] *ed.*; ~_∧H
	6	full.] *ed.*; ~_∧H
	12	priing.] *ed.*; ~_∧H
	15	back,] *ed.*; ~_∧H
	17	round,] *ed.*; ~_∧H
H5	6	freind.] *ed.*; ~_∧H
	7	gas'de,] *ed.*; ~_∧H
	8	amas'de,] *ed.*; ~_∧H
	10	mild;] *ed.*; ~_∧H
	13	mee] *ed.*; ~_∧H
	14	see.] *ed.*; ~_∧H
H6	2	jarr;] *ed.*; ~_∧H
	4	grace.] *ed.*; ~_∧H
	5	end:] *ed.*; ~_∧H

	8	slide.] *ed.*; ~_∧H
H7	28	Butt in hapiness] butt [*still*] in [*all*] hapines H

In H end punctuation is provided only for lines 2 and 28; the editor has supplied all additional end punctuation.

H8	1	woods] ⟨woods⟩ H
	4	increase,] *ed.*; ~_∧H
	6	gone.] *ed.*; ~_∧H
	16	loss,] *ed.*; ~_∧H
	18	end.] *ed.*; ~_∧H
	22	desire,] *ed.*; ~_∧H
H9	1–3	[*Love a god did slander beare / gainst his person, and his power / butt,*] musique H
	4	were] [*was*] H
	14	By which they] [*wher*] ⟨by which⟩ they [*may*] H

spy] [*descry*] H
15 Cease] [*s*]cease H

The editor has supplied all end punctuation because there is none in H9.

Poem Possibly by William Herbert, Earl of Pembroke

N2 10 denies;] *ed.;* ~_∧_N
17 rest;] *ed.;* ~_∧_N
24 bee;] *ed.;* ~_∧_N
The following substantive variants
are found in the copies W, X, Y, and
Z. (For identification, see headnote,
page 217.)
1 that] N, X, Y, Z; the W
2 Which hath] N, Z; That had
W, X, Y
4 full] N, Z; then W, X, Y
5 Nor] N, Z; ere W, X, Y
mee] N, Z; I W, X, Y
6 Nor once] N, Z; or W, X, Y
8 For] N; But W, X, Y, Z

9 As] N, W, X, Y; That Z
sort] N, Z; part W, X, Y
11 doe] N; can W, X, Y, Z
14 thy] N, Z; those W; these
X, Y
15 I] N, Z; oh W, X, Y
thy] N, Z; this W, X, Y
18 dost] N; didst W, X, Y, Z
19 can lodge] N; could dwell W,
X, Y, Z
23 againe] N, Z; *om.* W, X, Y
cowldst] N, Z; couldst well
W, X, Y
25 made] N, W, X, Y; forc't Z
28 Soe] N; Too W, X, Y, Z

APPENDIX: THE CORRESPONDENCE OF LADY MARY WROTH

I. LADY MARY WROTH TO QUEEN ANNE

Holograph manuscript of the Most. Hon. The Marquess of Salisbury, preserved at Hatfield House, Ref. no. 130/174; *HMC*, Salisbury, XXII, 3.
No date

Sir Robert Wroth wrote James I a similar letter concerning Loughton Hall, dated 1608: *HMC*, Salisbury, XX, 315. It is very likely that Lady Mary's letter was also written at this time because she refers to the "petition of mr. wrothes to the kinge"; her letter must have been composed prior to 1612, when Loughton Hall was reconstructed.

Madame:

The infinite favours which from you I have reseaved, although I must confess my self farr unworthy of the leaste of them, beesids knowing how willingly the kinge will heare your Majestie I thus farr presume as humbly to beeseech you thus much to bee pleased as to recommende this petition of mr. wrothes to the kinge, your Majestie beeing the only help wheron I dare rely, It may bee thought to bee a matter of profitt, and soe the harder to optaine, yett is itt noe loss to his Majestie att all: mr. wrothes sute beeing but this, that itt may please the king to grant him a longer estate in itt, to avoide all feare of having itt taken over his head, which iff hee may obtaine, he will build, and make the house fitt for both your Majesties to rest in, and will also make his chiefe dwelling ther, whe[r]as otherwise the house beeing soe olde, and in decay as itt's likely every day to fall doune, hee must bee forst to settle him self some els wher, beesids hee knowes, for itt hath pleased his Majestie some times to doe that honor to that poore place as to come thether, how unfitt a house itt is, and how nessessary itt were to bee mended, the kings sports lying soe aboute itt: Nether doth mr. wrothe desire this for nothing, but as your Majestie may parseave by the petition, hee offers such a fine as, six hundred pounde, which hee will beestow ther upon building, if hee may have longer time granted him for his Majesties service; which sum doth rise to as much as the kings commisioners doe lett leases for in reversion, beesids the loss hee doth indure, and will still willingly suffer, by letting the deere feede in his best grounds, to which by his lease hee is nott bound, but is content rather to lose a hundred pounde a yeere, then to trouble them, least itt might [any] hinder the kings sporte, and of this itt hath pleased his Majestie to take notiss att his beeing ther, wheras if hee should nott still be ther, his absence would bring both decay

233

to the deere, and to the redines of the kings sports, I am imboldened thus far to take this boldenes beeing therunto lisenced by your Royall favours to mee, as humbly to beeseech your Majesties furtherance in this busines, since itt will be much for my good, mr. wrothe having promised to ad itt to my jointure, all the rest of his lande beeing entailed, soe as hee can nott conveniently mend itt (yett butt very smale) with any lande soe well as with this: / This reason made ⟨me⟩ the more presume assuring your Majestie that in doing this for mee, youe doe itt for ⟨one⟩ who will live noe longer, then most truly to serve you, and even with my lyfe strive to deserve thes high, and unspeakable graces you dayly doe mee. / And this I beseech your Majestie to beeleeve of mee since I have vowed ever unfainedly to bee

> your Majesties most
> humble, and faithfull servant
> Mary wrothe

II. Lady Mary Wroth to Sir Robert Sidney

Holograph manuscript of the Rt. Hon. Viscount De L'Isle, preserved at the Kent County Record Office, Maidstone, Ref. no. U1475 C52; HMC, De L'Isle, V, 249–50.
October 17, 1614

This letter was miscatalogued by the HMC under the name of Lady Mary Wroth's servant, H. Lansbrooke, but it was first correctly identified by Margaret Witten-Hannah:

My Lord.

I most humbly thank you for your letter, and for that care you have of poore James who as hee is yours ⟨in blood⟩, soe I hope hee shall one day live to deserve your love to him; the Excectors for any thing I see meane to doe little; the marchant and I have had some cross words butt I hope all will bee well, if nott the fault shall ly on him, for the wardship your Lordship as I think doth take a just, and good course, wherin I beeseech you to persist, what soever John wrothe told you, if hee sayd hee had petitioned this master of the wards beefor Saterday last by this letter inclosed your Lordship shall find hee sayd amiss, for I having occasion to write about some other things to him moved his favor towards my son, and my self withall letting him truly know your powers as overseers, and ther unfittnes, I meane the tow younger John wrothes for medling in the wardship, I hope I have dun noe hurt in itt butt good rather, for the profitts ⟨of the lands⟩ your Lordship must stand upon them or els the poore child will have an ill account, they say directly that they have, and must have the lease of the land till hee come of yeeres, I trust as your Lordship hath carefully, and lovingly beegunn that soe you will bee pleased to proceed, for itt is now your part to bee his father being left booth ways in blood, and charge unto you, For me I wish I may butt bee able to deserve the least of your favors which I will indeavor with all my power hartely and truly to parforme; My Lady remembers her best love to your Lordship and desires you to excuse her nott writing having commanded mee to deliver thus much, and that she hopes shortly now to see you the time growing on to leave this place, and withall for the other busines which hath troubled her, and longs to have an end, yett non butt such as may best like you and bee fittest for your honor and house; My brother is nott heere when hee comes from Halstead I will speake with him and ever strive how I may still most deserve your favor, and his love; soe humbly desiring your blessing to mee, and James, I take my leave, and will ever bee

From Penshurst the   Your Lordships most obedient Daughter
17 of October 1614   Mary wrothe

III. LADY MARY WROTH TO SIR DUDLEY CARLETON

Holograph manuscript, *SPD*, James I, 14, 108 (56).
April 19, 1619

Sir.

The honor which I receavd from you att your beeing heere, and the respect I doe, and ever must beare you makes mee thus bold to write unto you and by thes lines to present my service unto you which I had rather have dunn my self if my fortunes had bin soe good as to have permitted mee to visitt those parts, butt I must nott expect any hapines I soe much desire never yett having receaved any cause to flatter my self with hope crosses still preventing mee yett shall they nott have power to make mee other then constant in my respect to my noble freind among which number I presume to hold you, and soe to ty my self ever to you as

                              Your most affectionate
Baynards Castle the   freind to serve you
19 of Aprill;/   Mary wrothe

IV. LADY MARY WROTH TO SIR DUDLEY CARLETON

Holograph manuscript, *SPD*, James I, 14, 108 (73).
April 25, 1619

Sir;/

The honor was soe much mine in injoying your presence att Loughton as to acknowledg itt I took the boldnes to present some rude lines unto you which I hope shall receave pardon for: the truth they caried with them, and the assurance of the constant respect I beare and will ever carry unto you; soe many ways manifested as they ingage mee into parpatuall debts unto you, which can bee never payd butt in wishes till opertunity may serve to make mee able to express what my hart desirs to serve you with, this latter favor and delicate present is such as I knowe nott whether I may bee glad of itt beeing soe rare and wellcome a juell to mee as by the estimation my injoyment is the greatest that may bee imagined for such a creaturs gaine, which shalbee cherisht with all care, and love by mee as yours, and mine; which with my help shall bee the presenter to you of some of those enimies you speak of by his owne quarell to them, or my desire that they should serve you as hers who will never bee other then faithfully

	Your affectionate
Baynards Castle the	freind and servante
25 of Aprill;/	Mary wrothe

V. LADY MARY WROTH TO THE DUKE OF BUCKINGHAM

Holograph manuscript, Bodleian Library MS Add.D. 111, ff. 173^{r-v}. *HMC*, 2nd Report, item 392, p. 60.
December 15, 1621

My Lord.
Understanding some of the strang constructions which are made of my booke contrary to my imagination, and as farr from my meaning as is possible for truth to bee from conjecture, my purpose noe way bent to give the least cause of offence, my thoughts free from soe much as thinking of any such thing as I ame censurd for; I have with all care caused the sale of them to bee forbidden, and the books left to bee shut up, for thos that are abroad, I will likewise doe my best to gett them in, if itt will please your Lordship to procure mee the kings warrant to that effect, without which non will deliver them to mee, besids that your Lordship wilbe pleased to lett mee have that which I sent you, the example of which will without question make others the willinger to obay; For mine owne part I ame extreamly grieved that I ame thus much mistaken, butt yett comforted with this that itt is an injury dun to mee undeservedly, although to bee accus'd in this nature is a great wrong unto mee; I beeseech your Lordship therfor thus far to right mee as to beeleeve this for truthe, and what I ame able to doe for the getting in of books (which from the first were solde against my minde I never purposing to have had them published) I will with all care, and diligence parforme; soe I humbly take my leave; from London the 15 of December 1621

Your Lordships humble servante
Mary wrothe

APPENDIX

VI. LADY MARY WROTH TO SIR EDWARD DENNY

Contemporary manuscript of the Most. Hon. the Marquess of Salisbury, preserved at Hatfield House, Ref. No. 130/117; *HMC, Salisbury*, XXII, 160.
February 15, 1621/2

Another contemporary copy may be found in the Clifton manuscripts at the Univ. of Nottingham, Cl LM 85/2; *HMC*, series 55, 7, item 124.

My Lord;

This day came to my handes some verses under the name of the Lord Denny's but such vile, rayling and scandalous thinges, as I could not beleeve they proceeded from any but some drunken poett; and that they [the] rather bycause they so feelinglie speak of that vice and sinne; but to think my Lord Denny who hath professed so much Religion, Justice, and love of worth, should fall into so strange a disposition as to slander and revile a woman-frend who hath ever honour'd him; I was loath to creditt it; especiallie knowing mine owne innocencie; which is as cleare and pure as new borne; what ever such like slanderous conceipts have layed upon mee. And much I doe wonder how noblenes can faile so farre, as to lett such rudenes witnesse against it selfe; or rather take that away; and leave base basenes in place of honour; otherwise before such proceedinges had bin, truth and worth would have had the matter questioned: but heere, is no such matter; violence and falsehood rules. When as had I beene asked, I would have trulie and constantlie sworne, that I no more meant harme to my Lord Denny or his house, then to my selfe. Nor did I ever intend one word of that book to his Lordships person or disgrace: and this I will yet say to justifie my selfe; but not in way of satisfaction; for too course waies are taken with mee to offer or give that, but by way of justification; yet bycause I will not follow ill example, I send your Lordship your owne lines, (as they were called to mee) reversed; and the first coppyi; as desiring your owne eyes should bee first witnesse of your reward for your poetrie, if it were yours. This is the course I take yet; although your Lordship certainlie knowes, I may take others; and am not by this barred from anie. I should have taken it, as an expression of your worth had you proceeded on just groundes; now I shall pittie your rash follie, and wish you amendment of understanding; and to take this as a mornings work.

The 15th of February.   Mary Wrothe.

19   example] examples No

VII. Sir Edward Denny to Lady Mary Wroth

Contemporary manuscript (possibly holograph) of the Most. Hon. The Marquess of
Salisbury, preserved at Hatfield House, ref. no. 130 / 118–19; *HMC*, Salisbury,
XXII, 160–61.
February 26, 1621/2

Other contemporary copies may be found in the Clifton manuscripts at the Library of
the University of Nottingham, Cl LM 85/1; *HMC*, Series 55, 7, item. 124; and in
the manuscripts of the Rt. Hon. the Earl of Denbigh, preserved at Pailton House, Ref.
no. C48/2a; *HMC*, Denbigh, V, 3.

Madam yesterday the XXVth of this february, I received from you an invec-
tive, with an inversion of rymes inclosed, which you suspect to be myne, but it
seemes were a Romanza from the father in lawe of Sirelius to Pamphilia, and so
indorst as I heer which, how they can concern either your Ladyship or mee I
cannot conceive, for yf I in your intention and construction wear not the father
in lawe to Syrelius nor you Pamphilia then that paper hath no relation to either
of us, and so am I unjustly taxed, But be the author who yt will the whole
wor[l]d conceves me to be ment in one of the weakest and unworthiest passages
of your booke for the application whereof, whereas your Ladyship censures me
for dishonorable and undue proceedings in not seeking first by question to
receive true information from you who could best give yt, I confesse in some
kinds of doubts it is so just a course, that yf I had fayled in yt, I should have
needed no other or so severe an accuser as my self. But Madam to aske yf yt be
daie when the sunn shyneth wear a question so vaine as you count your booke
inocent, which all the world condemns, and allthough by your protestation,
not for my satisfaction, but your owne justification you deny the thing so
lykewise I out of charity not flattery can repent, yf [*any*] I should have any way
justly offended you. Though a private negative; for a plaester to a broken head,
by a publick affirmative, and to be proved by divers witnesses of your own
Ranck and somme higher, is, but a small recompence to be the onely chosen
foole for a May-game, before all the World and especially before a Wise King
and Prince, with all the nobility, so many evidences being of power by the law
of God and man to leade a whole jury, and evict any one witnesse whatsoever
and therefore not so foule in mee to creditt yt as in you to deny yt, besides
whilst you pull me by the sleeve for this error of hasty creditt, you quite forgett
the hole of your own elbowe, which putt the case I writt that you say I did
where is this question before you condemne, wherfore I returne my wintch to
your galle and justly your own letter all ⟨whole⟩ back again to your self, and
whereas your Ladyship pleases to tax me with the odious vice of drunkennes
which, I utterly abhorre, I most humbly take yt for a great favour, and beseech
you to voutsafe me one more (though I cannott deserve yt) which is that you
would be pleased to be present at my execustion, and with that white inocent
hand of yours, take up and throwe, the first stone, so should I hope of long lyfe

from the equity of a righteous judge. For my own part Madame I could have borne your trampling uppon me or any other disgrace that had not produced me as a scorn to the eyes of my dread and dear soveraigne and master. And allthough in christianity I may hope the best of your protestation, yet yf your Ladyship be, not overweened to much of your own excellency, how can you not suspect your own forgettfullnes, when so many noble witnesses may be brought to aver that your own mouth hath published me to be the man whom that spitefull and scornfull passa[g]e did concerne, and for a close wher you tell me of what other courses you may take against me, alasse Madame I fear none and am confident that I shall answer what shalbee objected to me to your losse and disadvantage, for I knowe the dust will fly into your own eyes and the wind will be full in your own face; But lett your Ladyship take what course yt shall please you with me, this shalbee myne with you [*that*] to ever wish you well and pray that you may repent you of so many ill spent yeares of so vaine a booke and that you may redeeme the tym with writing as large a volume of heavenly layes and holy love as you have of lascivious tales and amorous toyes that at the last you may followe the rare, and pious example of your vertuous and learned Aunt, who translated so many godly books and especially the holly psalmes of David, that no doubt now shee sings in the quier of Heaven those devine meditations which shee so sweetely tuned heer belowe, and which being left to us heer on earth will begett hir dayly more and more glory in heaven as others by [*whome*] ⟨them⟩ shalbe enlightened, who as so many trophies shall appeare to her further exaltation in gods favour, with which prayer for you I end and rest

> Your most wellwishing
> frend
>   Edward Denny
> who for the great honor I bear
> somme of your noble allies and my
> deerly honored frends doe forbeare
> to write what I might./

Feb: the XXVIth

<table>
<tr><td>1</td><td>XXVth] [25] ⟨15th⟩ No</td><td>30</td><td>for] as De</td></tr>
<tr><td>2</td><td>suspect] suppose De</td><td>41</td><td>passade] passage No, De</td></tr>
<tr><td>8</td><td>word] world No, De</td><td>46</td><td>to ever] ever to De</td></tr>
<tr><td>17</td><td>have any way] any waie have De</td><td>47</td><td>may] may not De</td></tr>
<tr><td>18</td><td>a broken] broken De</td><td>53</td><td>shee so sweetly] so sweetely shee De</td></tr>
<tr><td>18</td><td>head] fore heade No</td><td>53–54</td><td>left to us heer] left heare to us De</td></tr>
<tr><td>27</td><td>where] soe heare De</td><td>56</td><td>prayer] praiers De</td></tr>
</table>

APPENDIX

VIII. Lady Mary Wroth to Sir Edward Denny

Contemporary manuscript copy of the Rt. Hon. the Earl of Denbigh, preserved at
Pailton House, Ref. no. C48/2b; *HMC*, Denbigh, V, 3.
Contains holograph signature
February 27, 1621/2

Other contemporary copies may be found in the manuscripts of the Most. Hon. the
Marquess of Salisbury, preserved at Hatfield House, Ref. no. 130/120; *HMC*, Salis-
bury, XXII, 161–62; and in the Clifton manuscripts at the Library of the University
of Nottingham Cl LM 85/4; *HMC*, series 55, pt. 7, item 124.

My Lord.

For any verses written from Sirelius father in lawe to Pamphilia, are no waie
concerning mee; ⟨but as the author of the booke⟩ nor did I take them so meant,
till I was tould you had taken that part to your self, us'd all ill and curst courses
you could ⟨and⟩ to the King against mee; made the rymes and acknowledgd
them perticulerly; and with all rage and spleene hath proceeded against mee./
Yet had I beene guiltie I should not have taken them ill; But let them who have
accused mee, of what ranck soever, averr it to my face, that ever I said it, or my
soule accuse mee that I meant it, and I will throwe the stone on my selfe, else
those that have raised this, let them take heede of meddling or casting the
stone; I will speake sincerely and justly, I never thought on you in my writing,
nor meant you ⟨or any nor did⟩ I [n] ever speake any such thing. But since you
accuse ⟨mee⟩ so farr, right your self, and rectifie your owne judgment, and
censure, Produce your wittnesses, and I will not feare to stand before the best
in my owne [*justification*] ⟨cleering⟩; when I beleeve they will shrink;/ For my
ranke below the Kings Majestie and his, I know how to appeare [cancelled
words] before the best in justification. Therefore that is no bugbeare to mee;
Let not them feare, and I shall with all cleerenes and truth wittnes my
innocency, and not now with words or submission (which I scorne) goe about
to give sattisfaction, but ⟨with⟩ true and loyall faith prove and justifie what I
have said: wherefore if you desire truth; knowledg of truth; or use of truth, let
mee know my accusers; bring us together, and be assured you shall find mee;
what my blood calls mee to be, and what my words have said mee to be. Feare
not to saie what you please, for beleeve it my noble allies will not thank you for
forbearing mee; nor [*when*] ⟨iff⟩ the tyme shall serve spare you for what you
have done. Therefore take your course and spare not mee: for any respects but
justice, who wilbe as you deserve from mee:/

The 27th of Febr: Your as well wisshing frend
    1621   Mary wrothe

---

2   but as the author of the booke] *om.* Sa, No
3   and] *om.* Sa, No

240

```
 4   the rymes and] these rymes Sa, No
 5   them perticulerly] them against me particularly No
 7  8   my soule] my owne soule No
11   nor meant you] I never meant you; repeated twice in Sa, No
11   or any nor did] om. Sa, No
14   cleering] justification Sa, No
14   they] others Sa, No
14   my] any No
15   cancelled] equall in truth; or near in bloud to the best Sa, No
16   before the best in justification] om. Sa, No
19   what] this Sa, No
24   iff] when Sa, No
27   27th] 29th Sa, No
```

IX. Sir Edward Denny to Lady Mary Wroth

Contemporary manuscript copy of the Rt. Hon. the Earl of Denbigh, preserved at Pailton House, Ref. no. C48/2c; *HMC*, Denbigh, V, p. 3. No date

Other contemporary copies may be found in the manuscripts of the Most. Hon. the Marquess of Salisbury, preserved at Hatfield House, Ref. no. 130/121; *HMC*, Salisbury, XXII, pp. 162; and in the Clifton manuscripts at the Library of the University of Nottingham Cl LM 85/5; *HMC*, series 55, pt. 7, item. 124.

Madam./

I will make no further replie to your distempers; I but still profess and ever be redie to justifie what in my letter I have averred. You may have heard I doubt not by some of your best frends what hath come to the Kings eares [⟨*by Lady*⟩] from your [*La*:] owne mouth touching mee in this busines, which, if you will not, I cannot make you heare./ For my owne part, my conscience tells mee, I have don, nor ever will doe you any wronge, I hate to be an enformer, the truth is too apparant and maye be too well proved at your owne pleasure, if my wordes have no credit of truth with your Ladyship./ Whereas your Ladyship bidds mee speake what I can or will, for your noble allies will not thanke mee for forbearing you, not spare mee when tyme shall serve for what I have don. Madam, I saie, you are a noble Ladie, And for those noble allies of yours, I will ever honor and serve them; when you have made the worst of mee you can devise unto them;/ Thus without your Ladyships further trouble I still must rest;/

> Your truly well wishing frend
> if you could think so
> Edward Denny

```
1   I] om. Sa, No
2   in my letter I have] I have in my letter Sa, No
```

7   too] *om.* No
12   them] *om.* No
13   still] *om.* No

X. Lady Mary Wroth to Sir William Feilding, first Earl of Denbigh

Holograph manuscript of the Rt. Hon. the Earl of Denbigh, preserved at Pailton House, Ref. no. C48/2; *HMC*, Denbigh, V. p. 3.
No date, but probably March, 1622

My Lord.
To justify my self as directly as I may, and in this (as in all things els) strive to show how much I ame your servante, beesyds imboldened by your favors, and honord by your commaunds, I presume to send thes things unto you, unfitt for your most judisiall eyes to beehold, and goodnes to read; and unseemly for mee to pubblish if innocensy guarded mee nott, butt cleernes in some part as never meant ⟨to⟩ him, and faulshood on his syde in his accusation concerning drink, makes mee ⟨willyngly⟩ cast my self upon the same Jury hee taulks of, and from thence humbly to beeseech right, I can nott merritt any such favor butt by Loyallty, and truth, which may, and shall speake justly for mee, your favor may make all well with his Majestie: which I [*must*] ⟨doe⟩ and ⟨most⟩ humbly beeseech; for my Lord Denny I hope hee sees his error, and my last sute shalbee unto your Lordship: that I may bee honord with the continuance of your favor which I will all true service strive to deserve, and ever bee as Firste in truthe to your commaunds as the most obliged servant you have, ever remaining

Enfield this   Your Lordships humblest
Wensday;/   Some things have   servante,
            past by message;/   Mary wrothe

XI. Lady Mary Wroth to Sir Edward Conway

Holograph manuscript, *SPD*, James I, 14, 139 (53)
March 7, 1622/3

Sir.
   This busines which I heere present unto you doth make mee ashamed for the poornes of my estate to aske itt, or to trouble my honorable freinds with itt, butt nessessity urgeth mee, and that must beg my pardon, or plead my excuse, I dare nott ⟨of⟩ my self beeing soe unprofitable a creature, and a stranger almost to you present this sute, butt beeseech your favor in itt beeing allowed by the lords out of compassion, and justnes of my cause, for my intent is fully, and directly to satisfy all men, the particular reasons moving mee to sue for this protection which heere from mr. secretary Calvert is brought to your

honor, my Lord of Annand will make you acquainted with all, I beeseech you Sir to give mee your furderance in itt, that itt may bee dunn with your favor, and as much speed as may conveniently bee, which shall ty mee always to remaine

Loughton the   Your humble servant
7 of March;/   Mary wrothe

XII. LADY MARY WROTH TO SIR EDWARD CONWAY

Holograph manuscript, *SPD*, James I, 14, 158 (65)
January 30, 1623/4

Sir.

I was soe much bound unto you for your favor, furderance, and finishing my busines this last yeere, as when I prove to you ungratefull I will leave living; butt such is the continuance of my ill fortune, as I must beefor I can deserve the first beg againe, and trouble you, for to you I only adress my self as most confident of your favor, since you soe freely promised itt, I ame therfor now most ernestly to desire you to procure mee the kings hand once againe, the Lords I have petitioned, and given theyr Lordships an note of such debts as I have this yeere payd under my hand, which amounte to almost the haulf I did owe, and purposing God willing to doe the like this yeere with the rest I humbly beeseech his Majesties protection the saflier to accomplish itt, which I will doe with my best ability, and truly satisfy every man; If you please Sir to ad this favor to your former, you shall ty mee for ever (though the gaine of soe unfortunate a creature is noe thing) ⟨to your service⟩ yett I have a just, and true hart which shall ever serve you, and bind mee to bee

                                                     Your unfained freind
Loughton the   to commaund
30th of January;/   Mary wrothe

	Li	
To mr. Hull	340	
To mr. Ellis Rothwell	130	
To Georg Hadrington	135	
To Richard Gibbons	105	
To Ralf Dell	66	
To mistress Berden	52	10
To Richard Browne	45	
To John Catherick	58	

Sir.
These are all discharged, having receavd either reddy monny, or taken land for such time as this wilbee payd, by which means I have lessen'd my estate much,

and yett will goe on in this course to satisfy the rest in the like manner soe I may have time by one yeers protection more in which time I hope to free my self of all debts yett owing

Mary wrothe

Li: pound sterling

XIII. SIR EDWARD CONWAY TO LADY MARY WROTH

Draft of letter, *SPD*, James 1, 14, 172 (59)

27 Sept. 1624

Right honourable/
It is a kende of misfortune to me to putte to sue to you for favor to others perhaps with your trouble or others whoe longe to desire your noble favor by all the dutys and servis that come from a heart that honours you.

This bearer Mr. Hardinge whoe hath bounde me by the best . . . good, and carefull teaching and guiding of a younge son of myne, takes his triall of my good will to him by becoming a suitor to your Ladyship; that you wolde be pleased to make him satisfaction of a deabte he claymes from your Ladiship, what contentment equity or favor you will be pleased [*able*] that shall doe to him I will reckon of as an obligation layed upon me and in all your commandments by a redy operation expres have unto you great worthe and noble courtesy to me who rests as

Your ladyships
faythfull and humble servant

---

1   kende: kind

XIV. SIR GEORGE MANNERS, SEVENTH EARL OF RUTLAND, TO HIS "NOBLE COSIN"

Holograph manuscript of His Grace, the Duke of Rutland, preserved at Belvoir Castle, Letter Book of Sir George Manners, f. 132; *HMC*, Rutland, Appendix IV, I, 520.
May 31, 1640

Although the manuscript does not identify Lady Mary as the correspondent, it does refer to "your Urania" and mentions Baynard's Castle, where Lady Mary often resided in London.

Noble Cosin,
   Callinge to remembrance the favor you once did me in the sight of a Manuscrip you shewed me in your study att Banerds Castell And heere meet-

inge with your Urania I make bold to send this enclosed and begg a favor from you that I may read with more delight. If you please to interprete unto me the names as heere I have begunn them, wherein you shall much oblige me. And I shall ever rest as always I have professed my selfe,

Madam

Your Ladyships affectionate
Kinsman and servant
Rutland

May 31 1640

If you send your letter
att any tyme to Sir Edward
Baesh att Stansted he
will safely convey them
to Belvoir whither I
am goinge.

INDEX OF FIRST LINES

247